The HarperCollins Guide to Euro Disneyland 1992

The HarperCollins Guide to Euro Disneyland 1992

HarperCollins*Publishers*

HarperCollins*Publishers*,
77–85 Fulham Palace Road,
Hammersmith, London W6 8JB

HarperCollins*Publishers*,
10 East 53rd Street,
New York 10022

Published by HarperCollins*Publishers* 1992
9 8 7 6 5 4 3 2 1

Copyright © HarperCollins*Publishers* 1992

Catalogue details for this book are
available from the British Library

ISBN 0 00 637773 4

Set in Palatino

Photoset by Rowland Phototypesetting Ltd,
Bury St Edmunds, Suffolk

All rights reserved. No part of this publication may be
reproduced, stored in a retrieval system, or transmitted,
in any form or by any means, electronic, mechanical,
photocopying, recording or otherwise, without the prior
permission of the publishers.

CONTENTS

1 Getting Ready to Go
When to Go	9
Planning Ahead	10
Sample Itineraries	11
How to Get There	12
How to Cut Travel Costs	13
Hints for Travelling with Children	14
Hints for Older Travellers	16
Hints for Handicapped Travellers	16
Hints for Single Travellers	17

2 Transportation and Accommodation
Travelling by Car	20
Travelling by Plane	22
Travelling by Train	23
Euro Disneyland Hotels	24
Off-Site Hotels	33
Budget Accommodation	35

3 The Magic Kingdom
Main Street USA	39
Fantasyland	41
Frontierland	43
Adventureland	46
Discoveryland	48
Shopping	50
Entertainment	54

4 Good Food and Entertaining Evenings
Magic Kingdom Restaurants	57
Festival Disney Dining and Entertainment Centre	63
Euro Disneyland Hotel Restaurants	64
Off-Site Restaurants	65

5 Sports
Golf	69
Tennis	69
Ice Skating	69
Boating	69
Swimming	69
Fitness	70
Jogging	70
Bicycling	70
Croquet	70
Volleyball, Soccer, Basketball, Pétanque	70
Horseback Riding	70

6 Day-trips from Euro Disneyland
Versailles	71
Fontainebleau	74
Chartres	79
Champagne	84

7 Mini-Guide to Paris
Special Places	102
Sources and Resources	110
Shopping (discounts, too!)	117
Nightlife	124
Eating Out	125

8 En Route
From England	141
From the South of France	143
From Spain	146
From Sweden, Denmark, The Netherlands, Belgium	150
From Italy	154
From Germany	156

INTRODUCTION

Somewhere on this planet, perhaps deep in a New Guinea jungle or an Amazon rainforest, there may be three or four people who have never heard of Disneyland or Walt Disney World. They stride through life totally unaware of Mickey and Minnie and Donald, of Sleeping Beauty Castle and the Haunted Mansion. It is unlikely that these people have small children at home.

As for the other 4 billion or so folks, they can roughly be divided into those who have visited the parks in California or Florida (or Japan), and those who would like to visit as soon as possible. Which brings us to the subject of the book you now hold in your hands: *The HarperCollins Guide to Euro Disneyland*. As of 12 April 1992, Walt Disney's magic, his beloved mouse, and all his friends are open for business on a vast site in Marne-la-Vallée, 20 miles (32 km) east of Paris.

There is a staggering array of facts and figures that can be tossed about in regard to the scale of this first European venture by the Disney forces. The park is one-fifth the size of Paris itself. It employs 12,000 people, or 'cast members', as they are called. The six resort hotels on the property have 5,200 guestrooms. France, or all of Europe for that matter, has never seen anything like it.

But no matter how familiar the world is with Disney's theme parks, we can state with confidence that the one thing anyone contemplating a visit to Euro Disneyland needs is a guidebook. This one in particular. Consider a few reasons why you need this book:

1) *It is NOT a small world, after all*. It may be possible to arrive at Euro Disneyland and, in a single day, visit Main Street, Frontierland, Adventureland, Fantasyland, and Discoveryland. In fact, we will show you how. But you would not have seen even a fraction of all there is to do here. This guide will help you plan your visit in a logical, step-by-step way, and will help you make the most of any stay, no matter how long or short.

2) *You need a place to sleep*. The resort's six hotels range from moderately priced lodgings like the *Cheyenne* and *Santa Fe*, with their Western-style architecture, to luxury digs like the *Disneyland* hotel, which boasts more amenities than many a European hostelry. There's even the Davy Crockett Campground, with 414 cabins and 181 campsites. We've described them all in detail so you can be sure of getting your money's worth.

3) *There are lots of other things to do outside the Magic Kingdom*. The Euro Disney Resort, as the whole enterprise is formally called, also includes the Festival Disney Entertainment Centre featuring uniquely-themed shopping, dining, and shows, plus a championship golf course. Beyond that, an endlessly fascinating country called France is right outside the park's gates. Within a short drive are such remarkable sites as Chartres, and the *caves* of Champagne; and Paris is but 40 minutes away on the special RER rail line. For all of these sites, and more, we've included special mini-guides, plus some driving routes that offer the very best of this wonderful region.

In order to attract Europeans who may not have visited the Disney parks in the United States, the flavour is naturally very American, with the Magic Kingdom based closely on those in Anaheim (California) and Orlando (Florida). Main Street USA, for example, evokes the nostalgic atmosphere of a bygone era in a typical American town. Frontierland has the runaway mine train from Orlando's Big Thunder Mountain. Adventureland has a version of the ever-popular Pirates of the Caribbean ride, while Fantasyland would certainly not be complete without It's A Small World. And Discoveryland has imported the 3-D film *Captain EO*, starring Michael Jackson.

Visitors to Euro Disneyland will notice that there's a greater emphasis on those legends and fairytales that originated in Europe. Sleeping Beauty's turreted castle, for example, is based on illustrations from a medieval book, and it's known here as Le Château de la belle au bois dormant. Snow White shows a bit more of her Germanic roots, and Pinocchio has a distinctly Italian attitude.

Even the land itself has been altered, at great expense, to make a favourable impression. Disney have imported a quarter of a million trees to enhance what was previously flat farmland. Some things, though, even Disney can't control. The weather in this part of France is notoriously grey and damp, so what they have done is managed very successfully to put almost 90 per cent of the theme park under cover, from the awnings over Main Street to the enclosure of many of the rides and attractions.

When it came to the 12,000 'cast members', the art of compromise has been invoked. Disney's hitherto unbendable rules are very precise. Such things as ponytails, jeans and smoking are all strictly prohibited. In France, where bank clerks routinely show up for work in denim and chain-smoking is common these rules were tantamount to a cause for revolution. The contretemps over attire reached an impasse when the Disney organization tried to impose their standard dress code of pink lipstick and tan tights for women – this in a country where the national uniform is bright red lipstick and black stockings. French employees, however, were clever enough to point out that Minnie Mouse herself wears black stockings. In the end, Disney showed itself to be unusually flexible and gave in to the much-loved Chanel red lipstick and black tights on its female staff.

Still, certain rules simply cannot be broken, including Disney's traditional ban on the consumption of alcohol in the Magic Kingdom. Not to worry, though, you can get a drink in all the other park locales.

Miles of newsprint have been devoted to the subject of whether the French themselves will want to visit Euro Disneyland. In some ways, however, it really doesn't matter. There are 320 million Europeans within two hours flying time of Paris, and advance ticket sales indicate that people from other countries are counting the hours until they see the park. After all, they will get Paris as well. For all its concern about foreign cultural invasion and its anxiety over the spread of 'Franglais', France has bent over backwards to help welcome this huge American icon to the doorstep of its capital. Assuming Euro Disneyland succeeds (and who could doubt it), a second and even a third park are likely to be built by the end of this decade. The total investment could be a staggering $4.4 billion!

Beyond the complex schemes and big business deals, though, is the simple joy of entering into the world of Disney. The smiles of recognition at seeing a familiar fairy tale come to life, the pleasure of being at what must surely be the world's cleanest man-made attraction, ultimately win over even the most stone-hearted non-believer. So pack up the kids and the camera. There's fun ahead, and with this book in hand, you've got a companion to guide you to the very best of it all. What are you waiting for?

1
WHEN TO GO

The most obvious times to consider visiting Euro Disneyland are Christmas and Easter, as well as the weeks that comprise the traditional summer vacation period. There are, however, good reasons to avoid these times since most families travelling with children are expected to visit then and the projected crowds could make one-hour waits at attractions commonplace. On the other hand, there also are good reasons to visit during busy seasons, particularly in summer. The weather is perfectly suited to a Euro Disneyland tour, the park stays open late, and night-time entertainment – such as the Main Street Electrical Parade and Fantasia in the Sky fireworks – is presented each evening. There are advantages and disadvantages to any time of the year, so in the end the choice of when to go is a very personal one.

The first 1992 Paris-area school holidays are from 25 April through 10 May. Though known as the Easter holidays, they do *not* fall around the Easter weekend (which is 17 April through 20 April). 1, 8, and 28 May are all holidays and the French tend to *pont* or bridge their holidays which means that for the 28 May holiday, for example, everybody will take off the day after to create a four-day weekend. The 1992 French school summer holidays run from 8 July through 14 September. Since July, August, and September are the best months weatherwise, you have to weigh the pluses and minuses of crowds versus sunshine. June is usually very pleasant which makes it a good month for visitors without children in tow. Other school holidays include All Saints' from 25 October through 4 November; Armistice Day on 11 November; and the Christmas and New Year holidays from 20 December through 6 January. Also bear in mind that French state schools are closed all day Wednesday and private schools are closed on Wednesday afternoons.

What worries the Euro Disneyland planners the most is the weather: the Paris area can be

EURO DISNEYLAND WEATHER

	Temperatures (°C)			Rainfall	
	High	Low	Average	Rain (mm)	Days of rain
January	6.3	2.1	4.1	55	17
February	7.9	2.6	5.2	43	14
March	11	4.5	7.8	52	16
April	14.5	6.7	10.6	49	15
May	18.4	10.1	14.3	62	16
June	21.6	13.2	17.4	53	13
July	23.9	15.2	19.5	58	11
August	23.6	14.8	19.2	46	11
September	20.8	12.6	16.7	53	12
October	16	9.4	12.7	55	13
November	10.1	5.2	7.7	57	16
December	15.1	8.3	11.7	55	16

Note that in this chart the Days of rain column does not mean that it rains all day. It is fairly rare to have a full day of rain in the Paris area, though January, March, May, November, and December are the wettest months.

OPERATING HOURS

	Weekdays	Weekends
12–19 April	9 a.m.–7 p.m.	9 a.m.–midnight
20 April–10 May	9 a.m.–midnight	9 a.m.–midnight
11–27 May	9 a.m.–7 p.m. (until 9 p.m. Wednesdays)	9 a.m.–midnight
28 May–18 June	9 a.m.–9 p.m.	9 a.m.–9 p.m.
19 June–6 September	9 a.m.–midnight	9 a.m.–midnight
7 September–23 October	9 a.m.–9 p.m.	9 a.m.–9 p.m.
24 October–1 November	9 a.m.–midnight	9 a.m.–midnight
2 November–18 December	10 a.m.–6 p.m.	10 a.m.–7 p.m.
19 December–3 January	10 a.m.–10 p.m.	10 a.m.–midnight
4 January–2 April	10 a.m.–6 p.m.	10 a.m.–6 p.m.

These times are subject to change without notice.

cold and uncomfortable during the winter months, and there's the added problem of fog. But Disney has kept this in mind, and the resort's walkways, attractions, and many activities will be covered. Euro Disneyland Railroad trains will be heated, as will the steamboats. In winter, warm hats, scarves, and gloves are recommended and an umbrella is a good idea. In summer, a hat to protect against the sun is a must. And, at any time of year, wear comfortable shoes.

During the months of November, December, January, and February the sun sets at about 4.30 p.m. The early closing of the park at 6 p.m. or 7 p.m. means that after-dark attractions such as the Main Street Electrical Parade and the fireworks will not be presented. At Christmas time, however, even though the days are short and the weather cold, special Disney entertainment including parades, fireworks, and special Christmas meals will go on regardless of rain, sleet, or snow.

Special events at Euro Disneyland

January: New Year's Eve Celebration (31 December). Parties are held in all the hotels, and there's an extra-large fireworks display over Sleeping Beauty Castle. Festival Disney has special shows at the Bluegrass Saloon.

April: Easter Sunday (19 April). A promenade-style Easter parade makes this holiday celebration special.

July: Independence Day (4 July). A special parade and fireworks mark this US holiday.

November: Thanksgiving (26 November). Special meals are offered in all the restaurants.

December: Christmas (20 December–6 January). A large perfect Christmas tree is erected in Town Square. Main Street is decorated to the nines and patrolled by groups of carollers. A special parade and show also are staged.

Planning Ahead

Organizing a trip takes time, but almost every traveller finds that the increased enjoyment is well worth the effort. The fact is that planning can become the most pleasant sort of 'armchair' exercise and children will enjoy their visit to Euro Disneyland all the more if they are involved in the planning process.

WHEN TO GO

The best strategy in organizing a Euro Disneyland visit is to make a list of the attractions and activities you most want to see, and assemble all the options from the various sources listed in this guide. Putting these in some practical sequence is the first order of business, and the only additional risk lies in trying to see and do too much in too short a period of time. Assuming that most visitors also will want to visit Paris, then one should ideally allow a minimum of five days to see the city and three days for Euro Disneyland.

In general, good sense and normal human stamina dictate that a guest can count on visiting seven or eight attractions per day. That leaves time for shopping, the inevitable queues at some attractions, and unhurried meals. During less crowded seasons, it's possible to accomplish significantly more.

Sample Itineraries

Here are some schedules that should help you organize your visit and see as much as possible in the time allotted.

One-day visit: This short a stay can probably only be suggested for local residents and Parisians. Remember that locals will certainly choose Wednesdays for visits since schools are closed. However, if one day is all you have, then study all available material in advance so that you're as familiar as possible with your destination's layout and offerings. Be sure to arrive early and move quickly while you're there.

On entering the park, you will be on Main Street USA. It's a good idea to wander down the street noting the attractions in which you might be interested, and then plan a serious visit to Main Street before leaving – perhaps after having enjoyed the 3 p.m. Main Street Parade. The best way for first-timers to get an orientation is to hop aboard the Euro Disneyland Railroad for a grand circle around the park. The train goes through the Grand Canyon Diorama, past Frontierland and the Rivers of the Far West, Adventureland, Fantasyland, and through Discoveryland. Having circled the park, perhaps the most evocative land to see first is Fantasyland. It draws from childhood fairy tales and legends, stories and songs which represent the heritage of many European nations and those which Walt Disney turned into some of his most famous animated films.

From Sleeping Beauty Castle, head for Snow White's Adventures, Pinocchio's Daring Journey, Peter Pan's Flight, and Alice's Curious Labyrinth. Young children will particularly enjoy It's A Small World, Lancelot's Carousel, and Dumbo, The Flying Elephant. The Mad Hatter's Tea Cups are for visitors with strong constitutions (and stomachs!). Have a bite to eat in one of the Fantasyland restaurants or fast-food spots, then head for Adventureland and see Pirates of the Caribbean – a well-tested and beloved favourite at Disney's United States parks. See Adventure Isle and the Swiss Family Robinson Treehouse. Then it's on to Big Thunder Mountain Railroad, a rollicking roller-coaster ride through gold mines. Phantom Manor may be too scary for younger children but it's a must for everyone else. After Phantom Manor, go for a ride on one of the Indian Canoes or the River Rogue Keelboats or hop aboard the *Mark Twain* or *Molly Brown* for a peaceful trip along the Rivers of the Far West.

Next stop is Discoveryland where Star Tours awaits to take guests on a ride through space aboard a flight simulator. The effects are nothing short of spectacular; they might be too frightening for small children, but teenagers will be enthralled. Then see 'From Time to Time', a beautiful CircleVision 360 film and 'Captain EO', a 3-D spectacular starring Michael Jackson. Kids and adults will enjoy driving at Autopia and teens will most enjoy a visit to Videopolis. At Orbitron, guests pilot their own flying machines through space.

At around 2.30 p.m., head back to Main Street USA and look around in the shops. Children will especially enjoy the arcade. Grab a space to watch the 3 p.m. parade. After the parade go back to where you left off and complete the circuit through the lands. At the end of the day visit Festival Disney and enjoy a meal and a show. Try Buffalo Bill's Wild West Show. There are two seatings each day at 5.30 p.m. and 8.30 p.m. in a 1,000-seat arena.

During the summer and busy seasons when the park is open late, it is possible to return to the Magic Kingdom after dinner and take in the Main Street Electrical Parade and the Fantasia in the Sky fireworks. After the pyrotechnics, visitors with energy can head to Festival Disney for some late-night dancing and entertainment.

Two-day, three-night visit: This is probably the minimum length of stay to be able to enjoy everything available at Euro Disneyland. There is ample time to visit each attraction and then return to your favourites for a second look. The second go-round usually rewards guests with details missed on a first pass. Follow our guidelines for the one-day visit, but linger a bit longer to enjoy the shops and atmosphere. Have a leisurely lunch and then finish the circuit on your second day.

Three-day, four-night visit or longer: A stay of this duration will allow guests to really enjoy all the attractions at Euro Disneyland and actually relax, too. Apart from a day by the hotel pool (indoor or outdoor), there are many other sporting opportunities available including tennis, boating, bicycling, pony rides, ice skating (at the rink at the New York hotel), and, beginning in the autumn, golf.

Admission

There are several admission categories at Euro Disneyland. The following chart shows ticket prices for visitors travelling with an organized tour. Note that multiple-day Passports (as the tickets are called) do not need to be used on consecutive days. Additionally, those guests travelling with an organized tour are guaranteed admission to the Magic Kingdom even if it is full. The gates will close when 40,000 to 50,000 guests have entered.

1-day Passport   200ff adults/150ff children*
2-day Passport   342ff adults/256.50ff children
3-day Passport   450ff adults/337.50ff children
5-day Passport   500ff adults/375ff children

* 3 to 9 years of age

General admission prices for guests travelling without a tour are slightly higher. The price for a one-day Passport is 220ff for adults and 160ff for children. Multiple-day general admission prices were not available at press time. Access to Euro Disneyland hotels and Festival Disney is free.

How To Get There

Reservations for Euro Disneyland vacations can be made in a variety of ways. To reserve in writing contact: Euro Disneyland S.S.A., Central Reservations Office, BP 105, 94350 Villiers-sur-Marne, France (fax: 33-1-4930-7100 or 33-1-4930-7170; telex: 232-642 or 232-647). Callers from many countries can reach telephone operators speaking a variety of languages by dialling 33-1-4941 and the corresponding number listed below:

Austria	4995	Ireland	4915
Belgium*	4935	Italy	4930
Denmark	4920	Luxembourg	4905
Finland	4975	Netherlands	4980
France	4941	Norway	4950
Germany	4990	Portugal	4965
Spain	4960	Sweden	4970
Switzerland**	4925	United Kingdom	4910

*French and Flemish
**French and German

WHEN TO GO

In addition, Euro Disney Vacances S.A., a wholly owned subsidiary of Euro Disney S.C.A., offers a full range of vacation packages to Euro Disneyland. The company is operating initially in the French market but will expand to other countries later this year. Euro Disney Vacances has produced a 24-page colour brochure which is available at travel agencies throughout France. Their holiday packages offer stays of two nights or more at one of the six hotels or the campground at Euro Disneyland. All packages include a passport for unlimited admission to the theme park for the duration of the stay. Guests who want to tour Paris as well can opt for packages that include accommodation, a rental car, and sightseeing excursions in Paris.

In the United Kingdom, the Paris Travel Service is distributing one million copies of an authorized Euro Disneyland Resort brochure to travel agencies. For information about these brochures contact the Paris Travel Service, Bridge House, Ware, Hertfordshire SG12 9DF (44-0-920-461000). P & O Ferries have the exclusive ferry rights from the United Kingdom and Ireland. There are Disney exhibitions on board the company's two superferries and eventually every ship in the fleet will carry a Euro Disneyland display.

Vingressor, Always, and Saga, SAS Leisur's tour operators, have the rights to market package tours throughout Scandinavia, including airfare. Euroway, a Malmo-based cruise company, offers Euro Disneyland package tours through 700 travel agencies in Finland, Sweden, and Norway.

Oad-Reizen, headquartered in the Netherlands, arranges motorcoach trips to Euro Disneyland lasting several days. They have already reserved 200 rooms per day for their customers in the resort's hotels. Oad-Reizen also has its own Euro Disneyland brochure.

Do you need a car?

If you plan to visit only Euro Disneyland then you certainly do not need a car. However, if during your stay you intend to take in the surrounding countryside and sites, then a car is essential. The Information Desks in each hotel, at Festival Disney, and on Main Street all offer tourist information about Paris and the areas immediately surrounding Euro Disneyland. (See our *Mini-Guide to Paris*, *En Route*, and *Within A Day's Drive* chapters for more details.) Reims and Epernay – Champagne country – are less than an hour to the northeast. Burgundy also is easily reachable to the southeast. Fontainebleau and its forest are just to the southwest of Euro Disneyland, also less than an hour away. See *Transportation and Accommodation* for information about car rentals and other forms of transport.

How to cut travel costs

Although vacations are not getting less expensive, forgoing periodic family getaways is no answer. If financial considerations are a primary concern, it's better to simply prune your vacation budget in three main areas.

Lodging: The chief rule of thumb is not to pay for more than you need. Budget chains such as Hotels Climat, Fimotel, and Novotel are all located near Euro Disneyland and can prove to be very economical though they do not offer many frills. *Gites* or *Chambres d'Hôtes* offer yet another option. Many are located in cosy farmhouses or private homes or even castles. Some of these rooms include an evening meal though it must be requested in advance. For information about Gites and Chambres d'Hôtes in the Euro Disneyland area contact: Tourism 77, Gites de France et de Seine et Marne, Maison Départmentale du Tourisme, BP 144, 77194 Dammaire-les-Lys, (phone: 33-1-64-37-19-36; fax: 33-1-64-37-34-93).

If swimming pools and other amenities matter, consider the non-budget chain establishments. Remember that cut-off ages (above which there is a charge for children sharing their parents' room) do vary. For example, in Novotels children up to the age of sixteen stay free when sharing their parents' room.

At Euro Disneyland there are two moderate-price hotels. The *Hotel Cheyenne* and the *Hotel Santa Fe* feature rooms that accommodate four and range in price from 550 ff to 750 ff depending on the season. These hotels offer the convenience of being right in the heart of things. Additionally, at *Camp Davy Crockett*, bungalows and trailers can be rented for 575 ff to 875 ff depending on the season. Camping spaces at this site are very reasonable at 270 ff year-round.

For additional listings of inexpensive lodging options see our *Transportation and Accommodation* chapter.

Transportation: Comparative shopping is vital. Consider transportation needs at your destination, then figure the total transportation cost. Calculate the cost of driving based on your car's mileage, current petrol prices, the distance you expect to cover, and the cost of accommodation en route, then figure out what you'll pay by bus, plane, or train. Don't forget to calculate the cost of getting to and from the airport or terminal and the cost of renting a car (if necessary).

Food: Eat hot meals in cafeterias instead of full-service restaurants. Visit more expensive establishments for a treat at lunchtime rather than dinner. In France, for example, most restaurants offer a set menu at lunchtime so there are no hidden costs to surprise diners at the end of a meal. Carry sandwich fixings and have lunches alfresco when possible. Look for lodging places with kitchen facilities: the savings on food, especially breakfast, may be more than the extra accommodation expense.

Helpful hints

Travelling can be hard work, but with a little know-how the way can be smoothed to make a vacation much more relaxing. Here are some hints for getting the most out of a Euro Disneyland vacation.

Hints for travelling with children

Once you tell children that a Euro Disneyland vacation is planned, the response is likely to be overwhelming. So it will take all your parental savvy to keep youngsters relatively calm until you arrive.

Planning: By far the best way to cope with excited youngsters is to allow them to participate in some part of the planning of the upcoming Euro Disneyland trip. Not only will it heighten their enjoyment once they arrive, but it will also provide visitors of all ages with a realistic sense of what to expect. Give each child a small part of the trip's preparations as his or her responsibility – choose what attractions to see in what order, where to have lunch each day, what other activities to include in your Parisian/Seine et Marne visit, etc. Just writing for brochures and pamphlets can be a very important job for a youngster and make him or her feel more a part of the general undertaking.

En route: Certain techniques can stave off children's tiresome 'Are-we-there-yets?' until you walk through the main gates. One ploy is to set up a series of intermediate goals to which they can look forward, if you're travelling by car. Younger children might anticipate getting to the bottom of a child-size (easy to open and close) suitcase stuffed with well-loved toys and games. Also be sure to pack snacks to quiet rumbling stomachs at those inconvenient times when there's not a decent restaurant in sight. Most important of all, plan for plenty of breaks along the way. All autoroutes have either cafeterias or snack shops and there are many stopping places off the road marked as *aires* where there are toilet and picnic facilities.

If you are flying, try to time your departure and return flights for off-peak hours and off-seasons, when chances are better that an empty seat or two will be available. Remember that newborn babies probably should not fly since their lungs may not be able to handle the altitude. Check with your doctor to be sure. Many airlines carry a large supply of books and games for children.

At the hotels and campsite: Some of the Euro Disneyland hotels offer in-room babysitting services. All the hotels have arcades, and children will particularly enjoy the *Cheyenne* where each room is fitted out with bunk beds. Children's menus are available at all the restaurants.

Inside Euro Disneyland: Having kids along is a hassle-free experience. And inside the park itself, the smiles that break out on the faces of the little ones as they greet Mickey, Minnie, and the other Disney characters, or steer a motorboat or a car, or gaze in wonder at all those moving dolls at It's A Small World will repay you a thousandfold for any fuss and bother en route.

Top attractions for kids: At Adventureland, kids will love Adventure Isle, the Swiss Family Robinson Treehouse, and Pirates of the Caribbean. Fantasyland is filled with attractions designed especially for kids. It's A Small World tops the list. There's Peter Pan's Flight, Snow White's Adventures, Sleeping Beauty Castle, Pinocchio's Daring Journey, Lancelot's Carousel, Dumbo, The Flying Elephant, Alice's Curious Labyrinth, and the Mad Hatter's Tea Cups. Frontierland's big attractions are Big Thunder Mountain Railroad and Phantom Manor, both of which will delight older youngsters and teens but may frighten children under the age of six or seven. Star Tours at Discoveryland is another thrilling ride recommended only for older children. Visitors of all ages will enjoy Captain EO, a 3-D musical starring Michael Jackson in a story of good versus evil. Another film worth catching is the CircleVision 360 From Time To Time. At Autopia, under-licence-age drivers can motor miniature racing cars over expressways and enter the Grand Prix. Park employees are able to give advice on the suitability of attractions for children. Don't hesitate to ask.

Strollers: These can be rented for 30ff plus a 20ff refundable deposit from the Stroller Shop on Main Street. If yours disappears while you're inside an attraction, just show your claim ticket and you will be given another. You may also take in your own stroller.

Baby care: Mother will be happy to know about the Baby Care Centre. It is adjacent to the *Plaza Gardens* restaurant on Main Street. For tots it has child-size flush toilets. In addition, there are changing tables, a limited selection of juices and baby foods for sale for a nominal fee, and facilities for warming bottles and food. A separate room with comfortable chairs is available for nursing mothers. The decor there (and in the rest of the Baby Centre) is soothing, and the hubbub of the rest of the park seems a million miles away. A stop for nappy changing constitutes a restful break for both parent and child alike, though changing tables are available in most ladies' rooms throughout the park as well. Disposable nappies and baby bottles also are sold at the Emporium on Main Street.

Lost children: If a child suddenly disappears or fails to show up on time, it's reassuring to know that Euro Disneyland's security force and all Euro Disneyland cast members are carefully trained to follow specific procedures with a lost child. The child is taken to Lost Children adjacent to Central First Aid at City Hall, where there are Disney movies and a variety of books to amuse lost youngsters. It should take no more than 20 minutes to locate a lost child. The security staff are equipped with walkie-talkies.

Hints for older travellers

The best advice for older visitors is to join a tour and let someone else worry about the details. Travel agents can help find one that best suits your interests. Inside the Magic Kingdom, group tours also are a good idea for older travellers. Three-hour guided walks are offered that cover the park and Festival Disney and the price (45ff) includes general admission to Euro Disneyland for the day, and then the run of the park until closing. Be sure to read all Euro Disneyland literature before leaving home so that the park's layout is somewhat familiar. In the park, don't be shy about asking for advice or directions from Euro Disneyland employees – they're happy to help out. Eat early or late to avoid mealtime crowds. Don't push yourself. Remember, too, that sightseeing takes energy and only healthy meals can provide it. Don't try to save money by scrimping on food. Prices for meals at Euro Disneyland are reasonable. One good tactic is to save Main Street's sights for late in the afternoon so that if you're early you can browse through the shops and attractions. Visitors who come in groups should allow plenty of time to return to their buses at the end of the day. After all, a lot of the fun of Euro Disneyland is just sitting on a bench and watching the people go by.

Lost adults: Travelling companions do occasionally get separated. If someone in your party disappears or fails to show up at an appointed meeting spot, head for Lost Children at City Hall near the *Plaza Gardens* restaurant. City Hall has a message book where members of a group can leave notes for each other during the day.

Hints for the handicapped

Probably the most effective means of assuring a smooth trip is plenty of advance planning.

At Euro Disneyland
A brochure is available at City Hall on Main Street which lists the many attractions, shops, and restaurants accessible to the disabled. Wheelchairs are available at the Stroller Shop on Main Street and cost 30ff plus a 20ff refundable deposit. All Euro Disneyland hotels offer rooms specially equipped for handicapped guests, as do most of the chain hotels in the area. Be sure to request one when making reservations. Guests arriving by car can park in a designated lot with easy wheelchair access.

Travelling by plane
Fortunately times have changed in the way that airlines deal with handicapped travellers. Vacationers are occasionally allowed to board aircraft in their own wheelchairs – provided the chair is narrow enough for the plane's aisles. More often, the passenger is transferred to a narrower airline chair at the loading gate and his or her own is packed away in the luggage compartment. Wheelchair passengers are helped on board before other passengers, and de-planed after everyone else. If you have a flight connection, it's especially important to notify airline personnel at the time you make your reservations of any special needs you may have. Note that airlines policies on motorized wheelchairs vary so check well in advance. Many European airlines now allow guide-dogs aboard the aircraft though some may require that the dog be muzzled. Canes and crutches, unless collapsible, must be stowed during takeoff and landing, but will be

returned to the passenger upon request during the flight. Again, let the carrier know in advance about your particular requirements.

Travelling by train
As when travelling by plane, it is important to give the French Railways (SNCF) advance warning if a disabled person is travelling within France. This can be done either when making reservations at least 48 hours in advance or at the station from which you are planning to depart. For general information regarding train travel for the handicapped call 33-1-3626-5050. The railway offers price reductions for both the handicapped traveller and a companion. The discounts vary according to the severity of the disability. You will be asked for an official document stating that you are handicapped and to what degree, in order to benefit from discounts.

For the hard of hearing: All train information is displayed on large panels at each station. Train number, destination, time of departure, stops, and platform or *quai* are clearly marked. Many Paris stations have two distinct sides – one for suburban trains marked 'Banlieue' and the other for main-line departures marked 'Grands Lignes'.

For blind travellers: There are rail employees on hand to assist blind travellers and the announcements are usually clear though they are in French only.

Remember that your ticket must be validated, or in French *composte*, which means that before going on to the platform you *must* put your ticket in a red or orange machine at the entrances to the station concourse and platforms. This is especially important since ticket collectors on board the trains can collect up to a 10% fine for unvalidated tickets.

On the TGV and Corail there are a number of spaces available for wheelchair-bound passengers who prefer to remain seated in their own chair. These are located next to the automatic doors and close to the specially equipped toilets. A transfer chair can also be provided.

Hints for single travellers

There's so much to see and do at Euro Disneyland that the park can be as enjoyable for solo travellers as it is for couples, families, and groups. College students may encounter peers all over the park as well. Since all the Euro Disneyland resort hotel rooms accommodate up to four guests – and are priced accordingly – staying outside the resort will probably prove more cost efficient. At Festival Disney, the bars and discos are perfect spots to meet other travellers as well as local men and women.

Other information

The Euro Disneyland Information Centres are located in City Hall on Main Street, at the Main Street Railroad Station, at the Frontierland Depot, and in Adventureland and Fantasyland.

Barbers and salons
A variety of services are offered at the salon at the *New York* hotel.

Alcohol
Euro Disneyland's Magic Kingdom is completely alcohol-free, a fact which many French find hard to appreciate. The hotels serve alcohol in bars and restaurants as do all the establishments at Festival Disney.

Lockers
Coin-operated lockers are available at the Main Street Station, located just beyond the turnstiles. The ready availability of these storage facilities makes it convenient to do your shopping in mid-afternoon when the stores are relatively empty and to stash your purchases before returning to the lands.

Lost and found

At any given time a survey of the shelves of Lost and Found at City Hall might turn up cameras, umbrellas, pushchairs, handbags, sunglasses, cigarette lighters, and lens caps. If you find an item while you're walking around the park, bring it to the Lost and Found. You'll be asked to fill out a card with your name and address; if the item isn't claimed by its owner within 90 days, you have the option of keeping it. Items not claimed by their finders are eventually sold to employees and the proceeds donated to charity. Don't despair if you've lost your favourite pair of sunglasses or bag of souvenirs: check the Lost and Found before leaving the park.

Mail

A post office is located at Festival Disney just alongside the train terminal. You can purchase postcards and stamps at the news stand, and postcards are for sale in gift shops all over the park. There are about 20 mailboxes in the park itself. Postcards and letters weighing up to 20 grams cost 2.50 ff within the European Community. Letters weighing 20 to 50 grams cost 4 ff. Letters and cards to the United States weighing up to 20 grams cost 3.40 ff; up to 50 grams cost 6 ff. Aerogrammes cost 4.50 ff. There are express services available as well. Note that all Euro Disneyland hotels offer faxing facilities.

Money

Cash, traveller's cheques, personal cheques, American Express, Visa, and MasterCard are accepted as payment for admission to Euro Disneyland, for merchandise purchased in shops, and for meals (except at food carts where only cash is accepted). Personal cheques must be imprinted with the guest's name and address and must be drawn on a French bank. Cheques must be accompanied by proper identification, such as a passport, an ID card with a photograph, or a driver's licence. There are foreign currency exchange machines on Main Street, at the Frontierland Depot, Adventureland, and Fantasyland. The customary maximum withdrawal is 1,800 ff per week per card. A currency exchange and an ATM (cash machine) are located at the post office at Festival Disney. Remember that French banking hours are generally 9.30 a.m. to 4.30 p.m. Mondays through Fridays.

Pets

With the exception of guide-dogs, no pets are allowed in the Magic Kingdom or in the resort's hotels. There is an Animal Care Centre where you may leave your pet during the day. The Animal Care Centre is located near the parking lot close to the main entrance. Blind travellers staying at Euro Disneyland hotels should be sure to alert the hotel at the time they make reservations.

Tipping

Euro Disneyland is not a place where bellmen stick out their hands even before they have put down your luggage. Instead they seem genuinely glad to help out. The standard 5 ff to 10 ff per bag is appropriate for lugging luggage. Check at each restaurant to see if service is included in the price of the meal. If it is not included, then a tip of 15% to 18% is considered appropriate in full-service establishments. Gratuities are not expected at fast-food restaurants. At the *New York* hotel salon, a tip of 15% is customary. Cab drivers in the surrounding area expect a 10% to 15% tip.

Weather

For detailed weather information on the same day, call 36-65-0277 for the Seine et Marne area and 36-65-0275 for Paris. For five-day weather information for the Paris and Ile de France area (where Euro Disneyland is situated) call 36-65-0000. Elsewhere in France call 36-65-0101.

WHEN TO GO

Helpful local information

The villages around Euro Disneyland have services and facilities that are easily accessible.

Car Repair
Ets Guillaumy, 22/25 Avenue Charles de Gaulle, Crecy-la-Chapelle (64-35-81-27). *Gregoire*, 18 Route de Paris, Villeneuve-le-Comte (60-04-27-07), offers 24-hour towing service for the Seine et Marne area.

Supermarkets
Intermarche, Crecy-la-Chapelle (64-36-96-22). It also offers a car wash and a 24-hour petrol station. *Franprix*, 43 Rue Général Leclerc, Esbly (60-04-31-55). Closed Monday mornings.

Butcher
Tradition Viande, 37 Rue d'Esbly, Coupvray (60-04-80-07). Closed Sunday and Mondays.

Delis
Carlier, 19 Rue Général Leclerc, Esbly (60-04-22-77). *Carlier*, 13 Rue de Paris, Coupvray (60-04-26-52). *J.P. Tissier*, 2 Avenue de la Mairie, Montry (60-04-22-01).

Bakery
B. Driot, 5 Rue St Denis, Coupvray (60-04-37-59).

Local markets
Visiting an indoor or outdoor French food market offers local colour and atmosphere. *Esbly* – Thursdays and Saturdays; indoor. *Meaux* – Tuesdays, Saturdays, and Sundays; outdoor. *Lagny* – Wednesdays, Friday, and Sundays; indoor. *Montry* – Tuesdays and Saturdays; outdoor. *Coulommiers* – Wednesdays and Sundays; outdoor.

Florist
2 Place de la Fontaine, *Villeneuve-le-Comte* (60-25-08-21).

Hospital
31 Avenue Général Leclerc, *Lagny* (64-30-70-70 or 64-30-68-68).

Pharmacy
Marie-Odile, Miral Aulnoy, Rue d'Esbly, Coupvray (64-63-16-76).

Doctors
Dr Michel Jaquet, 26 Rue de Lagny, Serris (60-01-21-21). The following specialists work at the Medical Centre, 6 bis Avenue Général de Gaulle, Esbly: *Ophthamologist* – Dr E. Bieder (60-04-60-80). *Ear, nose, and throat* – Dr G. Gaston (60-04-70-00). *Cardiologist* – Dr A. Shqueir (60-04-81-81). *Gynaecologist* – Dr R. Dupuy (60-04-61-49). *Dermatologist* – Dr J. J. Lemeur (60-04-67-00). *Paediatrician* – Dr P. Rangi (60-04-50-01). *Podiatrist/Chiropodist* – S. Benoist (60-04-50-40). *Physiotherapist* (60-04-47-98). *X-ray* (60-04-63-23).

Dentist
In *Esbly* – Dr L Courbe and Dr P Noublanche, 11 Rue du Général Leclerc (60-04-33-69). Dr J. P. Aubert, 10 Avenue Général de Gaulle (60-04-49-08). Dr P. Rosenzweig, 2 Rue Mlle Poulet (60-04-55-79). Dr C. Kalfon, 80 Rue du Général Leclerc (60-04-24-62).

2
TRANSPORTATION AND ACCOMMODATION

Euro Disneyland is situated about 20 miles (32 km) east of Paris. It is located just off the A4 highway from Paris to Nancy/Metz in Marne-la-Vallée which is actually a series of new towns in the department known as Seine et Marne. Seine et Marne is one of the eight departments which make up the Ile-de-France – that is Paris in the centre and seven departments encircling the city.

There are many ways to reach Euro Disneyland – by car, by train, by air – and this chapter describes the various means of transport and some tips on choosing the best route for your trip. This section covers rental cars, driving tips, train travel from Paris and within France, and air travel.

The second half of the chapter examines the many options for lodging, including the six hotels at Euro Disneyland itself and the Davy Crockett Campground (about 15 minutes from the park), and hotels and motels in nearby towns.

By car

From central Paris, head east to the A4 highway and follow the signs towards Nancy/Metz. Exit at Provins-Serris (D231) and follow the signs to Euro Disneyland. There is a parking lot with a capacity for 12,000 vehicles. You can also park at your hotel if you are staying within the Euro Disneyland Resort.

Rental cars

The major car rental companies in France have the same price structures (though drop-off charges do vary), and usually the best deal is a weekly rental with unlimited mileage. Many companies like Budget and Europcar (represented by National in the United States) have advantageous weekend rates, too. To rent a car in France, you need a licence and you must be at least 23 years old to rent the less expensive models and 25 years old to rent the costlier ones. Payment is made by credit card; some companies require a passport.

Europcar's main office is at 145 Avenue Malakoff, 75016 Paris (phone: 45-00-08-06). They have 15 branch offices around Paris, and one each at Orly and Charles de Gaulle Airports. Weekly rates are around 3,450 ff with unlimited mileage. Each additional day costs 400 ff.

Budget Rent-a-Car also is at the airports and has 21 offices in Paris. The advantage of using Budget is that there is no drop-off charge if you are leaving from a city other than the one at which you rented the car. Advance reservations are necessary and you must inform the agency of your plans. Budget's central reservations number in Paris is 46-86-65-65. They offer weekly rates of 1,495 ff with unlimited mileage.

Hertz has 17 locations within Paris, and an office at each of the capital's airports. Their

TRANSPORTATION AND ACCOMMODATION

main office is at 27 Place St Ferdinand, 75017 Paris (phone: 45-74-97-39 or 47-88-51-51 for central reservations). In order to benefit from the discounted weekly rental, reserve at least two days in advance. Rates for a week are 2,200 ff with unlimited mileage.

Avis has 11 offices in Paris: at each airport and at the main railway stations. The central reservations number is 46-09-92-12. Weekly rates are 2,250 ff with unlimited mileage.

Paris and Euro Disneyland

Petrol

Essence ordinaire is about 5.50 ff per litre, although all but the least expensive cars require *Super*, which sells for about 5.90 ff per litre. The French have finally got around to lead-free (*sans plomb*) petrol which costs from 5.12 ff to 5.70 ff depending on where you buy it. Beware, the most expensive garages are on the motorways or autoroutes. Diesel is also sold and is sometimes known as *gasoil*.

Tolls

(*Péages*, in French) All autoroutes have tolls. Exact change lanes are clearly marked *Automatique*. The tolls usually range from 4 ff to 10 ff. Drivers without exact change should position themselves in a lane marked with a sign of a man in a hat. The toll-takers in these lanes also accept credit cards.

Driving Rules

Seatbelts are mandatory throughout Europe – in both the back seat (if the car is fitted with them) and the front seat. Children under 12 years of age must ride in the back seat. Speed limits are 130 km (80 mph) on the autoroutes; 100 km (60 mph) on major national highways – these are numbered with an N in front and the road signs are green. In towns the speed limit is 50 km (30 mph). Be aware of the French law which gives 'priority from the right'. This means that when you are driving on the main road, if a vehicle pulls out in front of you on your right, you must yield to that vehicle. The same law applies at roundabouts.

Car Trouble

On the autoroutes, telephones are placed at one-kilometre intervals. Just pick up the phone and you will automatically be put through to the nearest breakdown service station. On other roads, dial 17 from a public telephone to reach the police. They can advise you of the nearest garage.

Sample driving times

Boulogne or Calais to Paris...about 3 hours
Rouen to Paris ....about 2½ hours
Geneva to Paris..................about 5½ hours
Lyon to Paris ....about 4 hours

By air

Independent travellers who choose not to book package holidays can be assured that getting to Paris by air is very simple. (For details about package tours see *Getting Ready to Go*.) Every national airline flies to Roissy/Charles de Gaulle or Orly Sud airports. Orly is about 17 kilometres south of the centre of Paris, and Charles de Gaulle is about 25 kilometres to the north. Euro Disneyland lies to the east of Paris. A shuttle bus takes visitors straight to the site.

Air France flies to all European capitals and their internal airline, Air Inter, has a vast network within France, with practically every city linked to Paris. Air France offers *APEX* fares. These are the least expensive fares and require that reservations be made at least two weeks in advance with a Saturday night stay necessary. *Vols vacances* fares are slightly more expensive, and can be booked without advance reservation requirements but a Saturday night stay is still necessary. *Vols visites* also are economy-based fares with the same restrictions as *vols vacances*. These fares are slightly less expensive but are only offered on weekends. *Classe affaire*, also known as club class, is a full fare. The seating is marginally more comfortable and the food marginally better. There are no restrictions on these fares.

Air Inter operates about 300 flights per day, most of which are one-hour trips to and from

TRANSPORTATION AND ACCOMMODATION

Paris. They fly from Orly West terminal and also from Roissy/CDG. For reservations phone 45-39-25-25. There are various price categories for the same routes. For example, *Rouge* (red) fares are in effect during business hours and tariffs are accordingly higher. *Blanc* (white) and *Bleu* (blue) fares cover the weekends and evenings and are somewhat less expensive. There also are discounts for couples travelling together and children under 12 fly for half price.

By train

Euro Disneyland is now a stop on the Regional Express Métro Network (RER). The station is located at the main entrance to the park near

RER routes to Paris

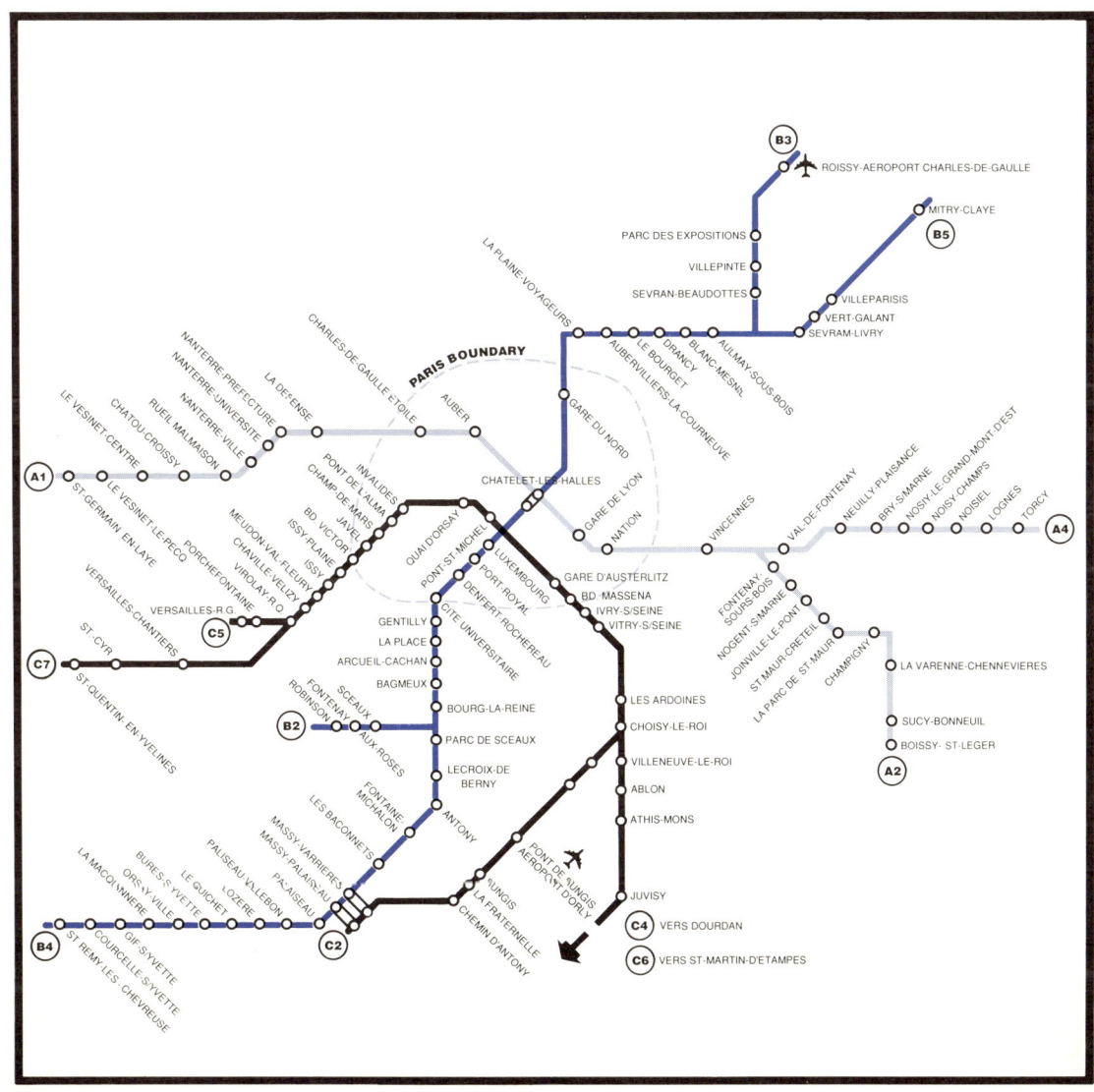

Festival Disney. These trains depart from Paris from the Etoile, Auber, Châtelet, and Nation stations. Travel time takes 45 minutes to an hour. In 1994, TGV (*Trés Grande Vitesse*) trains will stop at Euro Disneyland as well.

Trains in France are generally efficient, punctual, and clean. Residents of countries outside Europe and North Africa can purchase a Eurail Pass allowing them to travel all around Europe very inexpensively. Even without a pass, fares are fairly reasonable. For example, London to Paris (including sea crossing) is 590 ff for a first class ticket; 455 ff for second class. The Rome to Paris route is 882 ff in first class and 580 ff in second class. Madrid to Paris is 940 ff in first class and 635 ff in second class.

Visitors from Britain can benefit from the BritFrance Railpass. This pass is available for both first class and second class travel and can be used during any 5 days out of a 15-day period or any 10 days out of a one-month period. The cost for the 5-day pass is 1,600 ff in first class; 1,200 ff in economy. A 10-day pass costs 2,400 ff in first class; 1,800 ff in economy. Children ages 4 to 12 travel at half price and those under 4 years of age travel free. A France Railpass offers unlimited rail transportation throughout France in first class or second class for 4 days to be used within a 15-day period or 9 days to be used within a one-month period. Both types of passes also feature one day or two days of free bus and métro transport in Paris and free airport transfers via Orly and Roissy Rail. These passes also include discounts at some museums and tourist attractions. A 4-day pass costs 800 ff in first class; 600 ff in second class. The 9-day pass costs 1,345 ff in first class and 960 ff in second class.

French Railways (SNCF) offers first class or second class seating and couchettes or sleepers for night-time travel. Depending on the distance to be covered, trains feature either trolley service with drinks and sandwiches or restaurant cars. The TGV high-speed trains offer first class passengers meals at their seats. Reservations for seats and meals are required in advance. TGV trains are perfect for travellers without a lot of time. For example, the Paris to Lyon trip takes just two hours to and from the centre of each city. It takes over four hours to drive the distance, and by air, allowing an hour at either end for transport in and out of town, the trip takes about three hours. The trains are modern, comfortable, punctual, and, especially for first-timers, great fun.

The France Rail and Drive Pass, as its name suggests, includes rail travel and car rental. A 7-day pass provides 4 days unlimited train travel within a 15-day period, plus 3 days with an Avis car (least expensive models). The 15-day programme offers 9 days of train travel and 6 days with a rental car during a one-month period. The cost of a 7-day pass is 1,080 ff in first class and 900 ff in second class. The 15-day pass costs 1,800 ff in first class and 1,500 ff in second class. These prices are based on two people travelling together.

Accommodation

The six hotels that comprise the Euro Disneyland Resort were designed by American and French architects as themed attractions in and of themselves. Visitors familiar with Walt Disney World hotels in Orlando, Florida will find a similar feeling at Euro Disneyland. Some of the hotels were, in fact, designed by the same architects who worked their magic in the United States.

Each hotel's theme is reminiscent of a particular region of the US, ranging from Pueblo Indian cliff dwellings to New York City skyscrapers. There are nightclubs, theatres, indoor and outdoor swimming pools, a golf course, tennis courts, an ice skating rink, lakes for swimming and boating, bike trails, nature walks, a convention centre, a wooded camp-

TRANSPORTATION AND ACCOMMODATION

ground, and an entertainment centre called Festival Disney.

Additional convention facilities, single-family housing, other theme parks, including the Disney-MGM Studio Europe (opening in 1995), and more hotels are part of the master plan for Euro Disneyland that extends until the year 2017!

Five of the resort's hotels are situated around Lake Buena Vista. The sixth, and most elegant, the *Disneyland* hotel, provides a grand entrance overlooking the entire Euro Disneyland park. The hotels are equipped with central air conditioning and heating (except for the *Cheyenne* and *Santa Fe* where there are ceiling fans instead of air conditioning), direct dial telephones, electronic key access, a mini-bar, remote-control colour television sets with closed circuit movies and international channels, sprinkler and smoke detection systems, coin-operated guest laundries, and complimentary parking and transport within the resort. The luxury and first class hotels offer additional amenities including room service, in-room babysitting, and health clubs.

The hotel bathrooms tend to be small, particularly by European standards, and (as in the States) the toilets are not separate from the main bathroom. Most of the rooms have two double beds and can sleep four people. King-size beds are available at the *Disneyland* and *New York* hotels. The *Cheyenne* features rooms with one double bed and one set of bunk beds.

> **Cheers!** Despite the Magic Kingdom's no-alcohol policy, all the restaurants in the resort serve alcohol and there are many pleasant lounges and bars at which guests can enjoy beer, wine, cocktails, and speciality drinks.

Seasonal Calendar

High season is 12 April 1992 – 31 October 1992 and 18 December 1992 – 2 January 1993. Mid-season covers all weekends from 1 November 1992 – 17 December 1992 and all weekdays from 3 January 1993 – 10 April 1993. Low season covers all weekdays from 1 November 1992 – 17 December 1992, and all weekends from 3 January 1993 – 15 April 1993. Note that weekends are defined as Friday and Saturday nights only. Sunday nights are considered weeknights.

All rates are effective as of opening day, 12 April 1992. All Euro Disneyland rates are quoted in French francs and include room tax. Euro Disneyland rates apply to a family of up to four people per room. Credit cards are accepted as payment at all the hotels. Prices are subject to change without notice.

Disneyland

Situated astride the entrance to Euro Disneyland, the five-storey, 500-room luxury-class *Disneyland* hotel is evocative of America's grand hotels of the nineteenth century that brought travellers to places like Palm Beach, Florida and Coronado, California. There is one main building and two wings. Red-roofed turrets and wood-panelled walls dominate the architecture and bring to mind the Grand Floridian hotel at Walt Disney World in Orlando.

Guests are greeted by liveried doormen beneath a portico at the east end of the hotel. Inside, the lobby of marble and gold is rich with Victorian furnishings. Plush rugs in Oriental designs span the hallways; tasselled drapes, bevelled mirrors, and filigreed picture frames carry the theme in lounges and public rooms. The Victoriana, however, does not overpower: the spaces are light and airy, and the views over the theme park are spectacular.

The hotel offers in-room babysitting service; a coin-operated guest laundry; ice machines on every floor; an Information Desk offering Euro Disneyland tickets, restaurant and show reservations, and travel information about Paris and the surrounding areas; same-day laundry and dry cleaning service; 24-hour room service; shoeshine; turndown service; and complimentary valet parking.

The *Disneyland* hotel features 50 'Castle Club' rooms on designated floors. Each of these rooms overlooks Main Street USA, is somewhat larger than the hotel's standard rooms, and Castle Club guests have a private lounge where complimentary continental breakfast, beverages, and snacks are served; separate check-in and check-out desks; a concierge and free shoeshine service.

Rooms

The 500 guestrooms are decorated in soft pastels, with light wood furniture. The bathrooms have two sinks; in most cases they are just outside the bathroom. Most of the rooms have two double beds though some king-size beds are available. There also are 21 suites. Eleven rooms are specially equipped for disabled guests and some rooms are designated for non-smokers.

Rates

Room rates vary according to season and view. Standard rooms with park views cost 2,100 ff in high season and 1,400 in low season. Rooms without a Euro Disneyland view run 1,950 ff in high season and 1,300 ff during low season. Castle Club rooms are 2,750 ff.

Where to eat and drink

There are three restaurants at the *Disneyland* hotel offering a variety of dining options, and there is a lounge with a great view of Main Street USA.

California Grill: A casual but elegant setting in a light and airy environment. The menu changes seasonally. There is a private dining room for up to 12 people. The restaurant seats 170 diners and is open from noon to 3 p.m. for lunch and from 6 p.m. to midnight for dinner.

Inventions: A buffet restaurant offering an assortment of American regional specialities. A 'character breakfast', where guests have the opportunity to mingle with favourite Disney characters, is held here each morning. The restaurant seats 190 people and is open from 7 a.m. to 11 p.m.

Café Fantasia: A themed café that overlooks Disney Square. Its decor was inspired by the Disney film *Fantasia*. There is seating for 80; the café is open from 11 a.m. to 1 a.m.

Main Street Lounge: Speciality cocktails, wine, beer, and soft drinks are served at this spot overlooking Main Street USA. The lounge seats 80 and is open from 11 a.m. to 1 a.m.

What to do

A host of activities are available.

Swimming: A heated indoor swimming pool is located at the Disneyland Pool and Club.

Fitness: The Disneyland Pool and Club features aerobics classes, Nautilus exercise equipment, a Jacuzzi, sauna, steamroom, solarium, massage, and a snack bar.

Gamesroom: An arcade filled with a selection of popular electronic games.

Shopping: Galerie Mickey spotlights Disney memorabilia, merchandise with American logos, and giftware. Newspapers, books, and sundries also are available. Like the rest of the Euro Disneyland hotel shops, this one has an

TRANSPORTATION AND ACCOMMODATION

in-store display of animated characters in a setting appropriate to the theme of the hotel.

Transport

Euro Disneyland is just a few steps away. Free bus transport is available to the other hotels and recreational facilities.

New York

The hotel's eight-storey Manhattan Tower rises as the centrepiece of the resort area. Flanked by two guestroom wings, this 574-room luxury hotel and convention centre offers guests the essence of the Big Apple from Rockefeller Centre to Greenwich Village. The tower overlooks Lake Buena Vista and rooms offer exceptional views of the surrounding countryside. One of the wings is designed to resemble a large brownstone, the other to look like Gramercy Park row houses. At the rear of the complex is an ice skating rink (in winter) and reflecting pool. This hotel was designed by Michael Graves who is best known in Disney circles for his distinctive Swan and Dolphin hotels at Walt Disney World.

The hotel offers in-room babysitting service, a beauty salon and barber shop, a coin-operated guest laundry, ice machines on every floor, an Information Desk, same-day dry cleaning and laundry service, 24-hour room service, and free shoeshine. The *New York* features 130 Castle Club rooms which are larger than the standard guestrooms and have upgraded amenities. Castle Club guests enjoy a private lounge where a complimentary continental breakfast, snacks, and beverages are served.

Adjoining the hotel on the south side is the New York Coliseum Convention Centre, a state-of-the-art meeting facility themed to reflect a Wall Street business environment. The Grand Ballroom offers 1,600 square metres of column-free meeting space. It seats 2,000 theatre-style and 1,300 classroom-style. The modular design allows the ballroom to be divided into 12 sections. The Radio City Ballroom seats 500 theatre-style and 350 classroom-style. Banquets and dinner dances can be held in each ballroom. There also are four hospitality suites – the Wall Street, Columbus Avenue, Madison Avenue, and Park Avenue.

Communications services, television connections, video conferencing, satellite transmission, computer terminals, office equipment, multilingual secretarial services, a mezzanine with 16 projection booths, and translation booths are also offered.

Rooms

The 574 guestrooms are decorated in an Art Deco theme with contemporary customized furnishings. There is a blue-and-rust colour scheme, and artful touches include table lamps in the shape of skyscrapers. Most rooms have two double beds, though some king-size beds are available. All rooms feature a telephone in the bathroom, a hair dryer, a make-up mirror and a mini-bar. There are 13 rooms specially equipped for handicapped guests and designated non-smoking rooms are available. There are 36 suites scattered among the hotel's three buildings.

Rates

Lakeview rooms are 1,750 ff in high season, 1,450 ff during mid-season, and 1,200 ff during low season. Other rooms range from 1,600 ff in high season to 1,100 ff during low season.

Where to eat and drink

Two restaurants and two lounges evoke the atmosphere and taste of Manhattan.

Rainbow Room: A 1930s New York City dinner dance atmosphere is re-created in this restaurant which features live Big Band entertainment. A character breakfast (with Pluto, Goofy, Mickey, et al.) is served daily. The restaurant seats 200 diners and is open from 7 a.m. to 10 a.m. for breakfast; for 6 p.m. to 11 p.m. for dinner; and from 11 p.m. to 1 a.m. for late-night supper.

Park Side Diner: An all-day dining menu plus pleasant piano music makes this a perfect stop at any time. There are 200 seats; the diner is open from 7 a.m. to 11 p.m.

Rainbow Lounge: Adjoining the Rainbow Room, cocktails and after-dinner drinks are served. There are 60 seats. Open from 5 p.m. to 2 a.m.

57th Street Bar: Overlooking Lake Buena Vista, this 55-seat lounge also is open for continental breakfast from 7 a.m. to 10 a.m. Open for cocktails until 1 a.m.

What to do

There are many activities and sporting options.

Swimming: An indoor-outdoor swimming pool is located in the hotel's health club.

Fitness: The health club also features aerobics classes, Nautilus equipment, a Jacuzzi, sauna, solarium, steamroom, plus the pool and a snack bar.

Shopping: The Stock Exchange offers Disney merchandise and Big Apple logo items. Newspapers, books, cigarettes, and sundries also are sold. There is a window display of animated Disney characters in a New York setting.

Gamesroom: An arcade keeps youngsters mesmerized with the latest electronic games.

Ice Skating: Skate on the Rockefeller Centre rink during the winter months.

Tennis: There are 2 hard-surface tennis courts.

Transport

Euro Disneyland is just a short walk away. Free bus transport is provided to other areas of the resort.

Newport Bay Club

New York architect Robert Stern, who designed the Yacht and Beach Clubs at Walt Disney World, has similarly taken the New England seashore of the late 1800s and plopped it down across the Atlantic. The 1,083-room resort sits on the western shore of Lake Buena Vista directly across from the *New York* hotel. A large verandah, complete with rocking chairs, is a pleasant place to pass some time (in the warmer months) and there is also a lakeside promenade that's ideal for strolling. This first-class hotel features in-room baby-sitting service, a coin-operated guest laundry, an Information Desk, and room service. The *Newport* also has a small convention facility. The nautically-themed centre offers 230 square metres of space plus four function rooms that can accommodate private dinners, meetings, and receptions. Computer and office equipment, multilingual secretarial services, and a private desk for group check-in are among the other convention services offered.

Rooms

The guestrooms and suites feature a nautical design in white and blue with splashes of red. Most rooms have two double beds and some king-size beds are available. Extra in-room amenities include a hair dryer and a mini-bar. There are 23 rooms specially designed for disabled guests and designated non-smoking rooms are available.

Rates

Lakeview rooms are 1,250 ff during high season and 850 ff during low season. Other rooms run 1,100 ff in high season, 750 ff in low season.

Where to eat

The New England nautical theme is accented in the hotel's three restaurants.

Cape Cod: An American menu emphasizing natural farm products and fresh seafood is offered in a casual garden setting. There is seating for 320 diners and the restaurant is open from 7 a.m. to 11 p.m.

Yacht Club: Shellfish is the speciality at this restaurant with an open kitchen showcasing New England clambakes. The club seats 120 guests and is open for breakfast from 7 a.m. to 10 a.m. and for dinner from 6 p.m. to midnight.

Fisherman's Wharf: A cruise ship setting for 100 people with live piano music and wonderful lake views. Breakfast is served from 7 a.m. to 10 a.m. and cocktails are served until 1 a.m.

What to do

A variety of activities keep guests busy when they're not in the theme park.

Swimming: A glass-enclosed heated indoor pool plus an outdoor pool make swimming a year-round activity.

Fitness: A health club features aerobics, Nautilus equipment, a Jacuzzi, sauna, solarium, and steamroom.

Gamesroom: The arcade features a fine selection of video games.

Croquet: For a true taste of New England, pick up a mallet and head for the lawn.

Shopping: The Bay Boutique offers Disney merchandise and nautically-themed clothing and gift items. Books, newspapers, and sundries are sold. There is a delightful display of animated characters in a New England setting.

Children's playground: An entertaining array of slides, swings, and climbing apparatus can keep kids occupied for hours.

Transport

While it is possible to walk to Euro Disneyland, many guests may prefer to hop on a free bus to the park. Transport also is provided to other parts of the resort.

Sequoia Lodge

From the giant redwood country of America's Pacific Northwest comes the inspiration for this first-class hotel on the east shore of Lake Buena Vista between the *New York* and *Newport Bay* hotels. The rustic design is carried through in stone and wood. There is one large central building plus five smaller guest lodges housing the 1,011 rooms. A sixth building is home to an indoor-outdoor swimming pool and health club. Large conifers shade the walkways between the buildings giving the hotel the feel of a United States national park. The hotel offers in-room babysitting service, a coin-operated guest laundry, an Information Desk, and room service.

There are two meeting rooms, the Buffalo and the Coyote, available for small gatherings. Computers and business services are available.

Rooms

The guestrooms have a hunting lodge theme with dark wood furniture in a rustic setting.

There are either two double beds or two queen-size beds covered in colourful patchwork quilts. The colour scheme is carried through to the bathrooms, where an added advantage is that the sink is separate from the main bathroom. Each room has a hair dryer and a mini-bar. There are 21 rooms equipped for disabled guests and designated non-smoking rooms are available.

Rates

Lakeview rooms are 1,250 ff during high season and 850 ff in low season. Other rooms are 1,100 ff in high season and 750 ff in low season.

Where to eat and drink

A US national park theme is carried into the *Sequoia*'s eating and drinking spots.

Hunter's Grill: An open kitchen with a rotisserie features a selection of marinated meat and poultry. There is room for 325 guests and the restaurant is open from 7 a.m. to 10 a.m. for breakfast and from 6 p.m. to midnight for dinner.

Beaver Creek Tavern: An American barbecue menu featuring chicken, beef, and ribs as specialities. There are 125 seats and the hours are 7 a.m. to 10 a.m. for breakfast and until 10 p.m. for all-day dining.

Redwood Bar and Lounge: A lobby bar with a cosy fireplace features live piano music. Continental breakfast is served from 7 a.m. to 10 a.m. and cocktails are served until 1 a.m. There are 180 seats.

What to do

There are many activities to pursue.

Swimming: An indoor-outdoor pool is situated in a lushly landscaped setting.

Fitness: The hotel's well-equipped health club offers aerobics classes, Nautilus equipment, a Jacuzzi, solarium, steamroom, and sauna.

Gamesroom: The latest in electronic fun and games set in an arcade.

Children's Playground: An inventive area for kids to explore.

Transport

The hotel is within walking distance of Euro Disneyland. Free buses shuttle guests to other areas of the resort.

Santa Fe

New Mexico's Painted Desert and vintage movies about the Santa Fe Trail have inspired the design of this moderately priced, 1,000-room hotel (scheduled to open in July) located on the right bank of the Rio Grande. Stacked like adobe dwellings on the side of a sandstone cliff, 42 lodge-like buildings are painted in muted colours typical of the Southwestern desert landscape. Beams extend from the corners of each lodge. Architect Antoine Predock, known for his interpretation of Southwestern American architecture, has designed the hotel with four trails leading from the main lodge building to the guestroom buildings. Desert flora and props add to the Southwestern theme along the trails. There are, however, a couple of curious items here: an errant flying saucer and a smouldering volcano – neither of which is native to the American Southwest – are among the sights, and although we're not sure what they are doing there, if nothing else, they should serve as conversation pieces.

A large drive-in movie screen sits atop the main building. (Again, we're not sure why.) The public areas are centrally air conditioned, although the guestrooms are not. There is a

TRANSPORTATION AND ACCOMMODATION

coin-operated guest laundry, an Information Desk, complimentary parking, and luggage and bellman service.

Rooms

The 1,000 rooms all feature two queen-size beds and are decorated in a colourful Southwestern motif. Each room has a ceiling fan to compensate for the lack of air conditioning. There are 21 rooms specially equipped for disabled guests. Designated non-smoking rooms are available.

Rates

All rooms are 750 ff in high season and 550 ff during low season, regardless of location.

Where to eat and drink

Southwestern and Mexican influences accent the hotel's dining facilities.

La Cantina: Designed to resemble a New Mexico market, this food court features a variety of American and Tex-Mex specialities. Large enough to seat 325 diners. It's open from 7 a.m. to 11 p.m.

Rio Grande Bar: Speciality drinks, beer, wine, and soft drinks are offered in this lounge that features live entertainment. It seats 125 and is open from 11 a.m. to 1 a.m.

What to do

Children will especially appreciate the *Santa Fe*'s activities.

Children's playground: The Totem Circle features a variety of unique slides and climbing devices.

Gamesroom: The usual selection of video games can be found in the Pow Wow room.

Shopping: The Trading Post features Disney items and a line of merchandise with a New Mexico theme. Books, magazines, and sundries are sold. There is a window display of animated characters in a Southwest setting.

Transport

There is pedestrian access (about a five-minute walk) to the theme park as well as a free shuttle bus.

Cheyenne

Across the Rio Grande from the *Sante Fe*, this moderately priced, 1,000-room hotel evokes an Old West theme. The 14 brightly painted, wood-sided storefronts that house the guestrooms could have come straight from the set of a John Wayne movie. The imaginative design – inside and out – should delight young and old cowboy fans. Like the *Santa Fe*, only the public areas are centrally air conditioned. There is a coin-operated guest laundry, an Information Desk, bellman service, and complimentary parking.

Rooms

This hotel is best suited for families since there is a double bed and bunk beds (kids will love them) in each room. The beds are covered in gaily coloured quilts and the room lamp is in the shape of a riding boot. Every room has a ceiling fan which helps keep things comfortable during the warmer months. There are 21 rooms specially designed for handicapped guests and non-smoking rooms are available.

Rates

All rooms cost 750 ff during high season and 550 ff in low season.

Where to eat and drink

The Wild West is evident at the food court and lounge.

Chuckwagon Café: A group of counter-service restaurants feature barbecue specialities and hickory-flavoured smoked meats and poultry, just like those served along old western trails. Breakfast is also served at food stands. The seating area accommodates 325 guests. Open from 7 a.m. to 11 p.m.

Red Garter Saloon: An authentically re-created western saloon complete with live music. Drinks and light snacks are offered. Open from 11 a.m. to 1 p.m.

What to do

A unique playground hightlights the *Cheyenne*'s activities.

Frontier Fort: Actually a log fort, this playground has a look-out tower, a teepee village, and a covered wagon.

Gamesroom: An arcade features a selection of video games.

Shopping: The General Store sells Disney merchandise and western-themed clothing and giftware. Books, newspapers, and sundries also are sold. An animated character display decorates the shop's windows.

Transport

Euro Disneyland is accessible on foot (about a five-minute walk) or via complimentary buses.

Camp Davy Crockett

For those who love the great outdoors combined with the comforts of home, this 56-acre, wooded camping area – about a 15-minute drive from Euro Disneyland – is the place of choice. *Camp Davy Crockett* guests have two options available: to sleep in a log cabin or pitch a tent or campervan.

There are 414 log cabins which are fully equipped with kitchenettes, bathrooms, central heating, direct-dial telephone, daily maid service, and colour television sets. The kitchens feature a refrigerator, a microwave oven, an electric cooker, a toaster, and a coffeemaker. The cabins accommodate up to six people with one queen-sized bed, two bunk beds, and a hideaway double bed. A picnic area and a barbecue grill are right outside each cabin.

The second option is to pitch a tent or park a campervan at one of the 181 campsites. Each site has water, sewer, and electrical points, and the grounds are maintained daily. Campers have access to bathrooms with showers, toilets, vending machines, a coin-operated guest laundry, and baby changing facilities. There also is an Information Desk where Euro Disneyland tickets can be purchased and reservations made for restaurants and shows. Other travel information also is available.

Rates

Cabins are 875 ff during high season and 525 ff in low season. Campsites cost 270 ff year-round.

Where to eat and drink

When you're tired of cooking 'at home' you can head out for breakfast, lunch, or dinner.

Crockett's Tavern: A self-service restaurant featuring American home-style cooking. There also is a bar and a lounge. The tavern is open from 7 a.m. to 11 p.m. and can seat 120.

TRANSPORTATION AND ACCOMMODATION

What to do

An enormous range of activities should keep 'campers' (i.e. guests) happy here.

Swimming: An indoor water park and swimming pool features water slides, raft rides, a waterfall, a children's pool, a spa, a sun-tanning area, and a snack bar.

Bicycling: A variety of models are available for rent at the Camp Davy Crockett Bike Barn. (Golf carts also may be rented here.) Designated trails for cyclists abound.

Children's playgrounds: Kids' swings and slides are set up in several locations on the wooded property.

Gamesroom: An arcade houses a selection of electronic games.

Jogging: Several marked trails wind through this wooded campsite.

Nature trails: Self-guided nature walks give visitors an education about their environment.

Pony rides: Eight ponies call the Camp Davy Crockett Farm home. Other animals live here and welcome visitors who want a closer look.

Tennis: Two outdoor tennis courts are available on a first-come, first-served basis.

Basketball, volleyball, soccer, pétanque: Courts and fields for these games are all part of the camp complex.

Campfire programme: An evening by the campfire with music and marshmallows is featured nightly during the summer.

Shopping: The Alamo Trading Post features Disney merchandise as well as Davy Crockett logo items. Groceries and barbecue essentials also are stocked.

Transport

Four bus stops are scattered among the cabins and campsites. The buses are free and make the trip to Euro Disneyland in about 15 minutes. Guests also can drive their own cars and park in the main Euro Disneyland lot.

Off-site hotels

Numerous hotels surround the Euro Disneyland property. The following section first lists hotels that are members of major hotel chains. The next listing is of independent establishments in the Euro Disneyland area. The third section offers low-cost accommodation options near the theme park.

Climat hotels, Novotels, Ibis, and Fimotels are all modern and clean. They have their own restaurants, offer special discounts for children, and have their own parking lots. Some offer weekend discounts and many offer car rental deals as well. Note: Room rates at these hotels may increase by 5% during 1992.

Climat hotels

(Central Reservations phone: 33-1-64-46-01-23)

- Chelles; Route Claye 77500 (phone: 60-08-75-58). Off the A4 Lagny exit and about 18 kilometres to Chelles. 43 rooms. 310 ff.
- La Queue-en-Brie; Carrefour de Pincevent 94510 (phone: 45-94-61-61). Off the A4 Champigny exit. Then take the N14 to Sézanne. 56 rooms. 270 ff.
- Marne-la-Vallée Emerainville; 1 Rue d'Emery 77184 (phone: 60-06-38-34). Off the A4 Val Maubée exit. 37 rooms. 295 ff to 310 ff.
- Meaux; 32 Avenue de la Victoire 77100 (phone: 64-33-15-47). Take N36 off the A4

through Meaux towards Châlons-sur-Marne. 60 rooms. 250 ff.
- Melun; 338 Rue Raymond Hervillard 77000 (phone: 64-52-71-81). Via N6 or N105 off the A4. 42 rooms. 265 ff.
- Moisy-le-Grand; 5 Rue du Ballon 93160 (phone: 43-05-22-99). Off the A4 Champs exit. 51 rooms. 295 ff.
- Noisel; 3 Place Gaston Deferre 77186 (phone: 60-06-15-40). Off the A4 Val Maubée exit. 56 rooms. 300 ff.

Novotels

(Central Reservations phone: 33-1-60-77-27-27)
- Créteil-le-Lac; Route de Choisy RN 186 9400 (phone: 42-07-91-02). Take N86 off A4. About 5 kilometres from Porte de Bercy. 110 rooms; swimming pool. 435 ff to 475 ff.
- Fontainebleau/Ury; RN 152 77116 (phone: 64-24-48-25). South of Fontainebleau near A6 motorway. 127 rooms; Swimming pool, tennis. 440 ff to 495 ff.
- Marne-la-Vallée/Atria; Noisy Mont Est Rue de Centre; (phone: Central Reservations above). Off A4 Noisy-le-Grand exit. 143 rooms. 440 ff to 475 ff.
- Marne-la-Vallée/Collégien; Z1 les Portes de la Forêt 77090 (phone: 64-80-53-53). Off A4 Lagny exit. 126 rooms. 460 ff to 490 ff.

Ibis hotels

(Central Reservations phone: 33-1-40-25-50-50)
- Fontainebleau; 18 Rue de Ferrare 77300 (phone: 64-23-45-25). In the centre of town. 81 rooms. 300 ff to 325 ff.
- Marne-la-Vallée/Noisy; Maille Horizon 1 93167 (phone: Central Reservations above). Off A4 Noisy exit. 161 rooms. 300 ff.
- Melun; 81 Avenue de Meaux 77700 (phone: 60-68-42-45). Off N6. 74 rooms. 270 ff to 290 ff.
- Provins; Lieu dit Les Palis 77160 (phone: 60-67-66-77). Near N19. 51 rooms; 265 ff to 295 ff.

Fimotels

(Central Reservations phone: 33-1-40-25-50-50)
- Fontainebleau; 46 Avenue Franklin Roosevelt 77210 (phone: 64-22-30-21). Near N6. 67 rooms. 305 ff to 325 ff.
- Marne-la-Vallée/Emerainville; Boulevard de Beaubourg 77327 (phone: 60-17-88-39). Off A4 Val Maubée exit. 80 rooms. 350 ff to 370 ff.
- Meaux/Mareuil-les-Meaux; Avenue du Général de Gaulle 77100 (phone: 60-23-06-06). Off A4 Meaux exit. 47 rooms. 275 ff to 295 ff.

The following hotels are independent (non-chain) establishments and are located within an hour's drive of the Euro Disneyland area. Note that many are particularly recommended for couples, not for families.

Auberge du cheval blanc: Recently redecorated, this comfortable hotel has 10 rooms. There is a good restaurant. Recommended for couples only. 55 Rue V. Clairet Varreddes; Meaux (phone: 64-33-08-71). 280 ff to 300 ff.

Demeure de la catounière: An old private home transformed into a hotel. There are 22 large, well-equipped rooms, a heated swimming pool, tennis, and horseback riding. Recommended for couples only. Closed from 15 August through 1 September and from 18 December through 6 January. 1 Rue de l'Eglise; Meaux (phone: 60-25-71-74). 415 ff to 515 ff.

Grand Monarque: There are 45 rooms and 5 apartments plus a swimming pool and a tennis court. The recently-renovated rooms are small but well equipped and all windows

TRANSPORTATION AND ACCOMMODATION

face a lovely park. There is also a good restaurant. Avenue de Fontainebleau; Melun-la-Rochette (phone: 64-39-04-40). 380 ff to 480 ff for rooms and 650 ff to 700 ff for apartments.

Hostellerie du bas breau: Situated about 5 kilometres northwest of Fontainebleau, this 20-room place is quite elegant (see *Within a Day's Drive*). Closed from 1 January through 3 February. Recommended for couples. 22 Rue Grande; 77630 (phone: 60-66-40-05). 900 ff to 1,400 ff.

Hostellerie du moulin: Located in a converted flour mill, this hostelry has 10 rooms and each is named for a type of grain. The lovely restaurant serves regional food. Closed from 15 through 27 September and 20 December through 22 January. Recommended for couples only. 2 Rue du Moulin Flagy; 77940 (phone: 60-96-67-89). 225 ff to 390 ff.

Le Manoir Fontenay: Recommended for couples, this property offers a swimming pool and tennis court. There are 11 rooms and 3 apartments. The restaurant is highly recommended. The hotel is closed from 15 November through 8 April. Route des Coulommiers; Tesigny 77610 (phone: 64-25-91-17). 450 ff to 750 ff for rooms and 800 ff to 1,000 ff for apartments.

Le Richemont: A modern hostelry on the Marne River, offering good views of the cathedral and the old town. A restaurant is operated under separate ownership. The 42 rooms are small. Quai de la Grande Ile; Meaux (phone: 60-25-12-10). About 250 ff.

Nogentel: Located in the nautical centre of Nogent, this establishment is modern and offers a restaurant with a panoramic view. There are 61 rooms. 8 Rue du Port; Nogent-sur-Marne 94130 (phone: 48-72-70-00). About 450 ff.

Saphir: Modern and well equipped with an indoor swimming pool and a good restaurant, *La Canadel*. There are 105 rooms and 6 apartments. Avenue des Bêchères (D51); Pontault Combault 77340 (phone: 60-28-96-20). 415 ff for rooms; 700 ff for apartments.

The following is a list of budget-priced hotels in the Marne-la-Vallée region.

- Arcade Hotel and Restaurant: 110 modern rooms; restaurant; bar. Boulevard Newton Cité Descartes; Champs-sur-Marne (phone: 64-68-00-83). 310 ff to 340 ff.
- Auberge du Pré Long: 10 rooms; restaurant. 37 Quai du Pré Long; Lagny 77400 (phone: 60-07-73-99). All rooms 240 ff.
- Auberge St Nicolas: 14 rooms located just 500 metres from Euro Disneyland. 35 Rue du Général de Gaulle; Chessy 77144 (phone: 64-36-80-00). 140 ff per person.
- Les Balladins: 40 rooms with shower only; restaurant. 2 Allée Gaston Deferre; Torcy 77200 (phone: 60-17-63-09). All rooms 215 ff.
- Campanile: 52 rooms, restaurant with children's menu. Rue Bernard de Poret; Dammarie-les-Lys 77190 (phone: 64-37-51-51). All rooms 250 ff.
- Campanile Hotel and Restaurant: 164 modern rooms; restaurant with children's menu. 34 Rue du Général de Gaulle; Torcy 77200 (phone: 60-17-84-85). All rooms 320 ff.
- Château de Grande Romaine: 88 rooms and 2 apartments; park setting; 5 tennis courts; outdoor swimming pool; volleyball; sauna; restaurant. Lesigny 77150 (phone: 60-02-21-24). 450 ff to 550 ff for rooms; 650 ff to 870 ff for apartments.
- Confort: 20 rooms; restaurant. 639 Avenue Jean Juares. Dammarie-les-Lys 77190 (phone: 64-39-48-04 or 64-37-07-31). All rooms 280 ff.
- Confortel Hotel and Restaurant: 57 rooms with shower only. Avenue du Général Leclerc; Lagny 77400 (phone: 64-30-44-88). All rooms 240 ff.

- Confortel le Louisane: 42 rooms; restaurant with children's menu. Avenue André Ampère; Dammarie 77190 (phone: 64-39-30-33). 235 ff to 240 ff.
- Confortel Lousiane: 57 rooms; restaurant. Avenue du Général Leclerc; Lagny 77400 (phone: 64-30-44-88). 270 ff to 290 ff.
- Days Hotel and Restaurant: 96 modern rooms with full bath; 2 tennis courts, bar; restaurant with children's menu. 15 Avenue du Golf; Bussy St Georges 77600 (phone: 64-66-30-30). 430 ff to 500 ff.
- Devotel: 80 rooms; restaurant. 26 Rue de la Biberonne; Claye Couilly 77410 (phone: 60-26-18-00). All rooms 380 ff.
- Frantour: 85 rooms including apartments; restaurant; bar; fitness club; sauna; 12 kilometres from Euro Disneyland. 55 Boulevard du Mandinet; Lognes 77185 (phone: 64-80-02-50). 380 ff to 410 ff for rooms; 540 ff to 720 ff for apartments.
- Le Gonfalon: 10 rooms; restaurant; hotel and restaurant closed Sundays and Mondays and the month of January. 2 Rue l'Eglise; Germigny l'Evêque (phone: 64-33-16-05). 300 ff to 350 ff.
- Gril Hotel and Restaurant: 32 rooms; restaurant. 61 Rue Jacquart; Lagny 77400 (phone: 64-02-13-25). All rooms 250 ff.
- Hôtel de la Poste: 45 rooms; restaurant; 5 minutes from Euro Disneyland. 12 Avenue Charles de Gaulle; Esbly 77450 (phone: 60-04-55-77). All rooms 285 ff.
- La Louvesterie: 5 rooms and 3 apartments; swimming pool; sauna; restaurant. 10 Route de Faremoutiers; Saint Augustin 77515 (phone: 64-03-37-59). 450 ff to 500 ff for rooms; 700 ff for apartments.
- Le Plat d'Etain: 18 rooms; restaurant with children's menu; just 20 minutes from Euro Disneyland. 6 Place August Tinchant; Jouarre 77640 (phone: 60-22-06-07). 260 ff to 300 ff.
- Primavère Hotel and Restaurant: 52 modern rooms with full bath; restaurant. 34 Allée des Fresnes; Champs-sur-Marne 77420 (phone: 64-68-33-36). All rooms 255 ff.
- Le Relais de Croissy: 30 rooms; restaurant; closed weekends during winter. 1 Route de'Emerainville; Croissy Beaubourg 77183 (phone: 60-05-31-51). 170 ff to 260 ff.
- Le Réveillon: 47 rooms; golf course; restaurant; brasserie; 10 minutes from Euro Disneyland. Lesigny Ferme des Hyvermeaux 77150 (phone: 60-02-25-26). 270 ff to 290 ff.

3
THE MAGIC KINGDOM

Euro Disneyland, while inspired by the Magic Kingdoms in California, Florida, and Tokyo, is unique thanks to the European legends and fairy tales that figure prominently in this newest park. Euro Disneyland and the Magic Kingdom are actually synonymous since, for now, there is only one theme park (Disney-MGM Studios Europe is scheduled to open in 1995).

The Magic Kingdom has been described as a great festival and fair. The sight of the spires of Sleeping Beauty Castle, the gleaming woodwork of the Main Street shops and the tiny white lights that edge their rooflines after dark, and the crescendo of music that follows the parades, never fail to have their effect. Even when the crowds are large and the weather at its dampest, a visitor who has toured this wonderland dozens of times still can look around and think how satisfying this kingdom is for the spirit.

But the delight that most guests experience upon their first sight of the Magic Kingdom can quickly disappear when disorientation sets in. There are so many nooks and crannies, so many bends to every pathway, and so many sights and sounds clamouring for attention – not to mention 29 attractions and adventures and dozens of shops and restaurants – that it's all too easy to wander aimlessly and miss the best that the Magic Kingdom has to offer. So we seriously suggest that you peruse this chapter carefully before you make your own visit.

When Euro Disneyland's architects created Lake Buena Vista and the Rio Grande, there was enough soil to build up the level of the Magic Kingdom site, to provide proper drainage, to supply dry land on which to plant trees, and to accommodate a vast subterranean system of dressing rooms, computer banks, and connecting hallways where the magic of the Magic Kingdom is manufactured. A whole network of rooms houses Europe's largest working wardrobe, where thousands of costumes worn by the Magic Kingdom's cast members hang row upon row. The place looks like the world's gaudiest department store.

There are five sections or 'lands' in the Magic Kingdom – Main Street USA, Adventureland, Frontierland, Fantasyland, and Discoveryland. Each land's theme is carried through from the hosts' and hostesses' costumes to the food served in the restaurants, the merchandise sold in the shops, and even the design for the trash cans. Thousands of minute details contribute to the overall effect; recognizing these small touches makes any visit more enjoyable.

In order to spend your available time as efficiently as possible, it is important to know the lay of the lands *before* you arrive. The RER train station is just outside the main entrance to the park and the parking lot is located to the right of the main gates. The *Disneyland* hotel's ground level serves as an entrance to the 50 ticket booths. Once you've passed through the turnstiles, you are at the Main Street Railroad Station. Town Square is just beyond the station. The square feeds into Main Street USA. At the end of the street is the Central

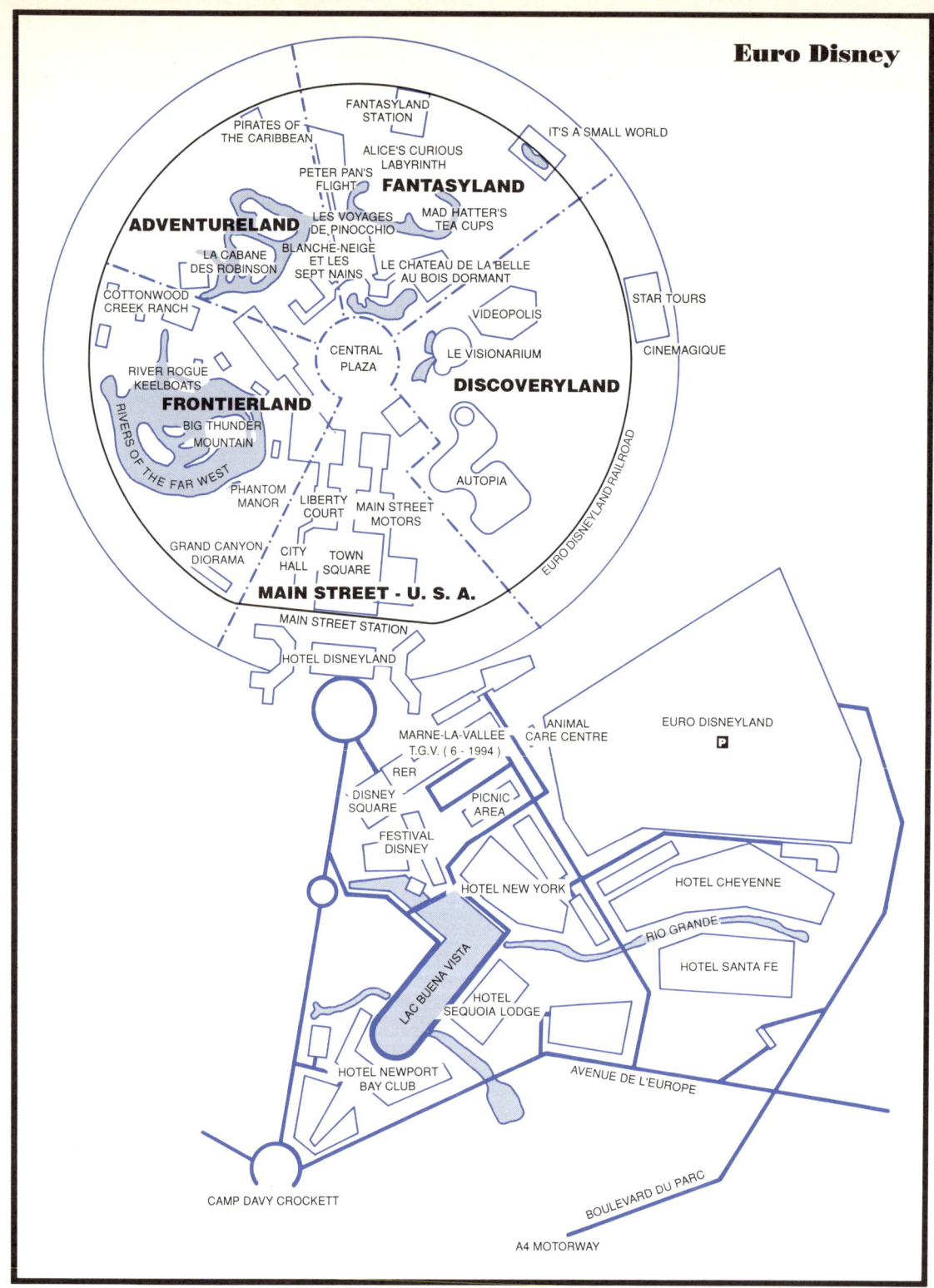

The Magic Kingdom and Resort Complex

Plaza from where paths lead to different areas of the park. One path leads to Sleeping Beauty Castle which marks the entrance to Fantasyland. If you are facing the castle, the first path on your right leads to Discoveryland; the next one on the right leads to the northern end of Discoveryland and its border with Fantasyland; the path just to the left of the castle leads to the border between Adventureland and Fantasyland; the next path leads to Adventureland and Frontierland, and the last path leads to Frontierland and back to the Main Street Railroad Station.

In theory navigating the park couldn't be simpler – in practice it's only too easy to get confused because of the many bends and curves in the pathways, the many entrances to each shop and restaurant, and the somewhat angular placement and architecture of many of the buildings. But if you keep mental notes of your own route, you won't lose your bearings. If you do manage to get confused, however, any park employee can help set you straight, and the map in the park's leaflet can help, too.

Main Street USA

This is the Disney version of turn-of-the-century, small-town Main Streets all over the United States – freshly painted, full of curlicued gingerbread mouldings and pretty details, and with its baskets of hanging plants and genuine-looking gaslights, a showplace both in the bright light of high noon and after nightfall, when the tiny lights edging all of Main Street's rooflines are turned on.

What's particularly interesting is that all the variety of frills and furbelows that a real, growing Main Street would have enjoyed have been assimilated into the Disney version. Most of the structures along the thoroughfare are given over to shops and each one is different – from the wallpaper and flooring to the layout of displays, the styles of chandeliers, and even the lighting level. Some emporia are big and bustling, others are relatively quiet and cosy; some are spacious and airy, others intimate and dark. Floors are made of black-and-white tile or of wood planks set in with wooden pegs; some are covered with Victorian patterned carpets. Where wallpaper is used, it is striped or gaudily flowered; in contrast some walls are panelled in subdued mahogany or oak. The effect is far more sophisticated than first-time visitors probably would have imagined, and it doesn't really matter that some of the 'wood' is fibreglass.

Inside and outside, maintenance and housekeeping are superb. White-suited sanitation men and women patrol the street to pick up litter and quickly shovel up any droppings from the horses who pull the cars from Town Square to the Central Plaza. The pavement, like all the Magic Kingdom, is washed down every night with fire hoses, and there's one crew of maintenance folks whose sole job is to change the little white lights around the roofs; another crew is devoted to keeping the woodwork primed and painted.

Finally some advice. Before heading down Main Street, stop at City Hall in Town Square and enquire about the times and places where live entertainment is scheduled to take place all around the park that day and night. And do your shopping in the early afternoon, rather than at the day's end when the shops will probably be jammed; purchases can be stored in lockers at the Main Street Station, or in the case of very large items, behind the information desk at City Hall. Other useful stops in Town Square include the Stroller Shop where children's pushchairs and wheelchairs can be rented. Also, reservations for guided tours can be made at City Hall.

At the other end of Main Street in the Central Plaza are the first-aid facilities, the Baby Care Centre, and the Lost Children area; all adjacent to *Plaza Gardens* restaurant.

Euro Disneyland Railroad – Main Street Station

This two-storey Victorian station is where guests can begin a grand tour aboard authentic steam-driven excursion trains. There are stops at Main Street, Frontierland, and Fantasyland. Three trains – named *W. F. Cody*, *C. K. Holliday* (these two are a nod to the Wild West), and *G. Washington* (a nod to the US president) – with five cars each make three round-trips every hour. Railway buffs will be interested to know that the trains run on narrow-gauge tracks. The 28-ton locomotives were made by veteran British boilermakers. Apart from the big round boilers, brass fittings, and giant diamond-shaped smokestacks, there are iron-bar cow catchers and a tender filled with fuel and water.

The passenger cars are replicas of early twentieth-century luxury trains, but Disney has left one side of each car open providing great views. Each car can carry 54 passengers. The individual cars have names and fall into three categories: the Far West – *Silverton*, *Durango*, *Wichita*, *Cheyenne*, and *Denver*; the Eastern Seaboard – *Coney Island*, *Atlantic City*, *Long Island*, *Niagara*, and *Chesapeake*; and Historic Sites – *Mount Vernon*, *Boston*, *Philadelphia*, *Yorktown*, and *Valley Forge*.

The trip begins at the Grand Canyon Diorama where one of the world's scenic wonders is brought to life: giant cliffs, cactus, pines, and sage brush that shelter bobcats, prairie dogs, hawks, and other animals help depict Arizona's natural setting and spectacle. The tiny silver thread of the Colorado River races between the canyon walls and a 78-metre-long mural portrays the canyon from sun-up to sunset. From the Diorama, the train passes through Frontierland and Fantasyland and provides views of the Rivers of the Far West, Skull Rock, and Sleeping Beauty Castle, and glimpses into the Pirates of the Caribbean and It's A Small World attractions.

Main Street Vehicles

Authentic re-creations of turn-of-the-century vehicles include a double-decker bus, a police 'paddy wagon', a produce truck, touring cars, a bright-red fire engine, and trolleys. The fire engine and trolleys are pulled by beautiful Percheron horses. All of the vehicles can be boarded for a ride down Main Street. Guests are let off near Sleeping Beauty Castle.

A word to the wise: Don't stand in line to get on if the wait is long. You'll get there faster and enjoy the sights more on foot.

Le Château de la belle au bois dormant (Sleeping Beauty Castle)

The fairy-tale castle with its turreted towers and multicoloured pennants is the centrepiece of Euro Disneyland and the main entrance to Fantasyland. Its design was taken from the original eighteenth-century edition of *Sleeping Beauty* and Walt Disney's 1959 animated film classic.

Thirteen colourful turrets soar 152 feet into the air. Through a technique known as 'forced perspective', the castle appears much taller. (In a real castle, blocks of stone near the top appear smaller than those at the bottom, simply because they are farther away.) The upper walls are tinted in shades of pastel pink with variegated blue tiles on the turret roofs. Spiralling pathways lead to a traditional wooden drawbridge and the inner courtyards and chambers.

The castle itself has three main elements: La Galerie, the Entrance Salon, and La Tanière du Dragon (the Dragon's Lair) in the catacombs beneath. A spiral staircase takes

THE MAGIC KINGDOM

visitors to La Galerie, where displays of Renaissance tapestries tell the story of Sleeping Beauty and her prince. Ancient tree trunks support giant stone archways, and the interior is finished in rough stone blocks accented by stained-glass windows. (A lift is available for handicapped visitors.)

The Entrance Salon is a grand path leading to the heart of Fantasyland at ground level and includes two shops: Merlin l'Enchanteur and La Boutique du Château (see farther on in this chapter for more details). A stairway of rough-hewn rock leads downward past an iron gate and stalactites and stalagmites to La Tanière du Dragon. In a shallow pool of dark water, almost hidden by fog, the dragon's tail twitches, his stomach growls, and he even drools a little. One eye blinks, his left wing and a giant claw swing, and then he falls asleep again.

Fantasyland

Walt Disney called this a 'timeless land of enchantment' and his successors term it 'the happiest land of all'. Although it's not precisely a kiddieland, it is the home of a number of rides that are particularly popular with younger children. The nursery-song cadences of 'It's A Small World' appeal to them, as do the bright colours of the trash baskets, the flowers, and the tentlike rooftops; and they delight in the fairy-tale architecture and ambience, reminiscent of a king's castle courtyard during a lively fair.

Children of all nationalities will find their favourite stories come to life. There are Sleeping Beauty and Cinderella from France; from Germany the Brothers Grimm story of Snow White; from Italy Pinocchio; and from Great Britain Peter Pan, Alice in Wonderland, and King Arthur's Knights of the Round Table.

Snow White's Adventures

This attraction retells part of the Grimm fairy tale, which Walt Disney made into the world's first full-length animated feature in 1937. Visitors ride in 14 six-passenger, hand-carved wooden carts on a journey that begins in the Castle of the Wicked Queen. The cars move on into the Seven Dwarfs' cottage and head for the diamond mine. Though basically a ride for children, Snow White features a skeleton that suddenly swings down in front of each car, the sinister eyes of waiting vultures, a Wicked Queen whose face in the mirror is transformed into a hideous witch, ominous trees that reach down with gnarled branches as if to grab the carts' passengers, a bevy of shrieking bats, and floating logs that turn into crocodiles – all of which can actually terrify some youngsters. At the end of the ride, the witch tries to pry a boulder over the edge of a cliff, but suddenly a flash of lightning sends her tumbling backwards out of sight. Believe it or not, this action-packed ride lasts approximately two minutes.

Pinocchio's Daring Journey

Based on Walt Disney's 1940 animated feature, this ride is a sort of small morality play. Passengers board what seem to be stationary cars where Jiminy Cricket, conscience personified, is host and guide. The 'play' is about Pinocchio, the creation of the toy maker Geppetto, who goes to Pleasure Island, a land of popcorn and candy-cane Ferris wheels, where a happy green worm lives in a fire-engine-red candy apple, to find the right way to live. Slowly, almost imperceptibly, the six-passenger rail cars move to the seamy world of Tobacco Road. Here the Mona Lisa wears a moustache, the candy is broken or half-eaten, and the brightly coloured Pleasure Island hues are supplanted by drab, dirty shades of brown and grey. This is the home of the Rough House and its perpetual free-for-all, and the poolroom where little boys turn into donkeys and the coachman sells them to the salt mines. Pinocchio escapes that fate, misses being gobbled up by Monstro the whale, and ends up back at home in the care of Geppetto – to live happily ever after. All of the above takes place on a ride that lasts about two and a half minutes.

Peter Pan's Flight

The inspiration for this attraction, one of the most beautiful at Euro Disneyland, was the Scottish writer James M. Barrie's play about the boy who wouldn't grow up, which appeared as a Disney animated film in 1953. Riding in flying versions of Captain Hook's ornate ship – which are suspended from an overhead rail – visitors swoop and soar through a series of scenes that tell the story of how Peter, Wendy, Michael, and John Darling are sprinkled with pixie dust, and heading for the 'second star to the right and straight on till morning', fly from the window of their nursery over the rooftops of London to meet Tinkerbell, Captain Hook, and the Indian Princess Tiger Lily in Never Never Land.

As in the movie, one of the most beautiful scenes – one that makes this attraction a treat for adults as well as for kids – is the sight of night-time London, dark blue and speckled with twinkling yellow lights, complete with the Thames, Big Ben, London Bridge, and vehicles that really move on the streets. The song that accompanies the trip is 'You Can Fly, You Can Fly, You Can Fly' by Sammy Cahn and Sammy Fain. The ride to Never Never Land lasts about two and a half minutes.

Lancelot's Carousel

This classic merry-go-round in the centre of the Castle Courtyard is one of two Fantasyland experiences that grow out of the longtime Disney fascination with King Arthur and his knights. The other is the daily Excalibur ceremony held in the courtyard (see the Entertainment section later in this chapter for details). There are 86 hand-carved horses that move up and down as the carousel spins. Unlike the carousels at the three other Disney theme parks, this one is a merry-go-round by virtue of the two ornate chariots for non-equestrians. Children are captivated by the movement and the music while adults will be charmed by the intricate detail and handwork of the horses, chariots, and decorations. There are nine hand-painted murals depicting scenes from *Sleeping Beauty*.

Dumbo, the Flying Elephant

Purely and simply a ride for kids. The character of the flying elephant was developed for the 1941 film *Dumbo*. One of the shortest of Disney's animated features (and one of the best), it starred a baby elephant born with inordinately large ears and an ability to fly that is discovered after he accidentally drinks a bucket of champagne. Faithful friend Timothy Mouse sits atop a mirrored ball in the middle of the circle of the ride's flying elephants.

Mad Hatter's Tea Cups

The theme of this ride – in a group of oversize pastel-coloured cups that whirl and spin as wildly as topsy-turvy tops – derives from a scene in the Disney studio's 1951 production of Lewis Carroll's *Alice in Wonderland*. During the sequence in question, the Mad Hatter hosts a tea party for his un-birthday. Unlike many of the other rides in Fantasyland, this attraction is not strictly for the younger set; the teenage crowd goes for it, too. Be sure to note the soused mouse that pops out of the teapot at the centre of the platform full of tea cups.

THE MAGIC KINGDOM

Alice's Curious Labyrinth

Another adventure from *Alice in Wonderland*. This outdoor maze of winding paths and topiary shrubs gives guests the opportunity to tumble down the rabbit hole into Tulgey Woods where bizarre birds honk, hammer, and wheeze. There are several Audio-Animatronic characters (computer-automated figures that look life-like), including the Cheshire Cat that offers such useful advice as 'You can go this way or that way'. Two gigantic leaves form the entry to the area where guests 'shrink' to the size of a dormouse through the use of magic mirrors, tilted scenery, and other optical illusions. There's time for picture taking and a refreshment stand for a snack en route. A leisurely stroll through the labyrinth takes about 20 minutes.

It's a Small World

Largest of the Fantasyland attractions, It's A Small World is a salute to the children of all nations, performed by a cast of charming doll-like AudioAnimatronic figures dressed in folk costumes. Originally created by Walt Disney for the 1964 – 65 New York World's Fair, with a tunefully singsong melody written by the Academy Award-winning composers of the music for *Mary Poppins*, this favourite of folks from 9 to 90 involves a boat trip through several large rooms where stylized Audio-Animatronic dolls – wooden soldiers, cancan dancers, balloonists, chess pieces, Tower of London guards in scarlet beefeater uniforms, bagpipers and leprechauns, gooseherds, little Dutch kids in wooden shoes, Don Quixote and a goatherd, yodellers, gondoliers, houri dancers, snake charmers, Japanese kite flyers, hippos and giraffes and frogs, hyenas and monkeys and elephants, hip-twitching Polynesians, surfers, and even dolphins – sing and dance to a melody that will run through your head for hours after you float out of their wonderland.

Frontierland

With the Rivers of the Far West lapping at its borders and Big Thunder Mountain rising towards the rear, this re-creation of the American Frontier encompasses the land of Texas cowboys, California Gold Rush miners, and native Indian chiefs, from the 1770s to the 1880s. Hosts and hostesses wear denim calf-length cutoffs, long skirts, or similar period garb. The shops, restaurants, and attractions have unpainted plank or stone or clapboard walls, and outside there are several wooden sidewalks – the kind down which Marshal Matt Dillon used to stride. To complete the scene (and mood), the paths and trails have hoof marks and carriage tracks subtly placed in various spots within the concrete. Guests step back in time and experience the legends for themselves as they pass through Fort Comstock to a frontier settlement.

Big Thunder Mountain Railroad

One of the most famous Magic Kingdom attractions, Big Thunder covers almost two acres astride the Rivers of the Far West. The trip lasts about three minutes and as any true roller-coaster buff could tell you, this ride is a relatively mild one – despite the posted warnings – but the thrills are there. The experience is not *so* extreme that you'll be left with a determination never to subject yourself to it again. The rush of adrenaline that comes with some of the sweeps and curves, as well as the attractive scenery along the 4,545 feet of track, give visitors the opposite reaction.

The adventure begins down sloping tracks into a dimly lit mine tunnel where hundreds of rats' eyes glow as the train passes phosphorescent whirlpools and waterfalls. Attempting to outrun the raging waters of Mill Creek, before they wash away the trestle over which the train must travel, guests can see the dangers ahead: a dangling ore car hangs over the water, the Mill landing dock is a pile of metal and wood, and flood water covers the track. Inside a canyon three howling coyotes and danger lights warn guests to duck. Then the cars pass into Big Thunder Mine, where the real rumbling starts. Lanterns jump, an overhead ore bucket sways, and vibrations are felt in the cars. There's a sudden explosion and a flash of fire. A huge timber swings down as the train plunges into daylight and the shattering sounds of the collapsing shaft can be heard back in the smoking mine. The final freefall occurs as the mine cars plunge into a cave filled with screeching bats. Next, guests splash down within the flooded caverns and finally to the depot for disembarkation.

The summit of the mountain, whose name refers to an old Indian legend about a certain sacred mountain in Wyoming that would thunder whenever white men took out its gold, is entirely Disney-made. It is constructed of textured concrete, tinted and aged to resemble the desert scenery of Monument Valley (a Navajo Indian tribal park in Arizona and Utah), considered one of the scenic wonders of the Far West. The props are authentic mining machinery and other Western memorabilia, collected by Walt Disney Imagineering (the Disney design team responsible for the park's attractions) historians from ghost towns, museums, and mine auctions throughout California, Arizona, and Utah.

Certain aspects of the ride are more convincing after dark. Optimally, you should experience it first at night, then go round again during the day. Since it is extremely popular, plan to take it in during the Main Street Electrical Parade (during the summer, at Christmas, and Easter) or just before the park closes when the lines are generally shorter. By day, go during the early morning hours or just before dinnertime.

Mark Twain and Molly Brown Steamboats

Steaming up the Rivers of the Far West is a perfect way to get a relaxing tour of Frontierland. These two gleaming Victorian-style steamboats are each 105 feet long and 28 feet wide and are powered by authentic steam engines with boilers heated by oil. They follow a steel guideway hidden at the bottom of the river. They were built in a Paris shipyard and brought to Euro Disneyland in sections and reassembled. Each boat has three decks, a pilot house, and lounges. The sternwheeler *Mark Twain* was based on designs developed for Disneyland and patterned after Mississippi River steamboats piloted by Mark Twain between St Louis and New Orleans during the late 1800s. The sidewheeler *Molly Brown*, named for the famous unsinkable Colorado prospector/saloon keeper, is much like the 'Frisco' ferryboats which plied the rivers of Northern California and San Francisco Bay for many years.

The steamboat trips take about 15 minutes and pass Smuggler's Cove, a dark and mysterious inlet surrounded by rockwork. There is a ramshackle structure with a shake roof and stovepipe chimney. The scenery changes as the boats enter a forest land of tall trees and rushing rivers. On the marshy mainland river bank of Wilderness Island is Joe's Landing. Joe is there sleeping and his dog stands guard. Past the dry dock, a family of moose can be seen. Other sights along the way include a deserted wagon with the skeletal remains of two half-buried oxen that provides a grim reminder of the dangers of exploring in the Old West. Then there's Boot Hill where the ghosts of Wild Bill Hickok, Calamity Jane, Wyatt Earp, and Billy the Kid are seen.

River Rogue Keel Boats

Like the boats piloted by Davy Crockett and Mike Fink on the rivers of Ohio and

Tennessee, these ark-shaped boats are powered by diesel engines. The free-floating craft are steered by Disney hosts. There are two – the *Coyote* and the *Racoon*. They make the trip around the Rivers of the Far West in about eight and a half minutes. It's a pleasant ride but very similar to the steamboat trip so don't plan to do both on the same day.

Indian Birchbark Canoes

Piloted by two guides and with the paddling assistance of up to 18 Euro Disneyland guests, the canoes provide a leisurely trip through the Rivers of the Far West and an opportunity to learn the art of canoeing perfected by the American Indian. There are six canoes and the length of the ride depends on the number and athletic abilities of the passengers.

Phantom Manor

This haunted house provides a retirement home for 999 friendly ghosts of gold barons, gun slingers, card sharks, and even some crowned heads of Europe. Slouched on a hilltop overlooking the Rivers of the Far West, the Victorian manor is crumbling. Its cupolas tilt precariously and chimneys belch green smoke. But that's only the outside. Within the manor, the Phantom himself beckons today's Euro Disneyland visitors to tour his house of horrors. Funereal music greets guests as they enter the dismal foyer. A secret panel opens to admit the fearless and fearful to an ornate candlelit chamber. Without warning, the doorway disappears and guests view an amazing transformation. The room is actually elongating – stretching walls and ghostly portraits. Suddenly all goes black, a corpse swings in the airless wind at the end of a hangman's rope. Next, wary visitors step on to an endless moving carpet and board two- and three-passenger 'doom buggies' hooded in black to protect riders. Giant shadows of bat's wings seem to engulf the intruders, pulling them irresistibly upward into the darkness. Spectators spy the illusive figure of the bride fading and reappearing. Around the first bend a mirrored hallway stretches to eternity and a storm-driven wind howls through the hall. Transparent shadows of a claw-fingered pianist drift across the keys of a piano accompanied by the caws of a raven.

The Phantom appears silhouetted in a window, and in the gallery above an oil portrait changes from a pair of happy newlyweds to a solitary bride. The carriage train invades the bride's sanctuary. Her portrait as a young woman hangs on the wall. But at the dressing table an aged crone peers into the mirror at her reflection – a giant fleshless skull. Outside the chamber, riders again perceive the Phantom leaning on his shovel beside an open grave. Suddenly tipped backwards, the buggy passengers turn into a subterranean tunnel – rat-infested caverns filled with decaying coffins. Ahead are some skeletons trying to reassemble themselves while others fall to pieces. A change of scene occurs as the buggies come out of the catacombs and into Phantom Canyon in the midst of an earthquake. The image of a ghost train can be seen rumbling through the sky. There's one more danger-filled passage past mirror-lined walls where passengers can see themselves engulfed by the outstretched hands of demons who live (almost) here. Guests find themselves in the wine cellar where they disembark on to another moving walkway and finally escape up a ramp towards daylight.

One of the biggest jobs of this attraction's maintenance crews is not cleaning up, but keeping things nice and dirty. Since the mansion's attic is littered with some 200 trunks, chairs, dress forms, shovels, harps, rugs, and assorted other knick-knacks, it requires a good deal of dust which has to be specially purchased. Cobwebs are bought in liquid form and strung up by an undisclosed Disney process.

Frontierland Shootin' Gallery

Silver bullets have given way to infrared beams at the completely electronic shooting arcade, with bullets seeking targets in a setting of Rocky Mountain plateaus. The 20 rifles emit infrared beams which trigger the targets drawn from Gold Rush mining days. Shooters can hear the bullets ricochet and when the aim is right, targets fall, spin, and explode with surprising results. Included are a dynamite shack, a windmill, a rustler's hideout, a prairie dog, exploding barrels, speeding ore carts, a vulture, a Peeping Tom and many more. There is wheelchair access to two of the rifles.

Frontierland Depot

The Frontierland stop on the Euro Disneyland Railroad is located in a two-storey building housing the trainmaster's office and a covered queue area. The depot has a peaked roof, a scroll-edge portico and clapboard sides. Inside is a working telegraph machine and a pot-bellied stove.

Cottonwood Creek Ranch

Located near the Frontierland Depot, this farm is home to longhorn steers, Western sheep, buffalo, cattle, bison, sheep, goats, ducks, and chickens.

Adventureland

For someone who grew up in Missouri more than 85 years ago, the very idea of the Amazon and the South Seas must have seemed terribly exotic. So it's not surprising that when Walt Disney was planning his Disneyland park, he designated one segment – Adventureland – to telescope all the far-off and mysterious destinations of the armchair traveller's world into this one compact area.

No single piece of architecture here comes directly from Polynesia, Southeast Asia, or the Caribbean, but every structure has a few characteristics of each of these areas and travellers in Adventureland get a definite feeling of being in a place that's nowhere in particular, but is unquestionably exotic and undeniably foreign.

Pirates of the Caribbean

One of the very best of the Magic Kingdom's adventures, this cruise through a series of sets depicting a pirate raid on a Caribbean island town is a Disneyland original and one of the last attractions that Walt Disney worked on himself. Guests glide in boats through 22 different scenes in the midst of incredible activity and realism. Departing from a stone dock, the boats wind through a West Indies island scene past a shipwreck, past the Blue Lagoon dining verandah, and through one side of another sunken shipwreck. Farther along, the boats are pulled by a chain and hoisted up a cargo ramp. Sounds of a battle can be heard in the distance. Suddenly a pirate, dagger in teeth, appears inches from the boat. Another pirate attempts to board by swinging on a rope from the ship's mast. A mighty flood threatens to engulf the visiting boat, shoving it over the brink and down a 30-foot waterfall right into the midst of an artillery battle between the pirate ship and port defenders. Cannonballs cascade into the waters around unsuspecting guests. Around a bend observers watch the plight of the town mayor suspended from a well rope above the cistern. Meanwhile, hostages are ransomed, drunken hecklers reel across the bridge, and the coxswain fires a warning shot. Farther along the wenches lead the pirates on a merry chase across balconies

THE MAGIC KINGDOM

and around fountains. Up ahead orange flames licking at rooftops can be seen, while the pirates are still singing 'Yo Ho Ho It's A Pirate's Life For Me'.

Two leaking casks threaten to spew rum into the passing boats, and others hanging overhead look as though they may fall on the passers-by. Drifting ahead, the boat enters a darkened tunnel and random flashes signal another moment of disaster. The roar of flames grows louder and the heat can be felt as the boat rounds the bend into the gunpowder room. It's on fire. Explosions and burning embers are everywhere. Then the boat is drawn into a misty cavern, but nature sends a raging rain storm against the slow-moving vessel, and through the rain guests see the remains of the pirates' skeletons and scarred walls. Seen next is the spectacular room full of pirate plunder of gold coins and jewels. The pirate skeletons all appear again, this time enjoying a drink at the bar.

The boats travel at a speed of two feet per second. Hundreds of authentic props and reproductions of sixteenth- and seventeenth-century weapons and furnishings have been collected to give this attraction ultimate realism. Two descents down water-covered ramps drop 15 feet and 8 feet respectively.

Adventure Isle

Castaways and treasure hunters from Disney films provide the inspiration for this island, which is divided into two sections. The southern half is the Swiss Family Robinson Treehouse, home of the shipwrecked family, and the northern half is the Treasure Island of Robert Louis Stevenson's novel. Skull Rock, Ben Gunn's Cave, and Spyglass Hill are on the Treasure Island side. The two sections are joined by a 100-foot-long suspension bridge above rushing waterfalls and a rocking barrel bridge across the cove of the shipwreck. Although completely surrounded by water, three other wooden bridges provide access to the island for visitors.

A tour of the Robinsons' banyan tree home lives up to every visitor's expectations. It is everybody's idea of the perfect treehouse with its many levels and many comforts. Quilts, mahogany furniture, candles stuck in seashells, even running water in every room. (The system is ingenious.) Climbing handmade stairs spiralling up into the giant branches, visitors discover the family room where a hand-pumped organ plays a tune, and the bedrooms. A lookout roost with spyglasses is at the top. Beneath the tree is the root cellar, a maze of tunnels where guests can climb between tangled roots. In a cove beside the tree is the wreckage of the *Swallow* which brought the family here.

Guests can cross over to Long John Silver's haunts and climb into the lookout tower on Spyglass Hill or descend to the caves below. Skull Rock, which seen from afar looks like a skull, is actually a granite monolith that provides mysterious passageways haunted by Captain Flint and his crew for brave visitors to explore. At Ben Gunn's Cave a hidden treasure awaits within the grotto. There are five entrances to the cave. The first one has a split pathway: one leads to a bottomless pit; the other to a rickety bridge. The second entrance also forks but both paths lead to the same colourful room filled with stalactites and stalagmites. (Take the lower road, it's longer.) The third path is on Spyglass Hill and leads to a bat-filled cavern overlooking a maze. A spiral staircase leads down towards the treasure. The fourth entry goes behind a waterfall into a room with five doors leading to still other tunnels. The last entry winds past grisly scenes filled with the skeletons of earlier intruders who suffered Ben Gunn's revenge just as they reached the treasure chest piled high with jewels. It is guarded by an assortment of bats.

Captain Hook's Pirate Ship is located in the

cove near Skull Rock and provides a playground for younger children. Below decks the galley offers snacks and beverages.

Discoveryland

Known in the United States as Tomorrowland, Disney planners changed the name for Euro Disneyland as they realized it isn't easy to portray a future that persists in becoming the present. Discoveryland is devoted to the dreamers, inventors, and science fiction writers who created flying machines, submarines, electric light, and space travel in their works of fiction long before they became reality. Visionaries like Leonardo da Vinci, Jules Verne, and H. G. Wells; inventors like Thomas Edison, Guglielmo Marconi, Madame Curie, and Alexander Graham Bell; and special effects wizards like George Lucas (of *Star Wars* fame) are given tribute here.

The only disappointment for devotees of Walt Disney World and Disneyland is the omission of Space Mountain, considered by many to be one of the world's great roller coasters.

Star Tours

Inspired by the sensational George Lucas trilogy of *Star Wars* films, Star Tours employs flight simulators used by commercial airlines and the military to train pilots to offer a very realistic trip through outer space. Synchronizing a stunning film with the virtually limitless motion of the simulator allows guests to truly feel what they see. (Note that when instructed to put on your seatbelt, do it; this is a rough ride.) It achieves a roller-coaster effect and physical impact unlike any attraction in the park. Signs outside Star Tours warn that passengers must be free of back problems, heart conditions, motion sickness, and other physical limitations to ride. Pregnant women and children under three are not permitted to board. Children under seven must be accompanied by an adult.

The adventure begins on a woodland path on the Moon of Endor. Guests walk past the 35-foot-tall Imperial Walker, and into a maintenance hangar. Here they meet R2D2 and C3PO preparing the StarSpeeder 3000 for its next flight. The droids are repairing damage caused during previous flights. A fuel leak and asteroid damage to the hull are among the problems. Guests board one of the five 40-passenger StarSpeeder vehicles, and are met by Captain Rex (RX24). It's his first voyage.

Flight ST-45 bound nonstop for Endor begins calmly. Within seconds, however, the StarSpeeder is catapulted into space and threatened by asteroid-like frozen ice fragments. The spacecraft pitches and rolls vertically and laterally. Passengers will gasp as the StarSpeeder is drawn into combat with a massive imperial star destroyer and then the Empire's dreaded Death Star battle station comes into view. Captain Rex panics. The ship rolls out of control towards the planetary city. Missiles and explosions continue as the craft swoops low. It dodges oncoming laser blasts and comes perilously close to the intergalactic warlords' fortress, before being rocketed up into hyperspace. Seconds later, the StarSpeeder decelerates and touches down, skidding into the landing bay.

Le Visionarium

Inside a futuristic-looking round building, *From Time to Time*, a CircleVision 360 film, completely envelops its audience. Breathtaking European scenery and famous moments in history are projected on nine giant screens. For the first time that a CircleVision 360 film is being combined with Audio-Animatronics technology, computer-generated special effects, and a story line. Another first is that well-known European movie and television personalities play roles in the film. Actor Michel Piccoli portrays Jules Verne and Franco Nero is cast as Leonardo da Vinci.

The story explores the drama, beauty, and cultural development of Europe over thousands of miles and centuries. Guests stand against leaning rails in the middle of the circular theatre so they can turn quickly to see the 360° panorama.

In making the film, the producers travelled all over Europe with a 400-pound turret of nine mounted cameras. It had to be transported (sometimes by hand!) to the top of mountains, set underneath aircraft, and carried in a variety of boats and vehicles, on to crowded thoroughfares and into sanctuaries normally disturbed by the slightest sound. They took the rig from France's Mont St Michel to the imperial palace of Vienna to the nineteenth-century Paris Centennial exhibition. In addition, a British meadow was turned into a medieval battleground, the rig was taken into the heart of the Kremlin while a 125-foot-high hot-air balloon in the shape of Mickey Mouse's head rose above Moscow's Red Square. Through the use of models and animation they created future time travel scenes in the twenty-second century.

Captain EO

Dazzling space photography, 3-D images that jump out at the audience, and the magic of Michael Jackson's music and dancing combine to make this musical fantasy a great experience. The film, which runs about 17 minutes, was produced by George Lucas, directed by Francis Ford Coppola, features original music and choreography by Michael Jackson, who stars as Captain EO, and Academy Award-winner Anjelica Huston as the evil queen.

Mythical space characters in the cast include Hooter, the little green elephant who sneezes wild musical notes; Fuzzball, an orange-haired space monkey with butterfly wings; the Geex, a golden, two-faced personality with shaggy heads named Idy and Ody; Major Domo, whose costume becomes a complete drum set; and Minor Domo, the rocker who turns into a synthesizer. The story is one of good versus evil and demonstrates how the magic of music can bring about happy endings.

Orbitron

This is the central hub of Discoveryland and it provides a fast-moving spin through space. Euro Disneyland guests pilot their own spaceships through an animated galaxy made up of polished metal spheres representing planets and constellations. With four levels of motion and the astronomical models moving in the opposite direction of the spaceships, the sensation of speed is increased. Pilots can control their height above the ground with levers. Twelve 'jet-powered' vehicles spin around the hub between 7 feet and 16 feet above ground level. The spacecraft have side fins and rear nozzles that resemble those made popular in the 1930s Buck Rogers and Flash Gordon films.

Autopia

Anyone who contends daily with London or Paris traffic may find it difficult to get excited about lining up to steer these small streamlined sports cars around an equally pint-sized highway. But those in the 6-to-15 age bracket adore the trip and can spend hours driving these cars along the twisting roadways. While actual speeds may be slow, Autopia cars create the illusion of greater speed by placing the driver right next to the tarmac.

Like a mini Grand Prix, the Autopia roadway twists and turns, and skilled manoeuvring around corners lets drivers maintain maximum advantage over other racers. Cars chase in single file over bridges, around hairpin bends, and down slopes.

Shops in the Magic Kingdom

Most visitors to Euro Disneyland don't come just for the shopping, but many are surprised at the array of merchandise available. Traditional souvenir items such as key chains, sweatshirts, T-shirts, lapel pins, buttons, hats, and the like, all emblazoned with Mickey Mouse, Pluto, Goofy, or one of the other Disney characters, don't tell the whole story.

The Magic Kingdom's boutiques and stores stock much more and it's possible to buy antiques and silver-plated tea services, escargot holders and cookbooks, mock pirate hats and toy frontier rifles, to say nothing of authentic vintage automobiles. Gold charms and filigreed costume jewellery, magic tricks, film, peanut brittle, and Droste chocolate apples are on sale in the shops along Main Street. In Adventureland you can buy items imported from around the world – hand-carved elephant statues from Africa, inlaid marble boxes from India, batik dresses from Indonesia, and much more. Shops stock items that complement the themes of the various lands (and so, in Discoveryland, you'll find contemporary wall hangings and futuristic-looking lamps). Every store offers a selection of items from the inexpensive to the costly. In many shops you can watch craftsmen at work – peanut brittle being poured at the Boardwalk Candy Palace on Main Street or a glassblower at Harrington's. Consequently, there's no need to spend a fortune to have a good time. It's a good idea, however, to set a spending limit for each member of your party in advance and try to stick to it. It will be tough if you've got kids in tow.

The shops are open during park hours.

Main Street USA

Town Square

Ribbons and Bows Hat Shop: Hats, caps, and chapeaux of every shape, size, and colour are available here. There are warm ones for the winter and sun hats for the summer, plus beribboned Victorian millinery and the ubiquitous monogrammed Mickey Mouse ears. Overhead fans provide the power for the sewing machines on which the monogramming is done.

Storybook Store: All the Disney favourites create a pleasant atmosphere in this cosy children's library which features a spiral staircase and an animated Tiger who stamps each book with his personal monogram. There are also colouring books and children's classics in standard versions or Disney editions. *Heidi*, *Black Beauty*, *Treasure Island*, *Charlotte's Web*, and *Peter and the Wolf* are among the most popular offerings. Compact discs, soft toys, and games are also available.

Discovery Arcade – Eastside Shops

Boardwalk Candy Arcade: Delicious chocolates are available in this old-fashioned, brightly-coloured, calorie-crammed paradise. A delight at any time of day, but especially when the cooks in the shop's kitchen are pouring peanut brittle on to a huge tabletop to cool, and the candy is sending up clouds of scent that you could swear were being fanned right out into the street. Some 18 to 20 batches are made each day. The sweet product is for sale in small bags, along with pastilles, jelly babies, marshmallow peanuts and nougats, mints, kisses, and dozens of other nemeses for a sweet tooth.

Disney Clothiers: Velvet drapes and an ornate fireplace set the mood for this elegant

THE MAGIC KINGDOM

boutique selling Disney character merchandise. This shop caters to fashion-conscious shoppers with a love for Disney gear. There is a vast array of men's, women's, and children's clothing and accessories, all of which incorporate Disney characters in some way. There are men's golf shirts with a small Mickey Mouse embroidered on the pocket, and satin-look jackets with Mickey (as the sorcerer's apprentice in *Fantasia*) embroidered on the back. Hats, ties, exercise clothing and dress shirts round out the adult selections. Children's items include socks, braces, shirts, trousers, and bathing suits.

Main Street Motors: Classic motor cars and powered cycles from the early part of the century, posters, and a kerbside gas pump set the mood. And the antique autos are for sale. There are four models from which to select.

Town Square Photography: Gleaming glass-fronted mahogany cases show off Canon, Minolta, Pentax, Nikon, and other 35mm cameras for sale at this shop near Town Square. Flashcubes, film, and other photo supplies also are available, and minor repairs can be made. Video camcorders (8mm) are available for rent (a deposit is required). The shop's display includes tintypes, daguerreotypes, and a Gay Nineties box camera. There is also a silhouette studio, where Euro Disneyland artists working at the rate of about one minute per portrait, make cutouts of guests' faces. The silhouettes make great souvenirs.

Harrington's: Fine china and Disneyana collectibles are on sale here, including porcelain table settings, figurines, crystal, and jewellery boxes. There are cut-glass bowls, vases, urns, and glasses. The store also features animation cells from Disney films, books, and ceramics. An engraver or glassblower is always at work.

Liberty Arcade – Westside Shops

Emporium: This is the Magic Kingdom's largest gift shop and it stocks a little bit of everything. Stuffed animals and toys, an array of dolls, T-shirts, sweatshirts, towels, handbags, Mouseketeer ears, sundries, film, and Parisian souvenirs line the shelves. The turn-of-the-century style of the store includes an overhead, cable-driven cash transport system. Don't miss the 15 animated window displays, including AudioAnimatronic figures and scenes from the most recent Disney film releases.

Harmony Barber Shop: The setting is quaint and old-fashioned, the shop is filled with vintage newspapers, pin-ups, calendars, and a pot-bellied stove. You can get a haircut and a shave and you may even find a shaving mug with your name on it. The local gossip is free.

Disney & Co.: The selection of fashionable T-shirts and souvenirs is not as vast as at the Emporium, but for those who prefer a less overwhelming atmosphere, this is the place to shop. The toys and souvenirs are displayed on a Victorian carousel and there is an antique band organ that plays music.

Fantasyland

La Boutique du Château: With a decor of wrought-iron and ornate oak casework, this shop has a royal look befitting a store situated in a castle – which it is. It's on the ground floor of Sleeping Beauty Castle and is stocked with a wide variety of holiday decorations and gifts, including special Christmas ornaments from many Old World towns. You can also admire Santa Claus trinkets, wooden soldiers, bells and drums, Christmas sleighs, plus trifles in velvet, and china to help decorate next year's tree or mantelpiece. The originality and variety of these gifts should come as a pleasant surprise to European customers.

Merlin L'Enchanteur: Filled with precious stones and jewels, this store also is located in the castle. There is a magical array of prisms, crystals, kaleidoscopes, sculptures, magic tricks, and jewels with mystic meanings. A stairway leads downwards past an iron gate into La Tanière du Dragon.

La Chaumière des Sept Nains: A charming shop in which visitors find a miniature forest of shadowy trees with a little wooden bridge over a babbling brook. One side of the shop features unusual Disney-inspired clothing, while the Seven Dwarfs' cottage at the other end is filled with toys and a menagerie of stuffed animals.

La Bottega di Geppetto: This establishment is a treasure trove of handcrafted wares from all over Europe. Carved wooden columns and stencilled designs from *Pinocchio* are part of the decor. There are thimbles, cuckoo clocks, toy soldiers, wooden angels, music boxes, mugs, cowbells, dolls, chess sets, and more.

Sir Mickey's: This shop features toys, souvenirs, and cuddly animals and characters from the most famous of Disney's films.

Le Brave Petit Tailleur: Mickey's film role as the brave little tailor sets the mood for this store offering Disney character hats, shirts, and other clothing.

La Ménagerie du Royaume: The Magic Kingdom's miniature zoological collection is found in this quaint shop. Fine carousel horses, figurines, statuettes, cuddly rabbits, dogs, and other pets are among the offerings. Wood-planked floors and stone-arched doorways create a medieval village atmosphere.

La Confiserie des Trois Fées: Try as you might to eat sensibly in the many health-food restaurants and salad bars at Euro Disneyland, sweets are unavoidable in the Magic Kingdom and the displays are indescribably tempting. At this shop which takes its setting from the woodland cottage of Sleeping Beauty, her three fairy godmothers, Merriweather, Flora, and Fauna, hover overhead encased in glass. They wave their magic wands to cast an enchanted spell. Aside from the fairy godmothers, the decorations here include murals, 3-D relief figures, and four-dimensional forest scenes including one tree which has lollipops growing from its branches. On sale are lemon drops, Boston baked beans, rock candy, swizzle sticks, red hots, sour balls, spice drops, fudge, and fancy chocolates. There also are peanuts, cashews, and other nuts for sale.

Adventureland

Adventureland Bazaar

Except for the fact that bargaining is impossible, this small marketplace is aptly named. There are five shops within one building. Goods from most of the exotic corners of the world are on sale. This market draws its style from the *Arabian Nights*, the casbah, Constantinople, palaces of the Middle East, and the Congolese jungle. As guests enter through an onion-shaped archway, they are greeted by the sounds of horns and drums. Next, see striped awnings and clotheslines hung with robes and sheets, little passageways crowded with brass platters and leather wine sacks, open bags of saffron, ceramic jars, ribbons, and a magic carpet or two. Aladdin's lamp is in the corner. Laughter is heard, wisps of smoke appear, and a green genie rises from the lamp only to disappear with a puff. The bazaar is sheltered by thick, turreted walls and walkways connect to Sleeping Beauty Castle on one end and Liberty Arcade on the other to protect visitors from inclement weather. A description of the five shops follows.

Les Trésors de Scheherazade: Items from the 1,001 nights make up the wares from Egypt, Persia, India, and many other mysterious lands. There are magic lanterns, brass bells, exotic dolls, and more. The decor features a shield bearing a blue rose, an astrologer's corner, swords enbedded in the ceiling, and a 10-foot camel woven out of reeds and bamboo.

La Reine des Serpents: Suspended from the ceiling is a mysterious Serpent Queen right out of the Arabian nights – the woman's face married to a serpentine figure was created by basketweavers. A giant honeycomb display adds to the theme. Soft toys, figurines, and miniatures are among the wares.

Echoppe d'Aladdin: The merchandise available is mainly Moroccan with leather goods, pottery, and North African clothing the major items. Trinkets and souvenirs also are available. A magic carpet carrying Tiger and Turtle is hung overhead.

Le Girafe Curieuse: This shop features a curious giraffe who has poked his long neck and head inside to nibble leaves and fruit from the tree that stands in the centre of the store. The merchandise includes safari items such as shorts, hats, cool shirts, plus casual clothing for any adventurer.

Le Chant des Tams-Tams: Tucked away in a quiet corner of the bazaar, facing the jungle, this intimate boutique takes its inspiration from East Africa. A caterpillar's footprints appear along the floor, up the wall, and on the ceiling. At the end of the trail is the caterpillar made of giant bristle brushes. Carved wooden animals, native basketry, and African souvenirs crowd the shop.

Trader Sam's Jungle Boutique: All the essentials for a safari – even souvenirs of the hunt for those who prefer armchair travelling. Trader Sam, friend to all adventurers, sits beneath a thatched roof supported by bamboo and recounts tales of his own journeys.

Le Coffre de Capitaine: Located inside the Pirates of the Caribbean building, this shop features replicas of muskets and cutlasses, ship models, figurines, and pieces of eight. The nautical theme includes barrels, ropes, and sea chests.

Frontierland

Pueblo Trading Post: An adobe outpost from the American Southwest features handwoven Indian baskets, pottery, silver and turquoise jewellery from the Zuni, Hopi, and Navajo reservations of New Mexico and Arizona. A native Indian in traditional tribal garb demonstrates basketweaving, rug making, and beading. Other items include suede and leather goods and antique Kachina dolls.

Tobias Norton: Two shops in one are here. The *Bonanza Outfitters* offers cowboy hats, boots, jeans, jackets, belts, and other essentials for would-be cowboys. At *Eureka Mining*, Western-themed toys and souvenirs are for sale along with decorative gifts, Indian-made jewellery, and snack food and sweets.

Woodcarver's workshop: As its name suggests, guests who come here can see a woodcarver at work on statues, name plates, or any other ideas a creative visitor wants.

Discoveryland

Star Traders: Located next to Star Tours, this is one of the best places in the park to obtain Disney-themed items. There are T-shirts, sweatshirts, jackets, back-scratchers, books, magazines, soaps, lollipops, key chains, pewter charms, you name it. Cuddly toys resembling every character are here – be sure to look at the giant Pluto and Dumbo. Along with the Disney items there are futuristic gadgets including solar panels for awnings and large video screens.

Constellations: Set in this shop in the Visionarium building where the film *From Time to Time* is shown. Here are collectibles (if you want them) from around the world.

Entertainment

One of the wonders of Euro Disneyland is that even after you've visited all the attractions, browsed in all the shops, and eaten in all the restaurants, there's still plenty to keep visitors coming back again and again. A nearly endless array of performers and performances is available continuously.

There are a number of musicians who stroll, march, croon, and pluck their way through the Magic Kingdom every day. So many groups perform so frequently that you don't have to try very hard to find them – especially during the summer, at Christmas time, and at Easter. But it's always s good idea to check in at City Hall for an entertainment schedule before making your way down Main Street.

Main Street Merriment

Character Cavalcade parades: More than 180 famed Disney characters, singers, dancers, musicians, and performers march through the Magic Kingdom two to three times every day. The lively procession features songs and storybook characters from Disney's most famous films as Mickey Mouse leads the way. Check at City Hall for exact parade times.

Main Street Electrical Parade: Disney's greatest night-time spectacle is a fantasy of twinkling lights, a score of floats, and dozens of dancers and marchers, wearing an extravagant display of sparkling electric costumes. The parade comes straight from Walt Disney World in Florida where it has been the most popular parade for the last ten years. Giant bugs whirl, glittering mice dance, and an elephant sprays himself with a shower of incandescent colours. Twinkling floats re-create scenes from such classic Disney films as *Cinderella*, *The Little Mermaid*, *Dumbo*, and *Alice in Wonderland*. Mickey Mouse, dressed in a sparkling red costume covered with sequins, leads the way atop a giant bass drum. More than half a million tiny lightbulbs are used in the parade. The parade is performed twice each evening during busy seasons, that is Christmas, Easter, and the summer months. Check at City Hall for exact times.

Euro Disneyland Marching Band: This 26-piece signature musical group performs daily in parades, gives concerts at the Main Street Railroad Station and at the Castle Stage, and leads the way for special events and ceremonies. Their colourful red-and-cream uniforms carry plenty of gold braid.

Town Band: Led by the Main Street USA mayor, the band is costumed as police chief, doctor, fire chief, lawyer, postmaster, judge, and banker, and plays favourite tunes from the turn of the century. Daily concerts are performed in the Town Square Gazebo. Euro Disneyland guests are often recruited as 'guest conductors'.

Main Street Quartet: The butcher, baker, grocer, and banker make up this colourful singing group which performs along the kerbs, on the horse-drawn trolleys, and on a bicycle-built-for-four. Their repertoire includes many barbershop quartet tunes.

Keystone Kops Saxophone Quintet: Silent movie tunes dominate the songbook of this active instrumental group which plays aboard their nineteenth century paddy wagon.

Pratfall and Son: Slapstick comedy by a pair of repairmen carrying ladders and gear as they perform Laurel and Hardy type comedy routines up and down Main Street – creating havoc wherever they go.

THE MAGIC KINGDOM

Home Run Gang: A trio of gum-chewing, loud teenagers selling newspapers, singing and dancing near Casey's Corner and the Main Street Auto Shop. Nearby, Casey's Ragtime Piano and Banjo duo add to the musical mayhem.

Plaza Gardens Trio: A 1920s-style Dixieland trio entertains diners at the *Plaza Gardens* restaurant in true New Orleans fashion.

Fantasyland fetes

Sleeping Beauty Show: The story of Sleeping Beauty unfolds with the help of a giant, leatherbound, three-dimensional picture book as more than 150 singers, dancers, musicians, and other performer gather at the Castle Stage two to three times each day. The 20-minute show is accompanied by melodies from the classic Walt Disney film.

Fantasy Festival Stage: The Fantasyland Railroad Station platform serves as a stage for performances by Kids of the Kingdom and other visiting instrumental and vocal groups.

Excalibur Ceremonies: Nine fanfare trumpeters and five drummers announce the 'Sword and the Stone' ceremonies each day as rituals taken from the pages of *Knights of the Round Table* and the Disney film *The Sword and the Stone*. The legend claims that whoever can pull King Arthur's magical sword 'Excalibur' from the anvil and stone which hold it fast, is a true knight and a true leader. Merlin himself assists in the ceremony. Guests line up for a try. Some fail but those who succeed receive a parchment scroll attesting to their faith and courage. Special effects include smoke, fireworks, and the release of doves.

Pearly Kings and Queens: Inspired by the Pearlies from *Mary Poppins*, this six-member troupe carries on the tradition of British street musicians which began in Victorian times. Their repertoire includes the film's songs 'Jolly Holiday', 'Chim Chim Cheree,' and 'Supercalifragilisticexpealidocious'.

Court Jesters: Three harlequin-costumed jugglers/acrobats/comedians perform on street corners throughout Fantasyland in a tradition dating back to medieval courts.

Stromboli's Marionettes: Staged in a 'gypsy' wagon near Pinocchio's Daring Journey, this puppet show recounts the tales of Snow White, Cinderella, and Pinocchio.

Troubadour: A Renaissance troubadour retells legends in song and verse as he plays a lute while strolling through the hallways and salons of Sleeping Beauty Castle.

Travelling Fairy-tale Troupe: Four strolling actors, each from a different country, tell stories and favourite fairy tales in their own language. Audience members can participate in acting out the stories.

Disney Characters: Mickey and Minnie Mouse, Pluto, Goofy, Donald Duck, and other Disney favourites walk around Fantasyland during the day to pose for pictures and greet guests. At Alice's Curious Labyrinth, the Mad Hatter, White Rabbit, Tweedle Dee, and Tweedle Dum make appearances regularly throughout the day.

Discoveryland doings

Videopolis: A high-tech entertainment centre where scores of large-screen monitors show the latest music videos or close-up views of live performers appearing on the Videopolis stage. This dance club features contemporary music in an atmosphere centred around Jules Verne's fictional heroes. Verne's cigar-shaped airship *Hyperion* thrusts its nose from the entryway, setting the theme. There are replicas of airships, hot-air balloons, atomic submarines, race cars, and speedboats, as well as models of nineteenth-century conveyances – both real and imagined. Bands perform regularly and when there is no live entertainment, music videos keep things rocking. There are two seating areas for non-dancers, both of which offer a fine view of the dance-floor action. Videopolis is open during park hours.

Les voyageurs: A 16-member silver horn fanfare group entertains in and around Videopolis and near the Discoveryland shops and attractions.

Parades: Weird and wonderful contraptions taken from the designs of Leonardo da Vinci, Jules Verne, and other dreamers, make up mini-parades through Videopolis and down Discoveryland's streets. They are helped along by some favourite Disney characters.

Robots: A pair of robots with synthesized voices entertain guests as they wait in line for Star Tours and Captain EO.

Frontierland festivity

Lucky Nugget Revue: A Wild West dance hall dinner show stars Miss Lil and Pierre Paradis, her Parisian boyfriend. While hunting for gold, Miss Lil struck it rich finding a lucky nugget. In no time she rustled up a troupe of cancan dancers and returned along with Pierre to Thunder Mesa and opened a saloon called – you guessed it – the Lucky Nugget. Along with Miss Lil and Pierre, the show features six cancan dancers and a comedian, Charlie McGee.

The 30-minute revue is performed during a two-hour dinner each evening. During the day, the Lucky Nugget serves snacks and features continuous musical entertainment. Reservations for the dinner show must be made in person on the day of the performance. Be sure to reserve early in the day.

Adventureland airs

Ali Baba's street musicians: A quartet of Persian pashas plays an unusual assortment of Oriental drums and horns as they stroll through the streets of the Adventureland Bazaar and set up impromptu concerts.

Pirate stuntmen: Four of Hollywood's best stunt performers lurk around Skull Rock on Adventure Isle, waiting to join Peter Pan and Captain Hook in hand-to-hand combat and show off their martial arts skills for guests queued up for Pirates of the Caribbean.

African tam-tams: This unusual foursome plays drums and wood percussion.

Blue Lagoon trio: A Caribbean island steel drum trio lends calypso, Brazilian, and West Indian rhythms to the mood of this restaurant overlooking the Blue Lagoon (see *Good Food, Entertaining Evenings*).

Dr Livingstone: Decked out with a gramophone, wicker suitcases, and 1920s safari attire, this character can be seen entertaining guests all around Adventureland.

4
GOOD FOOD AND ENTERTAINING EVENINGS

Euro Disneyland's Magic Kingdom (as opposed to those kingdoms in the US and Tokyo) has the distinction of being the first one at which fast food takes a back seat to more interesting dining options. But as in the US parks, there is absolutely *no alcohol* served inside the Magic Kingdom. French guests, in particular, may find this more than a nuisance when they discover they cannot order so much as a glass of wine with lunch or dinner or a beer to wash down a snack. Guests who prefer alcohol with their meal should head for the restaurants at the resorts or at Festival Disney where wine, beer, cocktails, and speciality drinks are served.

Each of the Magic Kingdom's restaurants offers that special Disney touch as a result of which there's always much more to a meal than just food. So despite the no-alcohol policy, most guests will find many enjoyable dining experiences all around the park.

This chapter is divided into four sections. The first one lists all the restaurants inside the Magic Kingdom. They are grouped by 'land'

and by the type of service they offer – table service, cafeteria service, counter service, or snacks (and take-out). The second section focuses on Festival Disney and its restaurants, shows, and shops. The third section lists the restaurants located in each of the resort's hotels. And the last section offers suggestions for dining in and around the Marne-la-Vallée region.

Main Street USA

Table Service

Walt's – an American restaurant
Artifacts on loan from the Disney Archives, including models, sculptures, and paintings from Walt Disney's own collection, provide the setting for a menu of steaks, seafood, and chicken. The Disney planners scanned the menus of 500 popular American restaurants and picked items and recipes to make up the choices here. There are nine dining rooms on two levels (seats on the first floor offer the best views of Main Street). Appetizers include goat cheese with red pepper sauce, cornmeal pancakes with *duxel* and *crème fraîche*, grilled wild mushrooms with herb vinaigrette, fried calamari, and grilled eggplant (aubergine). Clam chowder, corn chowder, black bean soup, and lobster consommé are the soup selections. Main entrées include stuffed breast of capon with spinach and mushrooms, mixed seafood

---

All Euro Disneyland restaurants offer children's menus and many cater to special dietary needs. Be sure to specify your particular requirements as soon as you are seated. Reservations are accepted at some of the restaurants. Check at City Hall for up-to-the-minute details.

Orleans, grilled salmon with honey mustard glaze, Maryland crabcakes, fresh lobster, and tournedos Cannery Row. Dessert offerings include hot fudge sundaes, fresh fruit cobbler, pecan pie, coconut cream pie, and candied ginger cheesecake. There are 200 seats indoors and 40 outdoors beneath awnings and umbrellas.

Cafeteria Service

Plaza Gardens
This Victorian-style dining spot has antique furnishings, carved woodwork, velvet drapes, and a lively jazz ensemble that performs daily. The open-to-view kitchen turns out roasted chicken and charbroiled specialities found at the lavish buffet tables. Among the offerings are Caesar salad, fresh fruit, melon and berries with cottage cheese, tossed salad, cold cuts, shrimp, poached salmon, chef's salad, Cobb salad (a California classic), fried chicken, Maryland crabcakes, steaks, and pork chops. Cheesecake, angel food cake, deep dish apple pie, devil's food cake, carrot cake, pecan pie, and brownies round out the dessert items.

There also is a Sunday brunch at *Plaze Gardens*. Fruit, cereal, yogurt, croissants, smoked salmon, rolls, bagels, English muffins, pancakes, french toast, and eggs benedict are on the menu as Disney characters entertain guests and pose for photos.

There is seating for 300 inside and 100 outdoors under umbrellas.

Counter Service

Market House Deli
Tasty pastrami, turkey, and corned beef sandwiches are the highlights at this eatery. Guests have a choice of rye, pumpernickel, or seven-grain bread, and side dishes include cole slaw, carrot salad, potato salad, and ratatouille. New York-style cheesecake tops the dessert menu. Other choices include Linzer torte and poppyseed cake. Children's box lunches also are available. The decor evokes an old-fashioned country store with crates of canned goods, coffee grinders, and a pot-bellied stove. A piano player provides entertainment. There is seating for 190 guests.

Victoria's Homestyle Cooking
As its name suggests, hearty fare from a cast-iron oven is on the menu. Fresh-baked chicken pot pie, seafood pot pie, and vegetable pot pie are the entrées, and apple pan dowdy and strawberry shortcake are offered for dessert. The setting is strictly American folk art and guests will find family portraits on the walls plus quilts and antiques scattered about the restaurant. A piano player provides the tunes. There is room for 100 diners.

Casey's Corner
The theme here is baseball. Hot dogs and soda are the mainstays of the menu but it's really the decor that is the top attraction. Memorabilia from America's favourite pastime are all over the place and there's a scoreboard that tallies the total number of sodas served. A pianist plays 'Take Me Out to the Ballgame' and other baseball tunes. The menu includes Chicago sausage, foot-long Coney Island hot dogs, and chili dogs; and snowballs (vanilla ice cream, chocolate sauce, and coconut), baseball batter sugar cookies, and Casey's brownies for dessert. There are 52 seats indoors and 'box seats' for 140 more outside.

Snacks

Coffee Grinder Snacks
A variety of teas, coffees, and ice creams are available at this snack shop on the east side of Main Street. The enormous coffee cup mounted on the roof, with its coffee aroma being fanned into the street, attracts strolling guests. There is no seating here – only take-out.

Gibson Girls
A pink ice cream parlour where old-fashioned 'soda jerks' serve up hot fudge sundaes, milkshakes, and some innovative ice cream flavours. Specialities include the Kitchen Sink sundae for four or more with a very sweet tooth. There is seating for 75 guests.

Cable Car Brake Shop
Croissants, cookies, and pastries from France and the US are served in an atmosphere reminiscent of Old San Francisco. In the morning, choices include almond-stuffed croissants, pastries, cinnamon rolls, large muffins, coffee cake, and yogurt. The all-day menu features fruit pies, tarts, muffins, cupcakes, and cookies. Coffee and tea are available, making this a good spot for a quick breakfast as you head into the park. There are 90 seats.

Cookie Kitchen
The aromas will reach you long before you see this shop. Through the window, guests can watch chocolate chip, peanut butter, oatmeal raisin, and Disney character cookies being made. There also are ice cream sandwiches and brownies. There is no seating.

Fantasyland

Table Service

Auberge de Cendrillon
The only *really* French restaurant at Euro Disneyland and the only one with a French chef. Cinderella's glass coach is the centrepiece for this pretty dining spot. It faces the main courtyard of Sleeping Beauty Castle and inside, scenic murals tell the story of Cinderella, her mean stepsisters, and the glass slipper. There are three dining rooms dominated by rustic beams, pine panelling, and rough plaster walls.

Appetizer selections include pâté in a crust, Baltic Sea herring in cream sauce, Parma ham, cheese omelettes, smoked salmon and blinis, snails in garlic butter, stuffed mussels, poached eggs in herb sauce, and scallops. Soup choices are fisherman's chowder and onion soup. Entrées from the seafood menu include turbot in champagne sauce, broiled lobster in a whisky sauce, monk fish with peppercorn sauce, and lobster Newburg. From the broiler come lamb chops, sirloin steaks, chateaubriand, and duckling. Regional specialities include pigs' knuckles and sauerkraut, chicken fricassee with mushrooms and fresh pasta, roast saddle of lamb, cassoulet of sweetbreads and veal kidneys in port, wild boar stew with noodles, grilled beef ribs, and steak tartare. Dessert choices include fresh apple sorbet, Black Forest cake, nougat ice cream, and crème brûlé. The menu is the same at lunch and dinner. There is also a children's menu and a fixed-price meal each day. There are 220 seats inside the restaurant and another 80 seats in a central courtyard.

Counter Service

Pizzeria Bella Notte
Pizza by the slice, speciality sandwiches, pasta (the pasta is in the shape of Mickey Mouse) dishes, and soft drinks are on the menu at this fast-food spot. The theme of the restaurant comes from the Disney film *The Lady and the Tramp*. The scent of freshly baked bread, oregano, and basil are sure to attract many a guest. There are several types of pizza including four cheeses, Margarita, and four seasons. Children's box lunches are available. Dessert options include mini cannoli and fresh strawberries with zabaglione sauce. There is room for 84 guests inside and 190 outdoors.

Toad Hall
The theme for this eatery comes from Disney's

The Wind in the Willows. The murals on the walls feature scenes from the movie. The exterior resembles a typical Cotswolds manor built of wood and stone. There is access to Peter Pan's Flight from inside the restaurant.

The menu is strictly British – fish and chips with vinegar, ploughman's lunch with a Scotch egg, warm roast beef on a toasted English muffin, bangers and mash, and steak and kidney pie. Dessert offerings include apple pie with a cheese crust and English trifle. The only thing missing from this English pub is the beer. There are 48 seats inside and 62 more outside on a covered terrace.

Au Chalet la Marionnette
Situated between Fantasyland and Adventureland, this restaurant features charming mock Alpine village architecture with a shingled roof, leaded glass windows, and finials carved in the shape of storybook characters. Behind the service counter guests can see the miniature rooftops of Geppetto's village, with tiny windows, flower boxes, and chimneys. A rustic fireplace and murals depicting scenes from *Pinocchio* complete the decor.

The menu features roasted chicken in a basket, grilled sausages, served on a choice of rye bread or a bun with sautéed onions and french fries. There also are hamburgers and chicken salad. Desserts include apple strudel, Linzer torte, Black Forest cake, and gingerbread cookies. One outdoor seating area is shielded by topiary hedges and another is shaded with sails rigged to the mast from a tall ship and dressed with relics from Geppetto's shipwreck. Cinderella and Prince Charming make regular visits to this restaurant. There is seating for 810 guests in several rooms.

Old Mill
Located next to It's A Small World, this tea shop has a revolving Dutch windmill, stone and timber walls, and a thatch roof. Guests snack on frozen yogurt with fresh fruit toppings, cookies, nuts, candy bars, granola bars, pastries, coffee, tea, and soft drinks while gazing out at the Small World gardens. There are 100 seats available.

Snacks

March Hare Refreshments
Halfway through Alice's Curious Labyrinth and next to the Mad Hatter's Tea Cups, this snack stand offers un-birthday party cakes and cupcakes, fruit punch, tea, coffee, and soft drinks. The seating area holds 300 guests and has oversize, brightly coloured chairs and tables. Alice and her friends make regular visits to join guests for a snack.

Fantasia Gelati
The Disney film *Fantasia* is the inspiration for this charming ice cream shop. Scenic murals, props, and set dressing from the movie provide the decor. On the menu are six flavours of homemade Italian ice cream served in a dish or in a coloured cone. Sundaes are also available. The snack shop shares the 190 outdoor seats at *Pizzeria Bella Notte* (see above).

Frontierland

Table Service

Lucky Nugget
The popular Lucky Nugget Revue, performed here each evening (see the entertainment section of the *Magic Kingdom* chapter), is fun to accompany a meal. Be sure to make your reservations here *in person* as early in the day as possible. In addition to the evening revue, there also is continuous daytime entertainment.

The lunch menu features marinated grilled chicken served with corn on the cob, prime ribs sandwiches, hamburgers, chicken taco salad platters, barbecued pork sandwiches, chili, nachos, and fresh fruit platters. Peanuts in the shell are served before each meal. The dinner menu features the peanuts, chips and dip, and a main course of prime ribs, roast chicken, or pork chops stuffed with cornbread, with a side order of chili beans, O'Brien potatoes, corn on the cob, or tossed salad. Desserts at lunch and dinner include mud pie and strawberry shortcake. A children's menu is available. There is seating for 350 guests.

Silver Spur Steakhouse
A display kitchen that turns out steaks and prime ribs is the focal point of this elegant Victorian restaurant. Appetizers include shrimp and black bean cocktail, onion soup, and a variety of salads. Entrée options list prime ribs, T-bone steaks, filet mignon, stuffed pork chops, surf and turf, and barbecued pork ribs. There are 300 seats.

Fuente del Oro
Counter service is offered during the day and table service at dinnertime. Sheriff Goofy, dressed in his Western wear, patrols the boardwalk outside the establishment. The decor features a Mexican fountain at the entrance and brightly coloured tiles throughout. The lunchtime menu offers beef, chicken, or pork fajitas, enchiladas with green tomato sauce, tacos, and chips with guacamole. The dinner choices include an appetizer platter with a taco, a tostada, and a quesadilla, grilled shrimp with rice, fajitas, and fresh fish. Desserts tempt with flan, mango and coconut sorbet, rice pudding, and fresh fruit. There also is a tasty, non-alcoholic strawberry Margarita. There is seating for 300 diners at lunchtime and 210 for dinner.

Counter Service

Last Chance Café
Hamburgers, hot dogs, barbecued pork, barbecued chicken, and soft drinks are the choices at this quick-service spot – perfect for a snack on the run. Desserts include carrot cake, cinnamon muffins, ice cream, brownies, and apples. The exterior is themed as a bandit hideout with 'wanted' posters and menu boards hung on its wood siding. The wooden sidewalks are straight out of a John Wayne classic. There is seating for 72 guests indoors and outdoors.

Cowboy Cookout
One of Euro Disneyland's largest restaurants, the speciality is barbecue. Located in a giant barnlike structure complete with a peaked hayloft and grain silo, the decor features antique quilts, braided rugs, wagon wheels, assorted barrels, a butter churn, horseshoes, and ranchers' gear. The menu offers barbecued chicken, steak sandwiches, hamburgers, chicken salad, and fresh fruit. The sandwiches are served with french fries and relish and side orders include corn on the cob, chili, potato salad, and cole slaw. Banana cream pie, apple pie, pecan pie, ice cream, chocolate pudding, and fresh fruit complete the menu. There is seating for 400 diners inside and an additional 260 seats outside.

Adventureland

Table Service

Explorer's Club
This restaurant is decorated with souvenirs of a variety of explorations, including weathered safari clothing, native masks, trophies of the hunt, and even the nose of a plane. Broad covered porches overlook a pond fed by two waterfalls flowing into the Rivers of the Far West and a sunken dining room allows diners to sit beneath a huge tree. There won't be any leaves falling on the tables though. The tree is entirly Disney-made and it comes complete with the sounds of animated tropical birds.

There is a stage where singers and dancers occasionally entertain.

The menu offers standard beef, chicken, and seafood dishes plus a rotating sampling of foods from the four corners of the earth. Speciality appetizers might include Turkish lamb and eggplant salad, seafood cocktail, curry puffs, and exotic fresh fruit. Entrées feature a New Zealand seafood platter, chicken curry Bombay, wild game stew, piri-piri prawns in coconut-lemon butter, grilled duck, and scampi and black walnuts. There is seating for 200 diners inside and 50 on the verandah.

Blue Lagoon
Situated under palm trees beside the lighted lagoon in the Pirates of the Caribbean embarkation port, this dining space offers a view of the boats headed for adventure at the popular pirate attraction. The Blue Lagoon Trio, a Caribbean steel drum band, entertains diners. The menu is inspired by chefs from the Caribbean and the South Pacific. All meals are accompanied by a Caribbean appetizer plate. Entrées worth a try include cashew chicken in a pineapple boat, roast pork calypso, and pollo con piña à la Antigua – served with a variety of tropical sauces and sweet potato fries. The restaurant also specializes in breads – fried yeast, anise, cheese, banana, and sweet potato are among the offerings. Desserts include mango mousse, a tropical fruit platter, and the Blue Lagoon volcano. There is seating for 260 guests.

Aux Epices Enchantees
This is another spot that offers counter service during the day and table service at dinnertime. The thatch-roofed building's entrance is guarded by two false elephant tusks, native masks, and shields and spears. Lunchtime offerings include spring rolls, chicken, beef, and pork satay, sesame stir-fried vegetables, a spicy seafood platter, and fresh fruit salad.

The evening menu offers dim sum (Chinese appetizers), a good choise for guests who want to sample a variety of tastes and textures in bite-size portions. There are egg rolls, port stew Mandarin, shrimp and port stir fry, shrimp pocket dumplings, stuffed wontons, Indonesian meatballs, caramel spareribs, barbecued chicken wings, roasted peppers, and steamed dumplings with curry. There is seating for 280 guests inside and 370 outside at lunchtime. Seating for 362 diners is available at dinnertime.

Snacks

Café de la Brousse
Adjoining *Aux Epices Enchantées*, this grass-roofed snack spot offers Moroccan specialities, including minced beef or vegetable brewat. Other choices are soup, Turkish meatballs, pita sandwiches, baklava, almond cookies, soft drinks, coffee, and tea. There is seating for 24 guests.

Captain Hook's Galley
Located on Adventure Isle, this eatery is situated in a pirate ship where guests place their orders through a gun port. Candied fruit, ginger and cinnamon cookies, macaroons, Captain Hook's citrus punch, coffee, tea, and soft drinks make up the snack menu. There are 75 seats or you can just place your order to take out.

Discoveryland

Counter Service

Café Hyperio
Named for Jules Verne's airship, this unique restaurant, the largest at Euro Disneyland, overlooks the Videopolis stage and dance floor and offers voyagers a quick trip to counters offering an inventive menu of hot foods

GOOD FOOD AND ENTERTAINING EVENINGS

and cold salads in three distinct categories. There are hamburgers, cheeseburgers, grilled veal sausage with onions, french fries, and batter-dipped fresh vegetables. The sandwich counter offers crudités in pitta bread, smoked turkey, ham and cheese, chef's salad, and fruit salad. The pasta counter features linguini or ravioli with marinara, bolognese, or vegetable cream sauce, lasagna, two kinds of pizza, and chef's salad. Soft drinks, coffee, and tea are available at each counter. There are 850 seats and most have a good view of the Videopolis entertainment down below.

Café des Visionnaires
Adjacent to the CircleVision Visionarium theatre, this restaurant has a glass roof giving a bright, open-air feel to the place. The menu features the usual burgers plus cous-cous, paella, salads, tuna fish, and fresh fruit. Dessert treats include fruit sorbet, tarts, and caramel and chocolate flan. There are 300 seats.

Festival Disney

A glittering village-like entertainment complex, located adjacent to the *New York* hotel on the shores of Lake Buena Vista, Festival Disney is a series of buildings filled with shops, restaurants, and a variety of clubs featuring shows, entertainers, and live music. The unique design of Festival Disney is dominated by the metallic façades of the buildings and the square columns that rise to a network of twinkling coloured lights overhead. It was designed by American architect Frank Gehry, who is currently designing a new cultural centre in Los Angeles.

The biggest attraction at Festival Disney is *Buffalo Bill's Wild West Show*, a re-creation of the original production which wowed Parisians during their Centennial celebration a century ago. The two-hour cowboys-and-Indians exhibition – there are 800 performers, including 47 horses, 12 buffaloes, and a bull – of riding stunts, marksmanship, and roping takes place in a 1,050-seat arena where a Western cookout-style dinner is served. There are two seatings daily at 6 p.m. and 8.30 p.m.

Evening entertainment is also found at *Hurricane's*, a disco with a Key West theme. The high-tech club is open from 9 p.m. to 3 a.m. nightly. The *Bluegrass Saloon* is a country-and-western nightspot featuring live country music and dancing. It's open from 5 p.m. to 2 a.m.

Dining at Festival Disney

There are six restaurants at Festival Disney, each offering a different atmosphere and menu – all with true American flavour.

Key West Seafood
This Floridian crab shack is situated on its own island inside Festival Disney and features an oyster bar and a variety of shellfish specialities. There are 300 seats inside plus seating for 160 more diners outside under a covered terrace. Open from noon to 3 p.m. for lunch and 6 p.m. to midnight for dinner.

Los Angeles Grill and Bar
From Key West to Southern California. This restaurant has an exhibition kitchen with an oven that turns out an interesting variety of pizzas. There is seating indoors for 275 and outdoors on a terrace for 200 more. Open from noon to 3 p.m. for lunch and 6 p.m. to midnight for dinner.

Dee Dee's Diner
A 1950s decor with a distinct automotive theme makes this eatery the perfect stop for a meal or snack, since browsing among some of the decorative touches can be as interesting as the food. Burgers, salads, and typical diner fare are featured. There is seating for 220 indoors and 60 outdoors. Open for breakfast, lunch, and dinner from 8 a.m. to 1 a.m.

The Steakhouse
A Chicago warehouse-turned-restaurant is the setting for this elegant spot specializing in prime meat and distinctive wines. Guests can personally choose their own bottles from the cellar. There are 200 indoor seats and another 150 seats on a covered terrace. Open from noon to 3 p.m. for lunch and 6 p.m. to midnight for dinner.

Champion Sports Bar
A fast-food menu is augmented by a large selection of speciality beers. There is also a full-service bar. There are 150 indoor seats and 250 seats outside. Open from 11 a.m. to 1 a.m.

Carnegie's
Straight from the Big Apple, a New York-style delicatessen with lox and bagels, and pastrami and corned beef sandwiches. There is seating for 50 both indoors and outdoors. Open for breakfast and all-day dining from 8 a.m. to 1 a.m.

Shopping at Festival Disney

The Disney Store
New York's Grand Central Station is re-created in this transportation-themed shop. Along with an electric train that rides on a track around the store, there are replicas of Lindbergh's *Spirit of St Louis* and the Wright Brothers' *Kitty Hawk* hanging from the ceiling. An enormous selection of Disney character merchandise is available.

Movie Magic: This is *the* place to find Hollywood souvenirs, movie memorabilia, and Disney Studios logo items. The shop is designed as a movie set.

Team Mickey: A running track, complete with hurdles, sets the stage for this emporium, which offers a wide range of sports clothing with Disney logos.

Surfin' Hawaii: Casual clothing, bathing suits, shorts, and other beachwear – some with Disney logos – are the stock in trade here. The decor resembles an Aloha surf shop.

Streets of America: Highlighting three of America's quintessential cities – New York, New Orleans, and San Francisco – this place has three sections, each with landmarks denoting the city. The Empire State Building and Times Square lead the way to New York; the French Quarter designates New Orleans; and the Golden Gate Bridge is the gateway to San Francisco. The merchandise includes high fashion clothing and other items evoking the flavour of each city.

Buffalo Trading Company: Western wear, saddles, boots, leathergoods, and replicas of Wild West memorabilia are the items stocked in this shop, which is designed as an old-time general store.

OTHER FESTIVAL DISNEY OFFERINGS

There is also a marina at Festival Disney where a variety of watercraft can be rented for a ride on Lake Buena Vista. Other facilities include a post office, a currency exchange counter, an ATM cash machine, and a tourist office offering advice on exploring the areas around Euro Disneyland.

Dining at the Euro Disneyland Hotels

Below is a complete list of all restaurants, lounges, and bars at the Euro Disneyland hotels. For more details about these establishments, see the individual hotel listings in *Transportation and Accommodation*.

GOOD FOOD AND ENTERTAINING EVENINGS

Disneyland
Café Fantasia
California Grill
Inventions
Main Street Lounge

New York
57th Street Bar
Park Side Diner
Rainbow Lounge
Rainbow Room

Newport Bay Club
Cape Cod
Fisherman's Wharf
Yacht Club

Sequoia Lodge
Beaver Creek Tavern
Hunter's Grill
Redwood Bar and Lounge

Santa Fe
La Cantina
Rio Grande Bar

Cheyenne
Chuckwagon Café
Red Garter Saloon

Camp Davy Crockett
Crockett's Tavern

Off-site Restaurants

The restaurants recommended below are within easy reach of Euro Disneyland. Remember that most of these establishments offer a set menu at lunchtime which is good value compared to the price you'd pay for the individual items ordered at dinner.

Restaurants in the major hotel chains offer fairly unadventurous fare but do offer quick service and children's menus. The dining places listed here feature traditional French cooking. All prices quoted are per person. Note: Major credit cards are accepted at most of the restaurants below, but when in doubt – call first to be sure. Reservation policies vary from season to season so it's a good idea to call ahead to secure a table.

Auberge de Conde: A pretty inn that has been in the same family for several generations. Recommended dishes include lobster flan with tomatoes and olives, salmon with chicory and apple cider, and veal kidneys with celery and cream sauce. There is a good selection of champagnes. Lunch prices range from 200 ff to 450 ff; dinner from 600 ff to 700 ff including wine. Closed Monday evenings and all day Tuesdays. 1 Av. de Montmirail; La Ferté-sous-Jouarre; Seine et Marne (phone: 60-22-00-07).

Au Faisan Dore: An old farm transformed into a pleasant restaurant. The decor is rustic with beams and a large, cosy fireplace. Specialities include fried lamb's tongue with tarragon and mushrooms, hog fish with saffron and orange sauce, flan with broccoli and peppers, and veal cutlet with spinach. During the summer, guests can dine at tables set up in a pretty garden. The *prix fixe* menus range from 170 ff to 260 ff; *à la carte*, from 360 ff to 400 ff. Closed Sunday evenings and all day Mondays, and from 8 through 25 August. 5 Av. Charles Bras; Emerainville; Seine et Marne (phone: 64-61-71-90).

Aux Vieux Clodoche: On the banks of the River Marne, this establishment has a lovely terrace open for dining during the summer. Inside is a cosy wood-beamed dining room with a fireplace. Menu items include foie gras, turbot with champagne sauce and morello cherries, and peppered fillet of beef. There is no fixed menu. Prices range from 300 ff to 350 ff. Open daily year-round. 18 Rue de Champigny; Chennevières-sur-Marne; Val de Marne (phone: 45-76-09-39).

Aux Vieux Remparts: This newly renovated hotel restaurant has a rustic dining room and a varied menu. Choices include crab soup with vegetables, roasted perch in wine sauce, and grilled or fried beef with marrow. The *prix fixe* menus are 220 ff to 330 ff; *à la carte*, 320 ff to 360 ff. Open daily year-round. 2 Rue Couverte; Provins; Seine et Marne (phone: 64-08-94-00).

Egleny: Perhaps some of the best French food on the outskirts of Paris. The decor is that of a charming bourgeois manor house. Worth a try are vol-au-vent with sweetbreads, foie gras in pastry, and prawns in leaves of bacon. The desserts are worth the trip all by themselves. The *prix fixe* menus range from 200 ff to 320 ff; *à la carte*, about 450 ff. Closed Sunday evenings, all day Mondays, February school holidays, and the month of August. 13 Av. Général Leclerc; Lagny-sur-Marne; Seine et Marne (phone: 64-30-52-69)

Gargamelle: A very pleasant dining place with a garden and terrace on the River Marne. The food is tasty and fresh – warm salad with seafood, fillet of beef with raisins and pepper, light and dark chocolate meringue. The *prix fixe* menus range from 100 ff to 250 ff; *à la carte*, 280 ff to 300 ff. Closed Sunday evenings and all day Mondays. 23 Av. Péguy; Varenne-St-Hilaire; Val de Marne (phone: 48-86-04-40).

Grand Monarque: Situated in the hotel of the same name in a lovely park, diners can enjoy their meal on a terrace in summer. The menu is short but good and includes spring roll with cucumber cream sauce, chicken fricassee with a delicate raspberry vinegar sauce, and a classic pear tart, plus a good selection of cheeses. The *prix fixe* menu is 165 ff; *à la carte*, about 300 ff. Open daily year-round. Av. de Fontainebleau; Melun-la-Rochette; Seine et Marne (phone: 64-39-04-40).

Hostellerie de la Dague: A hotel restaurant near the Fontainebleau forest, this rustic dining room offers classic French food. Sweetbreads and duck with morello cherries, anglerfish with shrimp, and fillet of beef Henri IV are among the choices. *Prix fixe* menus range from 65 ff to 235 ff; *à la carte*, from 280 ff to 320 ff. Closed Sunday evenings and 24 through 31 December. 5 Grande Rue; Barbizon; Seine et Marne (phone: 60-66-40-49).

Hostellerie de l'Aigle d'Or: This newly renovated farmhouse-inn has a beautiful terrace and garden overlooking Croissy lake. Recommended items include warm foie gras and lobster salad, duck with fresh pasta and spicy black figs, and rabbit with herbs and garlic. A *prix fixe* menu is available at lunch weekdays for 220 ff; *à la carte*, from 400 ff to 450 ff. Closed Sunday evenings and all day Mondays. 8 Rue de Paris; Croissy-Beaubourg; Seine et Marne (phone: 60-05-22-24).

Hostellerie des Pleiades: This hotel restaurant has a 1930s-style decor plus a patio and a lovely garden. Menu selections include sardines in cabbage and tomato pastry, fried salmon with orange sauce, and fillet of beef with foie gras. *Prix fixe* menus range from 170 ff to 250 ff; *à la carte*, 380 ff to 420 ff. Open daily year-round. 21 Grande Rue; Barbizon; Seine et Marne (phone: 60-66-40-25).

La Bonne Marmite: Especially pleasant on summer days, this dining spot is situated in a restored manor. The menu features tartare of smoked salmon with cucumber cream sauce, seafood with saffron, and sweet and sour duck. *Prix fixe* menus range from 140 ff to 320 ff; *à la carte*, 330 ff to 380 ff. Closed Tuesdays, Wednesdays, and February school holidays. Summer closings vary so be sure to call ahead. 15 Rue Général de Gaulle; Villeneuve-le-Comte; Seine et Marne (phone: 60-25-00-10).

La Breteche: Newly redecorated in peach colours with a lovely terrace open for dining in summer. Anglerfish and salmon carpaccio in olive oil and steamed turbot are among the best choices. The *prix fixe* menu is 150 ff; *à la*

GOOD FOOD AND ENTERTAINING EVENINGS

carte, about 400 ff. Closed Sunday evenings and all day Mondays. 171 Quai de Bonneuil; La Varenne-St-Hilaire; Val de Marne (phone: 48-83-38-73).

La Cle d'Or: A charming restaurant with a lovely garden for summer dining. The food is classic French – ragoût of oysters, prawns, and truffles, anglerfish with lentil sauce, and fillet of beef with foie gras are among the options. *Prix fixe* menus range from 170 ff to 260 ff; *à la carte*, 380 ff to 420 ff. Closed Sunday evenings in winter and 17 through 30 December. 73 Grande Rue; Barbizon; Seine et Marne (phone: 60-66-40-96).

La Gueulardiere: The setting is rustic and the food is classic. Menu items include sole and prawns with lobster sauce, and fillets of baby rabbit with mushrooms. *Prix fixe* menus range from 130 ff to 190 ff; *à la carte*, about 350 ff. Closed Saturdays and Sundays for lunch, February school holidays, and the month of August. 66 Av. Général de Gaulle; Ozoir-la-Ferrière; Seine et Marne (phone: 60-28-20-56).

La Musardiere: Decorated with a collection of glass and ceramics, this restaurant specializes in fish with refined sauces. The desserts are excellent. The *prix fixe* menu is 140 ff; *à la carte*, about 350 ff. 61 Av. du Mal-Joffre; Fontenay-sous-Bois; Val de Marne (phone: 48-73-96-13).

La Table Gourmande: A charming little wood-panelled bistro. Salmon tartare, fish soup, and a dessert of half-frozen coffee-flavoured cake with mint sauce are among the specialities. *Prix fixe* menus range from 150 ff to 320 ff; *à la carte*, from 360 ff to 400 ff. Closed Sunday evenings and all day Mondays, and 19 August through 5 September. 7 Rue de la Marne; Jablines; Seine et Marne (phone: 64-36-81-27).

La Table St-Just, a la Ferme St-Just: Set in an old farmhouse near Melun, this dining place features tartare of sea bream with truffles, mushroom pie with foie gras and smoked duck, and pig's trotter braised with morello cherries and foie gras. The *prix fixe* menu is 180 ff; *à la carte*, from 400 ff to 450 ff. Closed Sunday evenings, Mondays, and the month of August. 11 Rue de la Libération; Vaux-le-Penil; Seine et Marne (phone: 64-64-03-67 or 64-09-37-210).

Le Bas Breau: A member of the Relais et Châteaux association, this elegant yet cosy establishment attracts politicians and celebrities. It is near the forest of Fontainebleau. The menu changes seasonally but may include boiled egg with truffles, braised turbot with celery, rack of lamb with thyme, and potato cakes. Everything is superb. *Prix fixe* menus range from 290 ff to 350 ff; *à la carte*, from 650 ff to 750 ff. Closed the month of January. 22 Grande Rue; Barbizon; Seine et Marne (phone: 60-66-40-05).

La Canadel: Located in the *Saphir* hotel, this restaurant is decorated in a nautical theme. The menu includes sweetbreads with orange, bass with creamy sea urchin sauce, and wonderful desserts. The *prix fixe* menu is 195 ff; *à la carte*, about 400 ff. Closed weekends and the month of August. D51 Aire des Berchères; Pontault-Combault; Seine et Marne (phone 60-28-96-20).

L'Ecu de France: This charming dining spot on the Marne riverbank serves king-size prawns with a melted avocado and chicory sauce, fillets of red mullet with mushrooms and snails, and duck and lobster with cheese-filled ravioli. There is no set menu. Prices range from 360 ff to 400 ff. Closed Sunday evenings, all day Mondays, and 3 through 10 September. 31 Rue de Champigny; Chennevières-sur-Marne; Val de Marne (phone: 45-76-00-03).

Le Medieval: Newly restored, this rustic dining room has an attractive verandah and is decorated in pretty pale colours. Specialities include escalope of warm foie gras, sole in butter sauce, and fricassee of veal with mushrooms. *Prix fixe* menus range from 105 ff to 250 ff ; *à la carte* from 260 ff to 300 ff. Closed Sunday evenings, all day Mondays, and the month of February. 6 Pl. Honoré de Balzac; Provins; Seine et Marne (phone: 64-00-01-09).

La Moulin de Poincy: A restored mill situated in a flower-filled garden. The restaurant features salad of rabbit and snails, courgettes stuffed with prawns, salmon with olive sauce, and rack of lamb with mushroom mousse. *Prix fixe* menus range from 175 ff to 295 ff; *à la carte*, from 250 ff to 350 ff. Closed Tuesday evenings, all day Wednesdays, and during Christmas school holidays. Rue du Moulin; Poincy; Seine et Marne (phone: 60-23-06-80).

Le Pavillon Bleu: A riverfront setting offers diners a wonderful view while enjoying a meal of scallops with foie gras, anglerfish with fruit and caramel, or fillet of beef with a tomato sauce. During the winter months, game dishes such as duck with sweet orange sauce and venison with blackberries can be found on the menu. The *prix fixe* menu is 150 ff; *à la carte*, about 450 ff. Open daily year-round. 66 Promenade des Anglais; La Varenne-St-Hilaire; Vale de Marne (phone: 48-83-10-56).

L'Oree de Rubelles: This eighteenth-century establishment is set in a cosy park. The menu descriptions are a bit overwritten but the food is straightforward. Specialities include prawns in a crusty pie, salmon in a crunchy sauce, and wood-pigeon with cabbage and foie gras. *Prix fixe* menus range from 150 ff to 350 ff; *à la carte*, 380 ff to 400 ff. Closed Saturdays for lunch, Sunday evenings from 15 August through 30 April, and Monday evenings from 20 December through 4 January and 15 August through 9 September. 2 Rue de Solers North; Rublées; Seine et Marne (phone: 64-09-56-56).

Les Magnolias: The setting is unattractive, but the fare makes this restaurant worth a visit. The interior is bright and colourful. Recommended items include warm foie gras, prawn-filled ravioli, fillet of beef with shallots, and for dessert, a chocolate millefeuille. The *prix fixe* menu is 270 ff; *à la carte*, from 350 ff to 400 ff. Closed for lunch on Saturdays and all day Sundays from 1 through 8 April and 14 through 28 August. 48 Av. de Bry; Le Perreux; Val de Marne (phone: 48-72-47-43).

Relais de Barbizon: A simple restaurant with reasonable prices. Specialities include coq au vin, steamed pototoes, and tournedos. *Prix fixe* menus range from 125 ff to 155 ff; *à la carte*, from 180 ff to 220 ff. Closed Tuesdays, Wednesdays, and from 23 December through 9 January and 16 through 30 August. 1 Av. Charles de Gaulle; Barbizon; Seine et Marne (phone: 60-66-40-28).

5
SPORTS

Many visitors to Euro Disneyland will be surprised to find a wide variety of sporting activities available to them. Within the 4,800 acres of the resort are opportunities to play a round of golf, some sets of tennis, go boating, swimming, bicycling, and even ice skating (during the winter).

What follows is a guide to the athletic endeavours offered at Euro Disneyland.

Golf

The 18-hole, par-72 Euro Disneyland golf course, scheduled to open during the summer, is a tribute to Disney designers who have taken a flat, treeless area and transformed it into a hilly, landscaped course that looks like it's been here for years. Streams, lakes, waterfalls, and more than 1,000 trees, including maples, ash, and pines, help to make this a pleasant place to try your hand at golf. An additional 9 holes will be added during 1993. There is also a clubhouse with a snack bar and a pro shop where clubs can be rented.

Euro Disneyland hotel guests have priority when booking tee times, but the course also will be open to non-guests. Reservations should be made at your hotel's Information Desk. The course will open at 7 a.m. during the summer and at 8 a.m. the rest of the year. Green fees will be 550 ff per round on weekends and 385 ff per round during the week. Twilight rates and group rates will also be available. Special golf packages are planned, to be offered through travel agents.

Tennis

There are four hard-surface outdoor tennis courts – two at *Camp Davy Crockett* and two at the *New York* hotel. The courts are all lighted for night-time play. Reservations are required and can be made at hotel Information Desks.

Ice skating

The Rockefeller Centre Ice Rink at the *New York* hotel is a re-creation of the famous New York City landmark. The rink is open daily from 10 a.m. to 10 p.m. from November through March. Two-hour skating sessions cost 50 ff including skate rental or 40 ff if you bring your own skates. Children pay 30 ff with skate rental.

Boating

The Festival Disney Marina on Lake Buena Vista rents 'toobies', small motorboats in the shape of oversize tyres for two to three guests, for a relaxing ride around the lake. Toobies cost 30 ff for 15 minutes and 50 ff for 30 minutes.

Swimming

There are indoor-outdoor pools at the *New York* hotel, *Newport Bay Club*, and the *Sequoia*, and an indoor pool at the *Disneyland* hotel. There also is a pool and water park at *Camp Davy Crockett*. Guests staying at the *Santa Fe* and the *Cheyenne* can ask for a complimentary card at their hotel's reception desk that will allow them to swim at any of the pools.

Fitness

Health clubs offering aerobics classes, Nautilus equipment, Jacuzzis, saunas, solariums, and steamrooms are located at the *Disneyland* hotel, the *New York* hotel, the *Newport Bay Club*, and the *Sequoia*. There is no charge for use of the health clubs for hotel guests. *Santa Fe* and *Cheyenne* guests must, however, pay to use the facilities.

Jogging

There is a lovely jogging trail at *Camp Davy Crockett* and the promenade around the *Newport Bay Club* is perfect for a jog or a leisurely stroll.

Bicycling

Bicycles are available for rent at the *Camp Davy Crockett* Bike Barn. There are several designated bike trails through the campground.

Croquet

The *Newport Bay Club* is the place for a game of croquet out on the lawn. Mallets and balls are available at no charge.

Volleyball, Soccer, Basketball, Pétanque

Courts and fields for these activities are found at *Camp Davy Crockett*.

Horseback Riding

Pony rides are offered at *Camp Davy Crockett*. For more serious riders there are two stables very close to Euro Disneyland. *Le Relais d'Anny John* (phone: 60-25-09-25) is about 15 kms from the park in the Cressy forest near Villeneuve. *Cercle Hippique Corbins* (phone: 64-30-25-02) is also close by.

6
DAY-TRIPS FROM EURO DISNEYLAND

The site of the Euro Disney Resort is not only convenient to Paris, but also is within only a day's drive of some of the most compelling sites in France. Several of these prime sightseeing attractions are sufficiently close to the Disney site that an ambitious tourer can easily visit them and be back at Euro Disneyland by nightfall.

We have included only four of the most memorable of these day-trips: to the Sun King's remarkable residence at Versailles; to the stunning cathedral at Chartres; to the forest hunting haven of Fontainebleau; and a ride around the region that is responsible for all of the best champagne that delights the palates of the world's oenophiles.

These are drives which not only offer intense satisfaction and delight when you reach your destination, but often also provide a sense of the stunning landscape of the remarkable Ile de France and surrounding rural enclaves. Just as London and New York are (although marvellous) very poor barometers of the true temper of England and the United States, Paris is hardly very representative of the rest of France, despite its abundant attractions. So if your visit to Euro Disneyland was scheduled to include only a detour into the City of Light, we earnestly recommend that you add one of these day-trips (more would be better) to your travel plans. They will enrich and illuminate your experience in this area.

Versailles

By far the most magnificent of all the French châteaux, Versailles is about 36 miles (60 km) from the Euro Disney Resort and 14 miles (22 km) west of Paris. Louis XIV, called the Sun King because of the splendour of his court, took a small château used by Louis III, enlarged it, and really outdid himself. The vast, intricate, formal gardens, designed by the great Le Nôtre, cover 250 acres and include 600 fountains, for which a river had to be diverted. Once, the combined population of the palace and the court numbered close to 30,000. Louis kept his nobles in constant competition over his favours, hoping to distract them from any opposition to his rule. Though it's impossible to see all of Versailles in one day, don't miss the highlights noted below.

We have given the opening hours for each sight. Guided tours in English are available from 10 a.m. to 3.30 p.m. Admission charge (phone: 30-84-74-00). A spectacular illumination and display of the great fountains takes place on Sunday afternoons during the summer. For more information, contact the Versailles Tourist Office, 7 Rue des Réservoirs (phone: 39-50-36-22 or 39-50-53-90).

From Euro Disneyland, take the A4 (Autoroute de L'Est) about 21 miles (35 km) to the west to reach the southern section of Boulevard Périphérique (the road that surrounds

Paris) to the Boulogne exit (Billancourt). The N10 leads directly to Versailles.

The construction of Versailles nearly bankrupted France. About 6,000 people once lived in this incredibly lavish palace, and its vast gardens are spread over 250 acres. A river was diverted to keep the 600 fountains flowing. A gleaming monument to the French monarchy at its most ostentatious, Versailles epitomizes the excesses that sparked a revolution that changed the course of world history.

Its beginnings were modest enough. In 1624, Louis XIII ordered a hunting lodge to be built on a hill above the small village of Versailles, 14 miles (22 km) west of Paris. Versailles's evolution from this simple lodge to the grandiose palace of the Sun King and the seat of the French government from 1682 to 1789, was the result of a complex – and ultimately condemning – set of circumstances.

A full day is almost the minimum required for a visit here. If time allows, spend two days. The château is under continuous restoration, so be prepared for temporary closure of certain rooms from time to time. The château is open daily, except Mondays, from 9 a.m. to 5.30 p.m. (phone: 30-84-76-76 or 30-84-76-24). Admission charge for the château; no charge for the gardens.

Before crossing the wide avenue that passes in front of the château, notice the king's stables (*écuries royales*) and carriage house constructed by Jules Hardouin-Mansart. Once past the Louis XVIII gates, three successive courtyards lead up to the visitors' entrance: the Ministers' Courtyard and the Royal Courtyard, separated by a bronze statue of Louis XIV on horseback, which give way to the internal Marble Courtyard.

The main entrance to the right of the Royal Courtyard leads to a vestibule and ticket booth through which some 4 million visitors pass annually. To get the most from a visit, join an English-language lecture tour (leaves every 20 minutes from Gate C) or read up in advance.

Chapel: Built between 1699 and 1710 by Mansart, this masterpiece of white stone and multicoloured marble – punctuated by great gilded doors and the bas-reliefs of masters such as Puget and Vasse – was dedicated to St Louis. Its construction was vehemently opposed by Mme de Maintenon (mistress and subsequently second wife of Louis XIV) who, according to Voltaire, was preoccupied with the poverty of the people. This did not deter the Sun King, whose aim was to offer God the most magnificent of all chapels. Note the elaborate ceiling paintings dedicated to the Holy Trinity and the magnificent gilded organ loft.

Grand Apartments: Some of the château's most extraordinary rooms are found in this first-floor wing. Start at the Salon d'Hercule, named for François Lemoine's ceiling painting, the *Apotheosis of Hercules*. Next is the Salon de l'Abondance, which marks the beginning of the king's state apartments. Each of the following five rooms was dedicated to a Greek god: the Salons of Venus and Diana, with their Italianate marble decor; the Salon of Mars, with an early Gobelins tapestry depicting the life of the king; the Salon of Mercury, a card room where Louis XIV lay in state for eight days after his death; and the Salon of Apollo, the former throne room and the last of the king's state apartments.

Hall of Mirrors: Flanked on either side by the Salon de la Guerre and the Salon de la Paix, the Galerie des Glaces is, for many, the most memorable of all of Versailles's rooms. Extending along the west façade of the château, it measures 240 feet long, 33 feet wide, and 40 feet high. Seventeen tall, arched windows facing east are reflected in 17 sparkling mirrors on the opposite wall, each separated by red marble and gilt bronze pilasters. Gilded scrolls and cherubs, ornate candlesticks, crystal chandeliers, and a celebrated ceiling painting by Le Brun add to the pomp and splendour of this hall, once the scene of magnificent balls and the place the Sun King chose to grant audiences to ambassadors from Persia, Siam, and other distant lands. The Treaty of Versailles was signed in this gallery on 28 June 1919, putting an end to World War I. In 1923, John D. Rockefeller donated funds for repairing the roof of the Hall of Mirrors, thus initiating the restoration of this monument.

Queen's Apartments: The queen's bedchamber, her private suite, antechamber, and guard room were created for Marie Thérèse, first wife of Louis XIV. Most outstanding is the sumptuous bedchamber, unveiled in 1975 after an intensive 30-year-restoration. The elaborate floral motifs amid rococo ornamentation reflect the queen's love of flowers. It is said that royal gardeners replanted the garden outside these windows daily so that the queen would see a new assortment of blossoms each morning. Nineteen royal children were born in this room, including Louis XV and Philip V of Spain, and it was here that Marie Antoinette spent her last night at Versailles.

King's Apartments: The king's state and private chambers comprise a series of some 15 rooms arranged in a 'U' around the Marble Court on the east façade of the palace. Completed in 1701, these rooms clearly illustrated the evolution of the decorative style known as Louis XIV. Included at the 'public' bedchamber where the king's waking and retiring were attended by members of the court and the public, as well as his private bedchamber and rooms – the king's most secret quarters.

Museum of French History: Louis-Philippe converted the palace's south wing – the apartments of Louis XIV's brother and some of the royal children – into a museum. The centrepiece of the museum is the Hall of Battles where huge paintings, busts, and bronze plaques represent French history from the seventeenth to the nineteenth century. Also in the palace museum are the sixteenth- to nineteenth-century rooms, including many royal apartments recently opened.

Royal Opera: Louis XV commissioned this dazzling display of carved and gilded wood, colourfully painted imitation marble, and glittering crystal in honour of the marriage of his grandchildren, in particular that of the dauphin to Marie Antoinette on 16 May 1770. It was the first theatre in France to have an elliptical shape and levels graded in tiers. Built in just 21 months, it was designed by Gabriel with decorative motifs by Pajou. It was stripped during the Revolution and later used for Assembly and Senate meetings from 1870 to 1875; it was restored to its original splendour in the 1950s.

Gardens: Le Nôtre created the gardens between 1661 and 1668, with mechanical assistance for the fountains by Mansart and magnificent sculpture by Le Brun. The gardens spread over 2,470 acres and represent the pinnacle of French formal landscaping. An in-depth visit requires nearly as much time as a tour of the château and can uncover a multitude of delightful surprises. On summer Sundays, the fountains dance to a presentation.

Grand and Petit Trianons: Apparently not content with the size of the domain encompassed by Versailles's palace and its immense gardens in 1668, Louis XIV bought the small village of Trianon located at the edge of his gardens and ordered his architects to construct a pavilion for casual gathering and rustic fêtes. The resulting House of Porcelain, completed in 1670, was covered with blue and white Delft tiles. It proved too small and quaint for the king however, and in 1687 he commissioned a more glamorous, marble palace – the Grand Trianon – that remains today. Nearby is the Petit Trianon, a small masterpiece by Gabriel set in the midst of a botanical garden and a sort of experimental farm, commissioned by Louis XV in 1761

After the king's death, his son gave the Petit Trianon to Marie Antoinette, who went there frequently in an effort to escape the pressures and confusion of Versailles. She decorated its rooms in the style of the period.

Several other structures also are grouped in this area, including Le Hameau, a collection of cottages emulating the small hamlet of Chantilly. Though legend has it that Marie Antoinette amused herself here by playing the peasant, most sources refute this, saying that the queen's sense of propriety would have prevented such behaviour. What seems certain is that she enjoyed the simplicity and privacy afforded by this hidden hamlet. The Grand Trianon is open daily except Monday from 9.45 a.m. to 12.30 p.m., and from 2 to 5.30 p.m. The Petit Trianon is open daily except Monday from 2 to 5.30 p.m.

Eating Out
At the restaurants listed below, expect to pay 580 ff and up for a dinner for two in the expensive category; 340 ff to 560 ff in the moderate range; and under 340 ff for an inexpensive meal. Prices do not include wine or drinks, although service usually is included.

Le Trianon Palace: Versailles's most prestigious hotel, in operation since 1911, recently underwent an extensive renovation. There is a covered swimming pool and two terraces facing the château's park. The 130 rooms are furnished with antiques, and its elegant restaurant, *Clemenceau*, serves modern and classic cuisine. Restaurant closed on Sundays. Major credit cards accepted. 1 Bd. de la Reine, Versailles (phone: 39-50-34-12) Expensive.

Les Trois Marches: Warm, intimate decor, charming service, and highly original cooking mark this celebrated restaurant (two Michelin stars), which would be worth the trip even if you weren't visiting the palace. Chef Gérard Vié invents new recipes daily, but his foie gras is famous, as are his oysters and wild goose. The wines here, especially the burgundies, are excellent too. Closed Sundays and Mondays. Major credit cards accepted. 3 Rue Colbert, Versailles (phone: 39-50-13-21). Expensive.

Les Ibis: Set in a large park in an attractive residential area, the 20 rooms are simple but comfortable. The restaurant (closed mid-July through September) offers good food and a warm atmosphere. Major credit cards accepted. Ile du Grand Lac, Le Vesinet, via N321 (phone: 39-52-17-41). Moderate.

Fontainebleau

The first thing to know about the so-called Island of France (Ile de France) is that it is not an island at all. It is the region surrounding Paris to a radius of roughly 50 miles, and its name alludes to the fact that its boundaries are delineated by rivers and waterways which form an irregular circle around the area, while the mighty Marne and the regal, ubiquitous Seine coil and curve through its heart.

The rivers define the land here, lending their names to the valleys that lie between them. Officially, the Ile de France can be divided into eight sub-regions: Paris and seven *départements* (Seine et Marne, Yvelines, Essonne, Hauts de Seine, Seine St Denis, Val de Marne, and Val d'Oise) that wrap snail-like around the French capital, cradling it in a temperate basin.

Richly blessed with both natural and man-made treasures, the Ile de France constitutes what art critic and author John Russell described as 'one vast national park of fine living'. Russell added, 'I doubt, indeed, if there is anywhere in France a greater abundance of unexplored marvels.' This is the region of the French kings, of their regal châteaux, and the châteaux of their ministers and mistresses. The special quality of the light has inspired nearly as many painters (and often the same ones) as those who worked in Provence, while writers and poets have found their inspiration in the region's character.

Through this area passed Charlemagne, St Louis, Joan of Arc, and Napoleon, each leaving an imprint. Almost every illustrious Frenchman or woman has ties to the Ile de France. The homes of historical, literary, and artistic notables are here, many of these now memorials or museums honouring their famous former occupants.

No other region of France has a higher concentration of cathedrals and abbey churches, exquisite Gothic stone witnesses to a fervent religious past played out over centuries. The same locally quarried stone chiselled for these masterpieces also defines the châteaux and the other countless small gems that dot the countryside.

The modern landscape of the Ile de France is full of sometimes jarring contrasts: quaint market squares, medieval fortresses, deep woods, and the ever-present serpentine rivers juxtaposing the bleak industrial pockets and urban sprawl that can dishearten the casual traveller. But despite the encroachment of modern times and suburbanization, nature still firmly holds its own. Apart from the rivers and their soft green valleys, the most characteristic natural feature of the region are its tens of thousands of acres of majestic forests.

The restaurants in the Ile de France range in price from 580 ff and up for a dinner for two in the expensive category; 340 ff to 560 ff in the moderate range; and under 340 ff for an inexpensive meal. Prices do not include wine or drinks, although service usually is included.

From Euro Disneyland, first drive about 45 miles (75 km) southeast to Provins on D231.

Provins

Roses thrive throughout the Ile de France, but nowhere are they more prevalent than in Provins, dubbed the 'town of roses'. According to legend, it was Thibaut IV, King of Navarre, Comte de Champagne, and religious crusader, who imported the first rose to France on his return to Provins from the Holy Land in the thirteenth century. He brought it as a gift to Blanche de Castille, his cousin, and the mother of St Louis. The red 'rose Gallica', later *La Rose de Provins*, flourished in the fertile Brie plain and became the object of cults. It symbolized the prosperity and flowering of this town, which remains one of France's most important relics of the Middle Ages.

Today, Provins has barely 13,000 inhabitants, but during the Middle Ages it boasted 80,000 residents and was the third largest city in France after Paris and Rouen. Behind the city's wealth was the *Foire de Champagne*, a twice-yearly trade fair sponsored by the powerful Counts of Champagne that attracted merchants from all over Europe.

The Ville Haute (Upper Town), a fortification on a promontory jutting out over the valleys of the Voulzie and the Durteint rivers, was already a key post in 800 AD when Charlemagne sent his governors to oversee the settlement. The Lower Town was founded later in 1049, when one of the Counts of Champagne built a chapel in the chestnut forest below. Provins gained power and prestige, and by the tenth century it was minting its own currency.

Today, numerous vestiges of Provins's former prominence remain. The wide stone ramparts of the Upper Town – which date from the twelfth and thirteenth centuries – are reminiscent of the famous walled city of Carcassonne. Visit the St Jean and the Jouy gates, and walk along the ramparts or stroll down the quaint, interior cobbled streets. Near the edge of the Ville Haute is the pride of Provins, the Tour de César, a curious 150-foot-high stone tower built over the foundations of a twelfth-century dungeon. The wall at its base, added by the British in 1432 when they occupied the tower, was dubbed 'English Pie'. When the French recaptured the tower, they hurled the executed English into the moat, which henceforth became known as the 'English Pit'.

Nearby is the church of St Quiriace. Work on the present structure began in the twelfth century, and although church canons had hopes of creating a cathedral to rival the one in Reims and other great edifices, its completion was plagued by lack of funds; the façade wasn't added until nearly four centuries later. Shortly afterwards, a fire destroyed many of St Quiriace's early treasures, though the twelfth-century choir stalls remain, as well as the north and south doorways (built during the twelfth and thirteenth centuries).

Provins has an exceptional number of underground passages, some of which are open to visitors. Dug over 1,000 years ago, these passages formed a bizarre labyrinth, winding from the Lower to the Upper Town. Whether these were used as refuges, places of worship, or for meetings of the secret societies whose symbols are carved in the earthen walls is unknown. Guided tours in English of one portion of the passages begins at the twelfth-century palace of the Comtesses de Blois and Champagne, which was later transformed into a hospital, and now is empty. Note the thirteenth-century portal and the Renaissance stone altarpiece, donated by the Seigneurs de Chenoise in 1506. Below is the vast vaulted gallery from which tours exit. Check with the tourist association (Pl. Honoré Balzac; phone: 64-00-16-65) for details on days and times.

Also worth visiting is the church of St Ayoul, which stands on the site of the first chapel built in the Lower Town. Portions date from the twelfth century, though much of it was rebuilt during the sixteeenth century. The damaged Romanesque doorway has recently received a new bronze tympanum, the subject of considerable local controversy. If you visit in June, be sure to attend the colourful medieval festival that takes place every year in the Upper Town. (Check with the local tourist office for dates.)

Detour from Provins. Before leaving the area, drive 5 miles (8 km) southwest of Provins to see the St Loup de Naud church. A beautiful little building, it has a magnificent twelfth-century main door and is surrounded by sculpture that rivals Chartres's cathedral portals. In 1432, the English destroyed the monastery that stood here.

Eating Out

Aux Vieux Ramparts: Reputed to offer the 'best table in town', this hotel in the Upper Town has a garden and 25 modern rooms. The rustic, beamed restaurant is in the older part. Its menu features refined interpretations of local specialities, with a strong emphasis on fish. Reservations advised. Major credit cards accepted. 3 Rue Couverte, Ville Haute, Provins (phone: 64-08-94-00); hotel, moderate to inexpensive; restaurant, expensive to moderate.

Croix D'Or: Claiming to be the 'oldest inn in France', this thirteenth-century stone hostelry has a handful of spacious old rooms, some recently redecorated. It also has 2 dining rooms, each warmed by a great hearth. Restaurant closed Sundays and Mondays. Visa and Carte Bleu accepted. 1 Rue des Capucines, Provins (phone: 64-00-01-96). Moderate to inexpensive.

En route from Provins: Follow N19 about 19 miles (30 km) to Mormant and pick up D215 southwest to Vaux-le-Vicomte (about 8 miles/13 km), a seventeenth-century château and park that ranks among the most beautiful in Europe. The château was commissioned by Fouquet, minister of finance under Louis XIV. Unfortunately, M. Fouquet's exquisite taste required greater resources than his personal

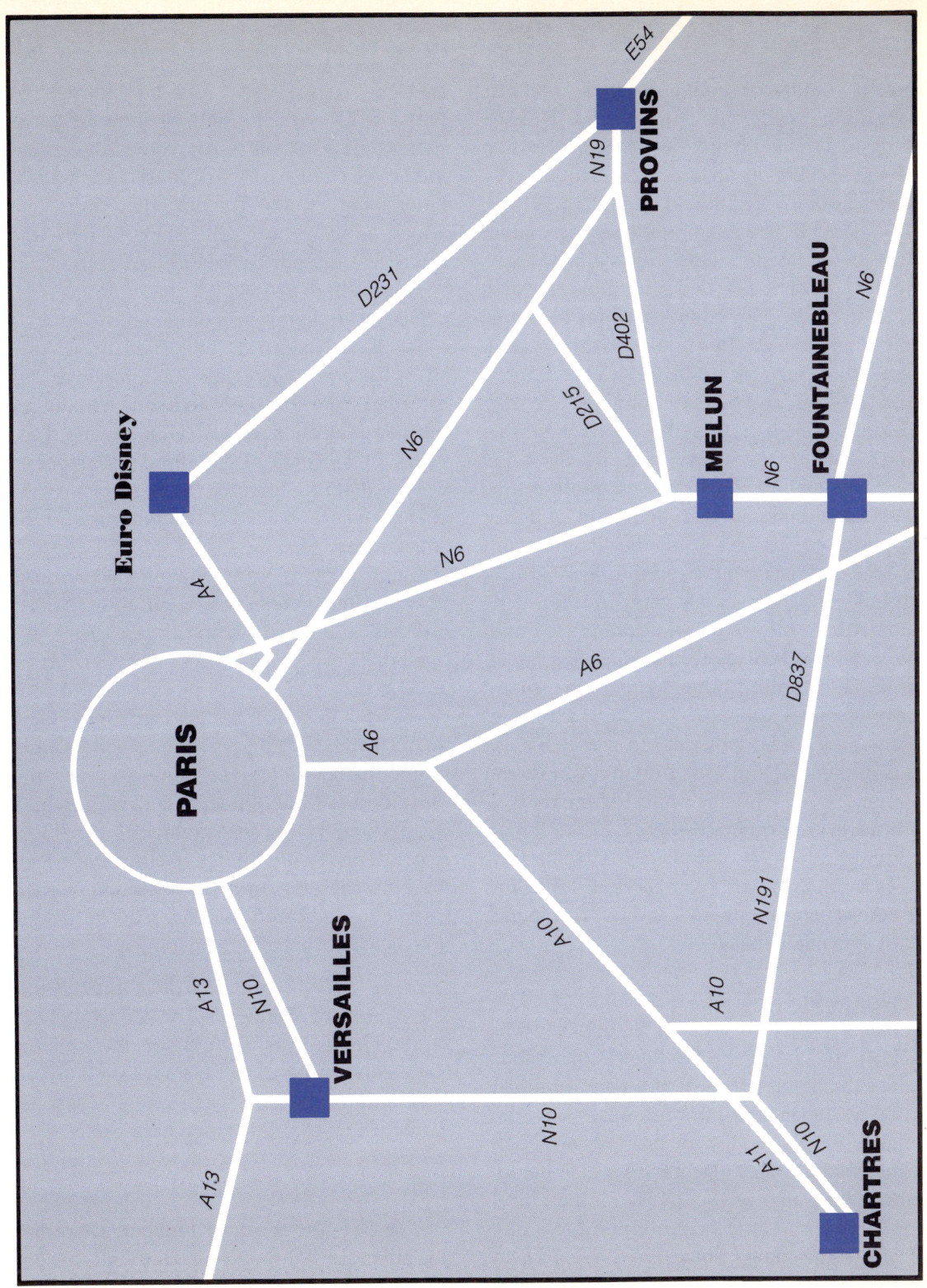

Route plans for day-trips to Versailles, Fountainebleau and Chartres

fortune could accommodate, so his access to state funds was convenient. To build Vaux-le-Vicomte, Fouquet hired the greatest talents of the day: Le Vau as architect, Le Brun as decorator, Le Nôtre as landscape architect. A total of 5 years, 18,000 labourers, and the equivalent of £6 million later, his château was finished. But Fouquet had committed the fatal error of creating an edifice grander in scope than his sovereign. In August 1661, he gave a fabulous dinner for Louis XIV. The decoration, the food, and the entertainment were so dazzlingly elegant that they provoked the king's jealous curiosity, and in no time Fouquet's embezzlement was exposed. A few days later, Fouquet was in prison and his property confiscated. But the magnificent château had whetted the self-indulgent king's appetite, and in the mid-seventeenth century, Louis XIV employed the same people to build his own dream palace at Versailles, the site of his father's hunting lodge. Many of the splendidly decorated rooms of Vaux-le-Vicomte are open to the public daily from 11 a.m. to 6 p.m. in summer, 5 p.m. in winter. Admission charge. Closed Christmas and 14 January to 2 February (phone: 60-66-97-09).

From Vaux-le-Vicomte take the N36 a few miles south to Melun. From there continue for 11 miles (18 km) to the N6 and the forest and town of Fontainebleau.

Fontainebleau

Here is the site of the fabulous Renaissance palace that is set within 50,000 acres of forest and was the ancient hunting preserve of the kings of France. Today the grounds are open to the public, and picnicking, hiking, or horseback riding among the trees, ravines, and ponds makes a perfect counterpoint to a day of city sightseeing. There are references to Fountainebleau as a royal hunting site as early as 1137. Philippe IX was born and died here, but it wasn't until the early sixteenth century that the palace itself was transformed by François I – with the help of some of Italy's most talented artists – from a twelfth-century medieval château to a Renaissance palace. Later kings made further alterations and added wings. Louis XIII was born here and Louis XIV signed the Revocation of the Edict of Nantes here in 1685.

Napoleon lived in Fontainebleau during most of his reign. He abdicated on 6 April 1814, but that wasn't his final goodbye. He returned from Elba in March 1815 to rally his troops again. In August 1944, following three years of German occupation, US General George Patton liberated Fontainebleau; the château was then used as headquarters for the Allied army.

Some people find Fontainebleau more beautiful than Versailles. It certainly is more intimate, full of surprising little corners. It's open daily except Tuesdays from 9.30 a.m. to 12.30 p.m. and 2 to 5 p.m. (the ticket booth closes at 4.15 p.m.); closed Christmas, New Year's Day, and 1 May (admission charge; phone: 64-22-27-40). Be sure to visit the Throne Room, the Queen's Bedroom (which was redone for Marie Antoinette), the Royal Apartments (with their Gobelin tapestries), the Council Room, and the Red Room, where Napoleon abdicated in 1814. The only sour note is the absence of furnishings.

Cour des Adieux or *Cour du Cheval Blanc:* The Court of Farewells, or Court of the White Horse, was named for the site for Napoleon's farewell to his guard on 20 April 1814, and for the equestrian statue of Marcus Aurelius that formerly stood here. An elegant horseshoe-shaped staircase leads to the first floor.

Salle de Bal: The work of Philibert Delorme, this splendid 100-foot-long ballroom, the site of feasts and celebrations, includes mythological paintings conceived by Primaticcio and painted by Dell'Abate.

Chapelle de la Sainte-Trinité: The medieval château's original chapel was consecrated by Thomas Becket in 1169. Its replacement, located to the left of the vestibule, was built by Philibert Delorme and was the site of the marriage between Louis X and Marie Leczinska in 1725.

Galerie de François: Named for the king responsible for the transformation of Fontainebleau, this long gallery dates from the 1530s and includes the original works of Italian masters such as Rosso and Scibec de Capri.

Appartements Royaux: These regal apartments are composed of several rooms, notably the Salon Louis XIII, the Appartements de la Reine (decorated by Marie Antoinette), and the Salle du Trône, the king's bedroom from the reign of Henri IV to Louis XVI – transformed into a throne room by Napoleon.

In addition, don't miss the Salle du Conseil, the Appartement de l'Empereur (including Napoleon's bedchamber and abdication room), and the Appartements des Reines Mères et du Pape. Before leaving, visit the *Musée Napoléon* and the extensive and beautiful gardens – particularly the Jardin de Diane created for Catherine de Medicis.

En route from Fontainebleau: Just a few miles (about 5 miles/8 km) on the edge of the forest lies Barbizon: made famous as an artists' colony in the nineteenth century by the likes of Honoré Daumier and Constant Musset, Alfred de Troyon, and George Sand. You can visit Rousseau's house at 55 Grand-Rue, just behind the Monument aux Morts (phone: 60-66-22-38). It is open weekdays except Tuesdays from 10 a.m. to 12.30 p.m. and 2 to 5 p.m.; weekends and holidays from 10 a.m. to 5 p.m.

Eating Out
L'Aigle Noir: An elegant, family-run establishment facing the château gardens and near the heart of the city. The style is Napoleonic – fittingly grand lodgings for visitors to the château of which the emperor was so fond. There are 57 rooms (5 suites); an elegant restaurant, an indoor pool, a workout room, meeting rooms, and an interior garden. Major credit cards accepted. 27 Pl. Napoléon Bonaparte, Fontainebleau (phone: 64-22-32-65; fax: 64-22-17-33). Expensive.

Hôtellerie du Bas-Breau: An elegant hotel that welcomes fashionable – and well-heeled – Parisians. In existence since 1867, it has housed such celebrities as Robert Louis Stevenson and Napoleon III. With modern bathrooms, an intimate bar, and a superlative restaurant (one Michelin star), it is expensive but worth it. An absolutely perfect place for a Sunday lunch. Closed January. Reservations necessary. Major credit cards accepted. 22 Rue Grande, Barbizon, via N7, N37, and D64 from Fontainebleau (phone: 60-66-40-05; fax: 60-69-22-89). Expensive.

Chartres

There are places in the world where the centre seems to hold, and Chartres is one of them. An enduring gift of the Middle Ages, the town wraps itself around its incomparable cathedral and unrivalled collection of stained glass and sculpture. To the traveller scaling the steep, winding streets and wandering along the banks of the river Eure, with its reedy waters and stone bridges, there are no jarring notes.

Since 1963, the municipality has been carefully restoring the town, shoring up timbers and gables and respecting the integrity of the original houses, but this city is not a museum. Though Chartres no longer is the bustling crossroads that supported the extravagant building projects of the thirteenth century, it still is a prosperous market town, sitting at the centre of some of France's richest arable land. On Saturdays, when the gardeners of the

Beauce region are out in force for the *Marché aux Fleurs* and farmers stack their produce under the arches of the covered market, crowds of shoppers mill around well-kept stores in the pedestrian zones. In the back streets, matronly neighbours in blue aprons gossip from their windows, and inviting courtyards offer glimpses of old iron pumps and greenery within. And on the feast days that draw pilgrims with their backpacks to special services at the cathedral, there may be a lean and tousle-headed ascetic pacing the cobbles and wrangling with himself, a shade of the many pilgrims who have passed this way.

In 1194, a fire razed the flourishing town, leaving only the crypt, parts of the façade, and a steeple of the cathedral. But the holy relic miraculously escaped damage, fuelling enthusiasm for the construction of a new building on the old foundations. The main body of the cathedral that stands today was completed between 1194 and 1225, financed by gifts from the crowned heads of Europe and the well-heeled merchants of the city. Chartres's status as a spiritual centre persisted into the fourteenth century, when the county became a dependency of the kings of France, many of whom became its benefactors, and in 1594 Henri IV of Navarre had himself crowned here, one of the few exceptions to the rule that French kings be crowned in Reims Cathedral.

Chartres *is* its cathedral. It is in its picture of medieval life that Chartres lives most intensely: in the clear gaze of its statues and the intense colours of its stained glass, undimmed by time.

From Euro Disneyland, drive about 21 miles (35 km) west on the A4 (Autoroute de L'Est) to the Boulevard Périphérique that surrounds Paris. Take the southern section of the boulevard to the exit for the A6 autoroute south. Signs will lead to the A10 and then the A11, which leads directly to Chartres.

Because it sits on a spur of elevated ground, Chartres looms on to the horizon whether you arrive by road or by rail (there are trains roughly every hour from the Gare Montparnasse in Paris). As you approach, the layers of the city peel off: sprawling twentieth century, sturdy bourgeois nineteenth century, then the unspoiled medieval core. It can all be seen from the highly decorated turrets of the cathedral's North Tower, a winding walk up narrow stairs (entrance inside the North Door); from May through September, 9.30 to 11.30 a.m. and 2 to 5.30 p.m. (shorter hours in low season); closed Sunday mornings and the month of January. Admission charge.

The stone bridges on the river Eure along the Rue de la Foulerie Frou and the Rue de la Tannerie in the Basse Ville (Lower Town) also give an unforgettable view of the city. Flanked by medieval buildings, the stream flows past tree-lined banks, carrying the eye up to the cathedral, and low walls provide a comfortable resting place for contemplation.

Chartres's Tourist Office, or Syndicat d'Initiative, is just to the left of the square in front of the cathedral at Pl. de la Cathédrale (phone: 37-21-54-03). Maps, pamphlets, and information are dispensed from 9.30 a.m. to 6.30 p.m. daily from May to October; closed Sundays and holidays off-season. From Easter through October, a currency exchange booth stays open from 9.30 a.m. to 6 p.m. daily, including Sundays and holidays, on the square in front of the cathedral. Off-season, call the tourist office ahead of time to be absolutely certain of an English-speaking guide. There are, alternatively, French tours at 10.30 a.m. and 3 p.m., except January and February. For self-guided tours of the Old Town, the tourist office also rents an hour-long cassette tape (in English, French, or German); it comes complete with a tape player and a map.

Chartres Cathedral

If the Parthenon sums up Greek civilization and St Peter's in Rome stands for the Renaissance, Notre Dame de Chartres is the last word in Gothic architecture. The cathedral of today is probably the fifth church to be built on the spot – fires and swords destroyed its previous incarnations – and because most of it was constructed within a period of 30 years (1194–1225), it has an unusual architectural homogeneity. Its two spires, which do not match and give it a lopsided look, are from completely different eras. The South Tower to the right (called the Clocher Vieux, or Old Tower) is in the Romanesque style, elegantly sober and unadorned to the tip of its steeple; it was finished in about 1160 for the previous cathedral and survived the fire of 1194. The North Tower to the left (the Clocher Neuf, or New Tower) is, at least at its base (which also survived the fire of 1194), older than the Old Tower, but its steeple in the convoluted Flamboyant style of the early sixteenth century was built by Jean Texier, or Jehan de Beauce, to replace a wooden one that burned in 1506. The twelfth- and thirteenth-century statuary surrounding the cathedral's three main doorways – the Royal Portal in the western façade and the porches of the northern and southern transepts – is a gold mine of information on the life and thought of the people of the Middle Ages, and its stained-glass windows are considered the most beautiful in France, a country where exquisite stained glass has been preserved in remarkable quantity.

As we went to press, excavations were underway in the square in front of the cathedral. Archaeologists already have uncovered traces from the *maisons canoniales*, where cloistered nuns lived during the thirteenth century. The digging was scheduled to go on for at least a year.

Note: Tourists are restricted from entering the cathedral during its most important masses. Visitors not attending mass will therefore not be permitted to go into the nave from Saturday at 7.45 p.m. until Sunday at noon.

Nave: The size of the building staggers even the blasé modern observer; there can be few structures, one feels, that enclose as much space. The nave is broader than any other in France. The ogival arches rise to 122 feet; and the walls, opened up by flying buttresses that carry the weight of the vaults, are studded with 27,000 square feet of mostly medieval stained glass, the most complete collection anywhere in the world. Brilliant reds, yellows, and greens puncture the deep aquamarine background that has come to be known as Chartres blue, telling the familiar Bible stories over and over again. It's best to come armed with binoculars (available at the *Optique des Changes*, 9 Rue des Changes; and at *La Crypte*, 18 Cloître Notre Dame) to appreciate, frame by frame, the detail of these luminous texts. Most prized are the three twelfth-century lancet windows under the spire of the west front, retrieved, like the famous Blue Virgin window by the choir (Notre Dame de la Belle Verrière), from the earlier Romanesque cathedral. They show the Tree of Jesse (on the right), scenes from the life of Christ (middle) and the Passion (left). It's well worth unravelling it all with the help of the detailed brochures available in English.

Choir: Like the massive baroque altarpiece, which is a little out of place here but striking in its sweep and movement, the ornate stone tableaux of the choir screen were an afterthought, embellishments on the Gothic. Begun by Jehan de Beauce in 1516 and finally completed in 1716, they show scenes in the lives of Christ and the Virgin, but are more eloquent about the courtiers and seamstresses of the Renaissance.

Chapelle de St Piat: The cathedral's treasure house, behind the choir, displays the famous relic of the Virgin's robe, as well as embroidered vestments and other precious objects given to the church. Closed during lunch, Sunday mornings, and January.

Crypt: The third largest in the world (after those of Canterbury Cathedral in England and St Peter's in Rome), the U-shaped crypt houses some interesting twelfth-century murals, statues rescued from the Royal Portal, and a carved Madonna that is a replica of one burned during the French Revolution. The crypt is the oldest part of the cathedral, most of it dating back to the eleventh century, but it contains an even earlier crypt (that of a ninth-century church) and parts of Gallo-Roman origin. Guided tours (the only way the crypt can be visited and for which there is a charge) leave several times daily from the Maison des Clercs, 18 Cloître Notre Dame, just across from the cathedral.

Royal Portal: The sculpted triple doors that make up the entrance in the western façade survive from the earlier cathedral and are considered among the finest examples of French Romanesque art. They present the stern and ethereal mid-twelfth-century vision of Christ in majesty, the figures elongated, the lines pure.

North Porch: The three arches here, carved in the thirteenth century, concentrate on the Old Testament and the prophecies of Christ's coming, with, in parentheses, the story of the Creation and a fascinating series showing the months, the arts, and the virtues as seen through medieval eyes.

South Porch: Also thirteenth century, the sculpture of the southern doorway (Portail du Midi) focuses on Christ, who is seen presiding at a vividly depicted Last Judgment, complete with sinners and demons, and surrounded by phalanxes of martyrs and confessors of the church. The grisly end awaiting sinners makes compulsive viewing, and there are some exquisite visions of the ideal courtly knight (watch for St George and St Maurice, outermost figures flanking the entrance).

Extra Special: Malcolm Miller, the well-tailored Englishman who conducts tours of the cathedral from Easter through November, has become something of an institution among English-speaking visitors here. Miller has made the cathedral his life's work, and his descriptions of the stained glass and sculpture have set audiences alight from Chartres to Kalamazoo. If he's not off lecturing somewhere else, try to catch him holding court during his 12.15 and 2.45 p.m. tours – imaginatively explaining the principles of medieval architecture by getting his audience to impersonate flying buttresses. Miller has been training a young man to take over when he's away, so even if you visit in January or February, a good English tour should be available. Private tours can be arranged in advance by contacting Miller in his superb medieval home at 26 Rue des Ecuyers (phone: 37-28-15-58).

Around the Town

Musée des Beaux-Arts: Behind the cathedral are the former Bishop's Palace, built during the seventeenth and eighteenth centuries, and the Bishop's Garden, which falls in terraces towards the river and provides a view over the Lower Town and beyond. The palace, now a fine arts museum, contains tapestries, furniture, and enamels, as well as an exceptional collection of ten paintings by the Fauvist Maurice Vlaminck, together with part of his collection of African sculpture. Closed Sunday mornings in winter and Tuesdays year-round; admission charge. 29 Cloître Notre Dame (phone: 37-36-41-39).

Enclos de Loens/Centre International du Vitrail: The fine ogival arches of this thirteenth-century cellar, down a small side street north of the cathedral, were built, unusually, for a secular purpose: wine was stored here by the priests. The spacious beamed attic houses the

Centre International du Vitrail (International Stained Glass Centre), which features displays of ancient and contemporary stained glass and permanent exhibitions that detail the history and techniques of stained-glass making. The art continues to flourish in workshops around town. There are also frequent temporary exhibitions. Open daily from 10 a.m. to 12.30 p.m. and from 1.30 to 6 p.m. Admission charge. 5 Rue Cardenal-Pie (phone: 37-21-65-72).

Eglise St André: This twelfth-century Romanesque church, deconsecrated since the Revolution, gave its name to Chartres's St Andrew's Fair, held in November (see *Special Events*). The back wall carried the stump of a bridge, now covered with greenery, that used to reach over the river Eure. Rue de la Brèche, just beyond Pl. St André.

Porte Guillaume: From the ruins of the city's last remaining fourteenth-century gate, fortified in the Hundred Years War and bombed by the Nazis, there are some bucolic views of the river. On the banks of the Eure, at Rue du Bourg Porte Guillaume.

Eglise St Pierre: If Chartres ever lost its cathedral, it would still be remembered for this late thirteenth-century church, once the church of a Benedictine abbey. The graceful ribs of its flying buttresses, each finished with a fearsome gargoyle, leave room inside for wall-to-wall stained glass (thirteenth to sixteenth century) and a unique impression of light and air. Pl. St Pierre.

Eglise St Aignan: Less elegant, and balanced on a single flying buttress, this sixteenth-century structure has an interesting sculpted doorway and exquisite Renaissance stained-glass windows, including one that shows the life of the Virgin (the fourth along from the entry). The highly decorative and colourful polychrome interior is a change from Gothic sobriety. Pl. St Aignan, off Rue des Grenets.

Eating Out

Chartres's restaurants, all in all, don't live up to the promise of the shopfronts of its butchers and bakers, but one or two illustrious names have come to nest here. At the lower end of the market is a cosmopolitan selection of Vietnamese and Algerian restaurants and pizza parlours, but variety may not make up for an absence of overall quality. Don't miss the local speciality, *marsauceux*, a soft-crusted cheese wrapped in chestnut leaves. Meals at the established and expensive restaurants cost 420 ff to 560 ff (and up) for two, with service usually included; at restaurants in the moderate range, 280 ff to 420 ff; and in inexpensive restaurants, 140 ff to 280 ff.

Henri IV: Jacques Corbonnois, trained by Maurice Cazalis, who was the doyen of Chartres's chefs, carries on his master's work. The panelled dining room specializes in a creation of duck liver with apples; there also are good sweetbreads, fish, and duck, and the pâtes and bread are made on the premises. The bill will be hefty and service can be a little flustered. Closed Monday evenings, Tuesdays, and the month of February. Reservations advised. Major credit cards accepted. 31 Rue Soleil d'Or (phone: 37-36-01-55). Expensive.

La Vieille Maison: Elegant dining in an old house near the cathedral. Bernard Roger, the unassuming chef, uses the freshest produce to create a varied menu; his favourites are poultry from nearby Brou, game and a sweetbread dish cooked with foie gras and homemade noodles. Closed Sunday evenings and Mondays. Reservations advised. Major credit cards accepted. 5 Rue au Lait (phone: 37-34-10-67). Expensive.

Le Bistrot de la Cathédrale: This restaurant-wine bar has a fine location facing the cathedral. Comfortably rustic decor, a tile floor, and an open, uncluttered atmosphere supply the backdrop for some imaginative country food and some good Loire wines. Closed Sunday evenings and Mondays in winter. Reservations advised in summer. Major credit cards accepted. 1 Cloître Notre Dame (phone: 37-36-59-60). Moderate.

Le Buisson Ardent: One of those fancy places that a bit too heavy on the decor for comfort, it offers two good *prix fixe* menus. There's also a cocktail bar and a tearoom. Closed Sunday and Tuesday evenings and Wednesdays. Reservations advised. Major credit cards accepted. 10 Rue au Lait (phone: 37-34-04-66). Moderate.

Le Moulin de Ponceau: The river Eure flows slowly by this idyllic spot for a long cocktail. In winter, there is a log fire and comfort; in summer, a wooden patio over the water. Snacks and a cocktail or an exotic punch do not come cheap, but the setting is impeccable. Closed Sunday evenings. 21 Rue de la Tannerie (phone: 37-35-87-87). Moderate.

Café Serpente: The proprietor has his hands on a prime location: the former post office building, classified as a monument and facing the cathedral. The place is done up as a turn-of-the-century bistro, with a moderately priced fixed menu. It also caters to the tourist in a hurry with a selection of fast food. Closed the first two weeks of January. Reservations unnecessary. Major credit cards accepted. 2 Cloître Notre Dame (phone: 37-21-68-81). Moderate to inexpensive.

Le Tripot: The chic local crowd eats here. Bunches of dried flowers hang from the rafters, an open fire burns in the winter, and the attempt to make rustic elegant succeeds. Straightforward country food is appetizingly presented, with multicoloured pickle jars and lots of salad greens, and there is a pleasing selection of good Loire Valley wines. Closed Sundays. Reservations advised. Major credit cards accepted. 11 Pl. Jean Moulin (phone: 37-36-60-11). Moderate to inexpensive.

Le Biniou: An unpretentious Breton *crêperie* that serves everything on a pancake, using such ingredients as fried onions, scrambled eggs, and fresh cream for the savoury versions, and Calvados and apple compote for dessert. Bowls of Breton cider help wash it all down. Cassette tapes alternate with an occasional group that plays live music, showing off the sounds of the Breton bagpipe that gives the restaurant its name. Closed Sundays and Mondays. Reservations unnecessary. No credit cards accepted. 7 Rue Serpente (phone: 37-21-53-12). Inexpensive.

Tartine Show: Fast food French-style, this high-tech eatery with a bright, open kitchen serves up everything imaginable on a 'raft' of good, country-style bread. In addition to these open-face sandwiches (called *tartines* in French), there are traditional sandwiches, plus salads, pastries, and drinks. Located just across the cathedral. Dinner daily; lunch Tuesdays through Saturdays. No reservations. Major credit cards accepted. 1 Rue Fulbert (phone: 37-36-28-07). Inexpensive.

Les Trois Lys: Another *crêperie*, this one nestles cosily in a crooked old half-timbered house by the river, in one of the oldest parts of Chartres. Pleasant atmosphere, affordable prices, and scenic surroundings make it worth the short walk down to the river and the Basse Ville. Closed Sundays and Monday evenings in off-season. Reservations unnecessary. Major credit cards accepted. 3 Rue Porte Guillaume (phone: 37-28-42-02). Inexpensive.

Champagne

Champagne. The word is magical, as charged with rich associations as the bottles of sparkling wine that bear that name on their labels. The world's most famous wine takes its name from the region 90 miles (145 km) east of Paris that produces it, though La Champagne, the region, is much less known outside France than *le champagne*, the celebrated bubbly product.

An elongated oval stretching 100 miles from north to south, Champagne offers visitors a surprising wealth of sights; foremost among them are its glorious Romanesque and Gothic churches, including the incomparable Cathedral of Reims; its great champagne houses, with miles of cellars housing millions of bottles of champagne in the making; and the vineyards themselves, more than 64,000 fertile acres spread across the landscape.

Yet perhaps the greatest charm of the region lies in the villages scattered throughout the countryside. Less than ten minutes outside urban Reims and off the often uninteresting, highways, it is possible to sample French provincial life, to step back, it seems, into the nineteenth century in villages crowded around medieval churches, and to drive along narrow, nearly deserted roads, through fields and vineyards looking as if time had cradled them ever so gently.

From north to south, the Champagne region has four vine-growing areas – the Mountain of Reims, the Valley of the Marne, the Côte des Blancs (Slope of the Whites), and the Region of the Aube – and the three centres of Reims, Epernay, and Troyes. The route we suggest begins in the cathedral city and champagne centre of Reims and circles south through the hilly vineyards and small villages of the Montagne de Reims before reaching Epernay. Next, it follows the valley of the Marne, which stretches east and west of Epernay, then turns south through the villages and vineyards of the Côte des Blancs. After a visit to the historic crossroads town of Châlons-sur-Marne, it continues south to Troyes, the former capital of Champagne, as well as an art centre.

There are many inviting restaurants in this part of France. A full meal for two, excluding wine and drinks, will run to about 580 ff or more in an expensive restaurant, 340 ff to 560 ff in a moderate one, and less than 340 ff in an inexpensive one. Service is usually included.

Take the A4 (Autoroute de L'Est) from Euro Disneyland almost 70 miles (110 km) directly to Reims.

Reims

This busy provincial centre is in many ways more French than Paris. For one thing, it is far more representative of the majority of French cities. For another, it offers a little of everything that the mind's eye tends to include in an image of France. It has a glorious cathedral, impressive medieval churches and elegant châteaux, sidewalk cafés and restaurants, stylish shops, the headquarters of famous wine firms – even barges floating downriver and a canal through the centre of town. Just outside the city are the celebrated vineyards of Champagne, as well as the not-so-celebrated battlefields of World Wars I and II, and many a place to linger for a lovely pastoral view.

Today, although quite a few things in Reims (pronounced *Rance*) are of historical or artistic note, most visitors include the city in their itinerary for one of two reasons – if not for both: the soaring Gothic Cathedral of Notre Dame and the ancient, labyrinthine cellars of the great champagne houses, full of millions of bottles of sparkling wine. These two tourist 'musts' rank with the best France has to offer. Notre Dame de Reims is commonly ranked with Notre Dame de Paris and Notre Dame de Chartres as the most sublime of France's cathedrals, and among the most magnificent in the world. Champagne is, considering its connotation of joy and celebration, doubtless the most famous wine in the world, and it comes only from this area.

For leisurely, ground-level viewing, try a 45-minute jaunt on the sightseeing train called Petit Train de Reims or a horse-drawn carriage ride. Both are offered during July and August and depart from the cathedral.

The Reims Office du Tourisme is at the Place du Trésor, just to the left of the cathedral (2 Rue Guillaume; phone: 26-47-25-69). Besides some useful free brochures, it provides a walking tour of the cathedral and central city on an audio cassette, which can be rented for about 15 ff.

Cathédrale Notre Dame de Reims

This magnificent cathedral is one of the most historic structures in France today. The first church on the spot was the Cathédrale St Nicaise, in which Rémi baptized Clovis I and crowned him King of the Franks in 496. The event became the basis of a later precedent, and from the coronation of Louis VII in the second church on the spot in 1137 to the coronation of Charles X in the third and present church in 1825, the kings of France, with few exceptions, were crowned here.

The cathedral is also one of the most important monuments of the French artistic heritage. After the second church was destroyed by fire in 1210, construction of the edifice seen today began in 1211, and was all but complete a mere century later (the towers were added in the fifteenth century). Consequently, the style of Notre Dame de Reims, conceived by master builder Jean d'Orbais and largely respected by his successors, is pure thirteenth century, representative – along with the cathedrals of Chartres, Paris, and Amiens – of the classic period, or the golden age, of French Gothic architecture. This unity endures, even though the cathedral suffered heavy shelling during World War I, which burned the roof, damaged the apse, and caused a section of the arches to fall down, requiring a long restoration. Also in this century, some of the statuary – either damaged or weatherworn – has been removed from the exterior and replaced by copies.

The cathedral's western façade is one of the most splendid conceptions of the thirteenth century. Its three deep doorways constitute a bible in sculptured stone, with the central doorway dedicated to the Virgin, the left door to the saints and martyrs, and the right door to Christ and the prophets. Among the glorious statues, note the groups representing the Visitation and the Presentation to the Temple in the central door and the two angels flanking the scalped St Nicaise in the left door. One of these, the *ange au sourire* (the smiling angel), is the most famous of the cathedral's many angels and also is known as the *sourire de Reims* (the smile of Reims). The upper part of the façade is ornamented with a gallery of colossal statues of kings.

Inside, the tall windows, the clerestory, and the spectacular stained-glass windows provide superb lighting for the nave. Much of the thirteenth-century glass, including the awe-inspiring rose window of the western façade and the rose window in the northern transept, was restored after World War I. Other windows are completely modern, including the six windows in the axial chapel drawn by Marc Chagall and executed in 1974. Not to be overlooked is the interior sculpture, as in the remarkable ensemble of masterly statues in niches surrounding the smaller rose window of the façade and in the very beautiful capitals of the columns.

No matter when you visit the cathedral, try to come back to see the façade and the stained-glass-lit nave in the early morning or at twilight. That is also the time when the face of the *ange au sourire* is most beguiling. For a lovely view of the spectacular flying buttresses, stand in the garden of the adjacent *Palais du Tau*. There's also an interesting view of the cathedral, and of surrounding Reims, from atop its towers (entry possible at 11 a.m. and 3, 4, and 5 p.m.). Two different light and laser shows are presented at the cathedral Thursdays, Fridays, and Saturdays from June through September. Sound and light presentations of the coronations also take place. They are shown on Saturday evenings at 9.30 p.m. from late June to mid-August. For information, call the tourist office at 26-47-25-69. Enter the cathedral from Pl. du Cardinal Luçon.

Champagne Cellars

After a visit to the cathedral, a tour of one or more champagne cellars is the second 'must' for visitors to Reims – especially for those who are not going on to the much smaller city of Epernay, which rivals Reims as a centre of the champagne industry. Reims is the home of a greater number of champagne houses, and some of its cellars are the oldest in the region, dating back to ancient times when the Romans excavated huge chalk pits (*crayères*) in the limestone base of the city, creating inverted funnels that they undoubtedly used as cooling pantries. These gigantic cones often were connected underground, and in recent centuries it was discovered that conditions in this netherworld were perfect for the ageing of champagne. Today, the underground tunnels have been expanded so that there are miles and miles of them, some with the bare chalk walls still exposed, some covered by brick, tile, and other materials. Of the more than a dozen champagne houses in Reims that open their cellars to visitors, a number are beyond the Place de la République in the Champ de Mars section of the city; others are beyond the Basilique St Rémi around Place des Droits de l'Homme and nearby streets, including Avenue du Général Giraud, Boulevard Henri Vasnier, and Rue des Crayères.

Before descending into any of these caves, be sure to have a sweater or jacket handy; a constant temperature of 45F to 50F is one reason the cellars are ideal for making champagne. Also be reasonably well shod, because in most cases you'll be doing a fair amount of walking in a damp and dimly lit environment. All the champagne houses listed below offer guided tours; unless otherwise indicated, visits are weekdays, except holidays and the month of August, and by appointment only (9 a.m. to noon and 2 to 5 p.m. are accepted hours). Most offer tours in English, but travellers should verify that an English-speaking guide will be available when setting up an appointment. There is no charge for the tours, which sometimes end with a free tasting.

Besserat de Bellefon: These are the most modern cellars, built when the company moved from nearby Ay to Reims in 1970. Allée du Vignoble (phone: 26-36-09-18).

Charles Heidsieck: Fifty rooms of pure chalk linked by galleries. The Gallo-Roman *crayères*, shaped like a bottle end, were rediscovered in the eighteenth century. Tours are not always available; call ahead. 3 Pl. des Droits de l'Homme (phone: 26-85-03-27).

Heidsieck Monopole: Eight miles of chalk cellars. 83 Rue Coquebert (phone: 26-07-39-34).

Krug: Here the cellars are standard, but the famous oak barrels used for the first fermentation are special. Write or call two months in advance for appointments. Krug family members conduct two-hour tours. Closed in July. 3 Rue Coquebert (phone: 26-88-24-24).

Lanson: Beautiful wine presses are one of the things that make this an interesting visit. Open weekdays and by appointment. 66 Rue de Courlancy (phone: 26-40-24-40).

Louis Roederer: The enormous oak tuns (casks) here are extraordinary. Make reservations to see them well in advance of a visit. Closed Friday afternoons, weekends, and July. 21 Bd. Lundy (phone: 26-40-42-11).

Mumm: No appointment required to tour the 11 miles of gigantic cellars, open weekdays from 9 to 11 a.m. and 2 to 5 p.m., year-round. The tour is very informative – one of the best. 34 Rue du Champ de Mars (phone: 26-88-29-27).

Piper-Heidsieck: No appointment is required here either, where part of the visit is aboard an electric train. Open daily from late March to mid-November; weekdays only the rest of the year. 51 Bd. Henri Vasnier (phone: 26-85-01-94).

Pommery: Fascinating cellars: Down 116 steps are 11 miles of avenues with crossroads, statues (including a fourteenth-century Virgin), bas-reliefs, and extraordinary *crayères* that form pyramidal wells reaching through smooth white walls to daylight. Open all year; appointments required on weekends and public holidays. 5 Pl. Général Gouraud (phone: 26-61-62-63).

Ruinart Père & Fils: The pyramidal *crayères* date from the second century BC and are the only ones in the region classifed as a historic landmark. Closed weekends and holidays. 4 Rue des Crayères (phone: 26-85-40-29).

Taittinger: An interesting historical slide show precedes the tour of cellars set up in the crypt of the former abbey of St Nicaise and remarkable for their pointed arches. Other cellars are in beautiful triangular *crayères* from the third and fourth centuries. Open daily from March through November; closed weekends in winter. No appointment necessary. 9 Pl. St Nicaise (phone: 26-85-45-35).

Veuve Clicquot: No appointment is necessary to visit these extraordinary funnel-shaped *crayères*, which date from Gallo-Roman times. There are 15 miles of underground galleries with splendid bas-reliefs carved into the walls. Open daily, except Sundays, from 9 to 11 a.m. and 2 to 5 p.m., April through October. 1 Pl. des Droits de l'Homme (phone: 26-40-25-42).

Eating Out

L'Assiette Champenoise: Still one of the best in town. The fish preparations are exquisite, the daily specials are a sure bet, but the desserts are forgettable – except for the bittersweet chocolate cake. Michelin has awarded it one star. Open year-round. Reservations necessary. Major credit cards accepted. 40 Av. Paul Vaillant Couturier, Tinqueus (phone: 26-04-15-56). Very expensive.

Boyer Les Crayères: Nary a pilgrim leaves this temple of haute cuisine in less than a state of bliss. It isn't just the best restaurant in the region, it is one of the best in France (which to some gastronomes means the world). And even after Gérard Boyer and his wife, Elayne, have earned innumerable accolades, including a three-star rating from Michelin, they keep getting better. The greeting here is sunshine – some say the best welcome this side of heaven – and there is a warmth and glow in the restaurant that quickly converts to the comfort and contentment of its diners. The menu is seasonal, brilliantly inspired, and loaded with foods that have a special affinity to Champagne. Try the *escalope de foie gras*, the delicate and elegant fish dishes, the cabbage stuffed with langoustines, Boyer's famous truffle in puff pastry, the no less famous *salades du Père Maurice*, the local cheeses, and save room somehow for the riches of the dessert cart. Closed Mondays, Tuesdays at lunch, and mid-December to mid-January. Reservations necessary. Major credit cards accepted. 64 Bd. Henri Vasnier (phone: 26-82-80-80). Very expensive.

Le Chardonnay: This was the site of Boyer's original restaurant. When they moved to new quarters across town, they left behind Dominique Giraudeau, a young chef with impeccable training, who continues to offer fine fare here. This restaurant earned its first Michelin star in its first year and now unfailingly served meals that are the equal of (or superior to) many two-star operations. Try the steamed shrimp in a champagne-vinegar sauce, duck breasts with wild cherries, and exquisite desserts, especially the sherbet and the orange

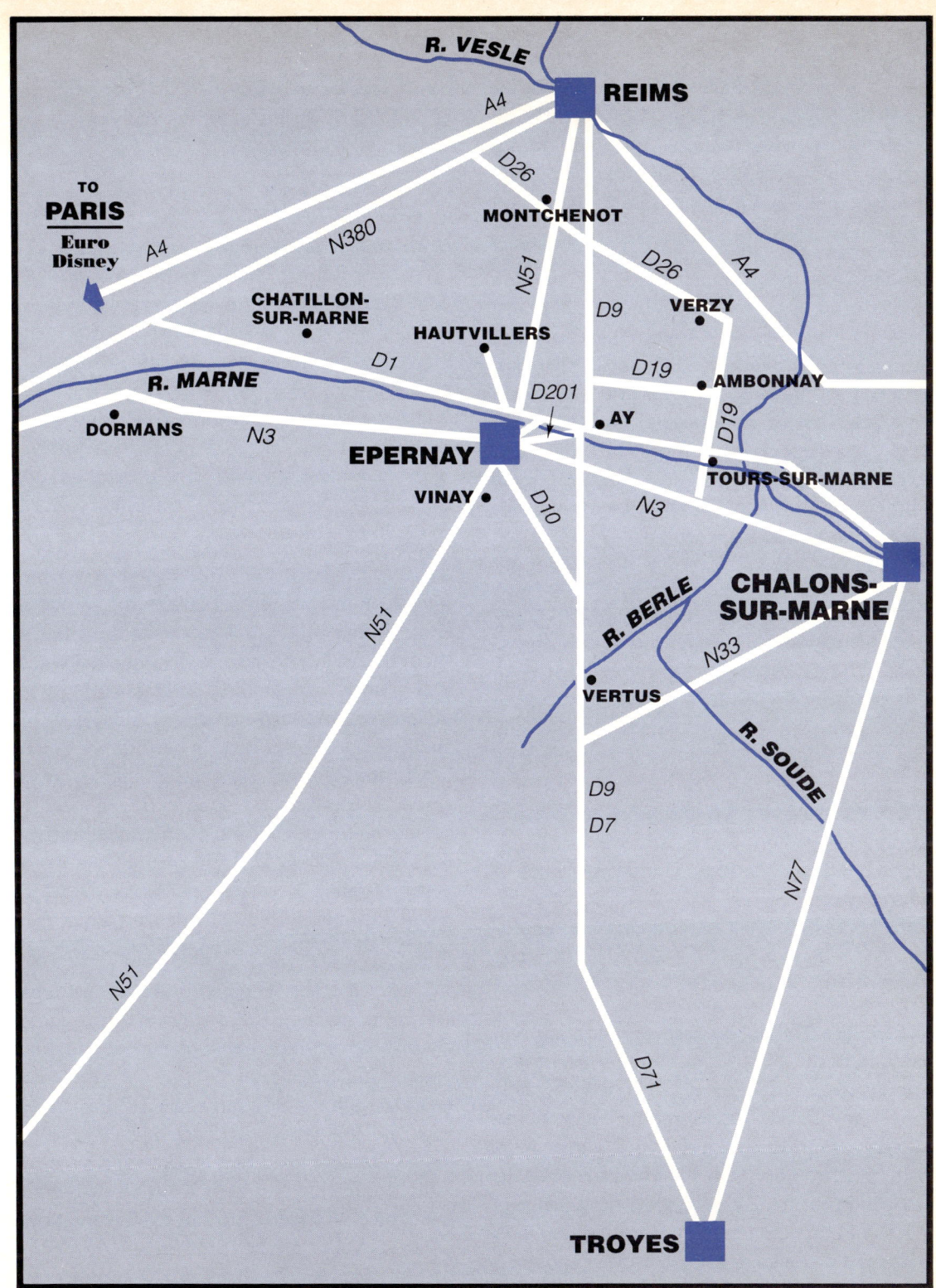

Route plan for tour of La Champagne

flan. Closed Saturdays at lunch, Sundays, most of August, and from 22 December to mid-January. Reservations advised. Major credit cards accepted. 184 Av. d'Epernay (phone: 26-06-08-60). Expensive to moderate.

Le Florence: This luxurious restaurant offers refined cooking characterized by delicate sauces, and some locals feel it offers the best food for the money in town. It's especially strong on fish dishes (crayfish, lobster, turbot, oysters), tantalizing desserts and a remarkable selection of champagne. One Michelin star. Closed Sunday evenings from November to Easter and from 20 July to 11 August; terrace dining in summer. Reservations advised. Major credit cards accepted. 43 Bd. Foch (phone: 26-47-12-70). Expensive to moderate.

Cinnamons: Local gastronomes in the know tout this restaurant, located just a few blocks from the cathedral, for chef Christian Clement's fine cuisine and the sincerity of Mme Clement's welcome. Specialities include *timbale de caille et son suprême à la crème d'ail* (timbale of quail with creamed garlic) and *duo de sole et saumon rose au beurre de Bouzy* (sole and salmon in red Bouzy wine and butter sauce). Closed Sunday evenings, Mondays, a week in February, and 22 July to 25 August. Reservations necessary. Major credit cards accepted. 36 Rue Chanzy (phone: 26-47-26-01; fax: 26-82-61-73). Moderate.

La Côte 108: A bit out of town, and first impressions here can be disappointing – the dining room is large and seems to lack ambience – but the food will make you forget the decor. In the autumn, there are wonderful *feuilletés* with wild mushrooms. Fish always is cooked to perfection, and dishes of wild duck *magrets* (slices of boneless breast) or lamb medallions with garlic cloves are superb. The balanced *menu dégustation* is a feast. Closed Sunday evenings, Mondays, and from 20 December through January. Reservations advised. Major credit cards accepted. In Berry au Brac, 7½ miles (12 km) from Reims via N44 (phone: 23-79-95-04). Moderate.

La Garenne: Chef Laurent LaPlaige was awarded his first Michelin star in 1990 at this restaurant in Champigny, just 4 miles (6 km) outside of Reims. His specialities include *filet de St Pierre grillé au jus de homard* (grilled fillet of John Dory with a light lobster sauce) and *ragoût de rognons de veau au Bouzy* (ragoût of veal kidneys in a red Bouzy wine). Closed Sunday evenings, Mondays, a week in February, and three weeks in August. Reservations necessary. Major credit cards accepted. On the RN31 route to Soissons (phone: 26-08-26-62). Moderate.

Au Petit Bacchus: Old and new mix harmoniously in this recently opened wine bar/lunch spot located on a small street behind the cathedral. Ceiling beams, wood-panelled walls, and rose marble tables add warmth to an otherwise modern motif. Daily specials chalked on blackboards announce light lunchtime platters, including cheese trays, smoked salmon, and such extravagances as caviar. As the name hints, wines take priority; the *cave* is excellent. Open from 11 a.m. to 8 p.m. daily. Reservations advised. Major credit cards accepted. 11 Rue de l'Université (phone: 26-47-10-05). Moderate.

Au Petit Comptoir: The bistro trend continues, and like many of France's starred chefs, Gérard Boyer (see *Les Crayères* above) has opened his version. A cosy, casual spot in the heart of Reims's old market area, it has all the requisite elements – a frosted glass façade, marble tables, zinc bar, and well-prepared, refined fare that can be had for an extremely fair price. Closed Sundays. Reservations advised. Major credit cards accepted. 17 Rue de Mars (phone: 26-40-58-58). Moderate.

Le Vigneron: Local cuisine *par excellence* is the stock in trade of the two small dining rooms in this seventeenth-century house. The rooms are decorated with old posters and a collection of rare wine labels; the atmosphere is friendly and very French. Try the Reims ham with grapes, pike in a champagne sauce, and *potée champenoise* (a stew of smoked ham, bacon, sausages, and cabbage). The wine list is reasonably priced and features an extensive selection of champagne and local still wines. Closed Saturday lunch, Sundays, and two weeks in August. Reservations unnecessary. Major credit cards accepted. Pl. Jamot (phone: 26-47-00-71). Moderate to inexpensive.

Waida: A popular pastry shop with a classic 1930s tearoom, complete with ceiling fans, inlaid woods, and an Art Deco stained-glass backdrop. Open daily from 7 a.m. to 8 p.m.; closed Sundays from 1 to 3.30 p.m. Reservations unnecessary. Major credit cards accepted. 3–5 Pl. d'Erion (phone: 26-47-44-49). Inexpensive.

En route from Reims

The Montagne de Reims, the first of the wine-growing areas of Champagne, is a gentle, wooded rise between Reims and the valleys of the Vesle and the Ardre to the north and Epernay and the valley of the Marne to the south. Route N51 cuts across it from north to south – between what is known as the *petite montagne* to the west and the *grande montagne* to the east – and connects Reims and Epernay somewhat as the crow flies. But the vineyards and wine villages, lying against the slopes, lead from one city to the other by a more circuitous route. Take N380 from Reims towards Château Thierry, then turn left on to D26 – the road to follow for the next 23 miles (37 km), as far as the village of Ambonnay.

The D26 first follows the flank of the 'small' mountain whose vineyards are the most acidic in the region. Leave the road briefly to see the church with a square steeple and lovely interior in Ville-Dommange and, nearby, the small twelfth- to sixteenth-century chapel of St Lie, surrounded by a quiet cemetery marked with two World War I *casemates* (bombproof shelters with openings for the guns). Pause for the view of Reims and its cathedral, the Reims plain, and the Tardenois woods, then drive on to Sacy, which has a beautiful twelfth-century church, and follow D26 through Ecueil, Chamery, and Sermiers to Montchenot, which has a splendid view of the flatland and also of Reims.

Eating Out
Auberge du Grand Cerf: With one Michelin star, this restaurant is rapidly becoming among the best in the area, with a chef who tends to avoid traditional dishes in favour of more inventive nouvelle ones. For a perfect marriage with champagne, try the warm oysters or the scallops in puff pastry. Any fish dish is recommended. Also recommended are the beautiful salads made of whatever is freshest in the market, duck liver fritters, lamb with ginger and mangoes, and the pastry cart. The *prix fixe* menus give a good sampling of what's best. Closed Sunday evenings, Wednesdays, late February to early March, and the last two weeks of August. Reservations advised. Major credit cards accepted. On the N51, Montchenot (phone: 26-97-60-07; fax: 26-97-64-24). Expensive to moderate.

En route from Montchenot

After crossing N51, D26 begins to follow the flank of the 'big' mountain. Villers Allerand, which contains a church from the thirteenth and fourteenth centuries, is the first village down the road; then comes Rilly-la-Montagne, which counts a number of champagne producers among its 1,000 inhabitants. Fittingly, the town's church has sculptured stalls depicting *vignerons* (vine growers). Rilly is the starting point for walks on 900-foot-hight Mt Joli, one of the few places where the Montagne de Reims comes to a point, and thus one that affords a wonderful panorama of the plain of Reims.

Next on D26 is Chigny-les-Roses, where there's an interesting Renaissance door to the sanctuary of the church, and Ludes, whose fifteenth- to sixteenth-century church has a statue of the Virgin and Child holding a bunch of grapes. Ludes also has the champagne cellars of Canard-Duchêne (phone: 26-61-10-96; fax: 26-61-13-90), which can be visited. These beautiful, long, and scrupulously clean chalk cellars, with attractively arched galleries, are open weekdays (10 a.m. to noon and 2 to 4 p.m.) year-round except August and holidays. Tours in English are available; call or fax two weeks ahead.

An area of first-rate vineyards begins at Mailly Champagne. To visit the champagne cellar of the village's cooperative Société des Producteurs phone: 26-49-41-10. It is open year-round for visits weekdays from 9 a.m. to noon and 2 to 5 p.m., from 9 to 11 a.m. and 3 to 5.30 p.m. on Saturdays, and 3 to 5.30 p.m. on Sundays. There is a charge for the visit and tasting. The vineyards of Verzenay, less than 2 miles (3 km) away, produce exceptional wine, but the town is also well known for its old windmill, probably the only one left in Champagne, which was used as an observation tower during World War I. In nearby Verzy, follow the road on the right (D34) into the forest, leave the car in the parking lot, and walk to the observatory of Mt Sinai. From this very panoramic spot, the highest point in the Montagne de Reims (928 feet), General Gouraud watched the progress of the battle of Reims in 1918. For an interesting – and unusual – sight, take the forest road to the left of the modern chapel of St Basles on D34 to reach the Faux de Verzy, a bizarre landscape of twisted beech trees with corkscrew-like branches, some 1,000 years old.

Beyond Verzy is Villers Marmery, where you can detour 3 miles (5 km) off D26 – crossing highways A4 and N44 and the village of Les Petites Loges – to Sept-Saulx, the site of a fine restaurant and hotel.

Eating Out

Cheval Blanc: In the middle of a quiet village, this charming, vine-covered inn offers views of a park and of the Vesle river. There are 2 suites and 19 well-equipped rooms (all with colour TV sets and decorated with antique furniture), as well as a tennis court. The large and comfortable dining room has an elegant country look and even a fireplace for roasting meats over an open flame. The atmosphere is friendly and cordial, the service attentive, and the food rates (and earns) stars (one from Michelin). Try the fish dishes or the lamb with fresh mint. The wine list is among the area's best. Closed from mid-January to mid-February. Reservations necessary. Major credit cards accepted. Rue du Moulin, Sept-Saulx (phone: 26-03-90-27; fax: 26-03-97-09). Expensive to moderate.

En route from Sept-Saulx

Continuing on the D26, you come to Trepail, where the small church has columns decorated with sculptured animals, before reaching villages that are known for their fruity red wines. One of these, Ambonnay, is picturesquely set amid the vines with a church that has an elegant Romanesque steeple and a pure, well-preserved interior. Another, Bouzy – reached by switching from D26 to D19 at Ambonnay – is famous for its non-sparkling Bouzy *rouge* (as well as for the particularly suggestive sound of its name to speakers of English). Louvois, with a twelfth-century church, lies just northwest of Bouzy. Here, where the vineyards end, you can look through eighteenth-century wrought-iron gates and be rewarded with the classic prospect of an impressive château standing in the midst of a vast park. Much of Château Louvois, which belonged to a chancellor of France and the father of one of Louis XIV's ministers, was destroyed during the French Revolution, so except for its outbuildings, most of what you see dates from post-revolutionary days.

From Louvois to Epernay on D9, our route leads through farmland and woods and the villages of Tauxières, Mutry, Fontaine-sur-Ay, and Avenay-Val-d'Or. This last is worth a stop to see the Flamboyant Gothic portal and rich interior of St Tresain, a beautiful church built in the twelfth and sixteenth centuries. Then you'll be among lovely vineyards again, but by now belonging to the Vallée de la Marne. Following D9, D1, and D201, you will shortly be in Ay, a small town that is the home of champagne houses, then Epernay, with even more champagne houses; its importance in the production of champagne belies its size. You can stop to visit Ay at this point, but since it is an appropriate starting place for a tour of the villages and vineyards of the Marne, stretching east and west of here, you may want to visit Epernay first, returning to Ay as you take to the road later.

Epernay

In the heart of the vineyards, strongly provincial in character, and dotted with parks and gardens, Epernay (about 16 miles/27 km from Reims) rivals Reims as the capital of the king of wines. It is small (pop. 29,000) compared to Reims, and it lacks the other city's architectural richness. The great champagne firms established here are its main attractions. Miles and miles of champagne cellars (*caves*), where millions of bottles of bubbly now are ageing, have been hewn out of the chalky soil under Epernay, and the major champagne houses offer tours of their facilities. The Office du Tourisme (7 Av. de Champagne; phone: 26-55-33-00) distributes a brochure giving the firms' hours; several of the most famous houses are right on the Avenue de Champagne. Remember that the cellars have a constant temperature of 45F to 50F, so bring a jacket or warm sweater. Appropriate shoes also are recommended, in part because some cellars are damp and may be slippery, in part because the tours usually involve a bit of walking underground, occasionally in rather dark surroundings. All tours are free, and it is not unusual for them to end with a taste of the product, though this is unpredictable. Tours in English are offered by most firms, but if you are travelling in the off-season, it might be best to call ahead to make sure a guide is available.

Of the major houses open to the public in Epernay, Moët et Chandon (20 Av. de Champagne; phone: 26-54-71-11) is the largest and has the most extensive cellars – 17 miles of galleries. Although they are not the most beautiful cellars, Moët's explanation of the making of champagne is extremely good, hence it is one of the most popular tourist spots in all of France. The cellars are open weekdays (10 a.m. to 12.30 p.m. and 2 to 5.30 p.m.) year-round, and also on Saturdays (10 a.m. to noon and 2 to 5.30 p.m.) and Sundays (9.30 a.m. to noon and 2 to 4 p.m.) between 29 March and 31 October. Nearby, Mercier (70 Av. de Champagne; phone: 26-54-75-26) conducts the tour of its 11 miles of cellars aboard an electric train. The cellars are open from 1 March to 1 October daily, from 10 a.m. to noon and 2 to 5.30 p.m. except Sundays and holidays, when closing is at 4.30 p.m.; they are also open from 1 November to 12 December. Neither Moët et Chandon nor Mercier requires an appointment, but at Perrier-Jouet (26 Av. de Champagne; phone: 26-55-20-53), which has 6 miles of brick, chalk, and stone cellars, an appointment is requested. It is open from 1 May to 15 September, weekdays from 9 a.m. to noon and 2 to 5 p.m. only. The 6 miles of cellars at De

Castellane (57 Rue de Verdun; phone: 26-55-15-33) can be seen weekdays except holidays and August from 10 a.m. to noon and 2 to 6 p.m.; and the dark and spacious cellars of Pol Roger (1 Rue Henri Lelarge; phone: 26-55-41-95) also are open weekdays, except August, by appointment only.

Eating Out

Les Berceaux: The cooking is good, the atmosphere that of a country dining room. Try the turbot in champagne sauce or thin veal with *chanterelles* (wild mushrooms). Closed Sunday evenings, also Mondays from November to March. Major credit cards accepted. 13 Rue des Berceaux, Epernay (phone: 26-55-28-84). Expensive to moderate.

La Terrasse: The menu is limited, but it represents good value. Closed Sunday evenings and Mondays. Major credit cards accepted. 7 Quai de la Marne, Epernay (phone: 26-55-26-05). Moderate to inexpensive.

Le Chapon Fin: It can't claim the most elegant dining room, but it's a nice place to try a few local dishes such as *andouillettes* (small sausages made with chitterlings) *au champagne*. Closed Wednesdays and the last two weeks in August. Visa accepted. 2 Pl. Mendès-France, Epernay (phone: 26-55-40-03). Inexpensive.

Le Palmie: For a fine couscous, with a local red wine. The restaurant is run by Moroccans. Closed Mondays. Reservations advised. Major credit cards accepted. 2 Pl. Carnot, Epernay (phone: 26-54-54-71). Inexpensive.

En route from Epernay

You can tour the vine-laden slopes and graceful landscapes of the winding Marne Valley by taking D201 directly into Ay, crossing the Marne and the canal that runs along it. Or, for a more comprehensive trip, take N3 east, crossing the Marne some miles down the road via D19 into Tours-sur-Marne, and return west towards Ay via D1. If you opt for the detour you will see several towns: Tours-sur-Marne, a town with an old priory and, near the tree-lined canal, the headquarters of Laurent Perrier, whose ancient cellars and collection of rare, large champagne bottles are open weekdays, except August, by appointment only (phone: 26-58-91-22); Bisseuil, famous for its red wines and with a church worth visiting for the beauty of its vaults and columns (ask for the key at the house next door); and Mareuil-sur-Ay, which offers a good view of the vineyards, a twelfth-century church, and the headquarters of Philipponnat, whose cellars can be visited weekdays, except August, by appointment (phone: 26-52-60-43).

Ay

This quiet town of 5,000 stands on the banks of the canal across the Marne almost 2 miles (3 km) north of Epernay. Because the vineyards of the area are on slopes of undulating ground in a particularly felicitous position, its wine has been renowned for centuries and was supplied in earlier days to the kings of France and England and to a Renaissance pope. Ay (pronounced *Ah-ee*) suffered serious damage during the war, but it still has some preserved fifteenth- and sixteenth-century churches and several half-timbered houses, including a wood-panelled one on Rue St Vincent that is described as once having been the press house of Henri IV. The champagne cellars of Bollinger (4 Bd. Maréchal de Lattre; phone: 26-55-21-31), Deutz (16 Rue Jeanson; phone: 26-55-15-11), and Ayala (2 Bd. du Nord; phone: 26-55-15-44) can be visited by appointment on weekdays only. There is also a museum containing a collection of tools relating to the cultivation of the vine.

En route from Ay

As you head west on D1, celebrated vineyards are on your right; the left is dominated by a developing suburb of Epernay. In Dizy, turn right on to N51 (the main road to Reims) and drive up the rising road to Champillon. Here is a splendid, not-to-be-missed panorama of the Marne Valley vineyards. Nearby Hautvillers can be reached directly from D1 back at Dizy via N386 or through the tiniest of back roads from Champillon.

Eating Out

Royal Champagne: Set high in the countryside, this small hotel looks down on the vineyards, the Marne Valley, and Epernay. Its 22 small rooms, set off from the main building – formerly an eighteenth-century coaching house – are furnished beautifully, and most of them have a terrace with a vineyard view. Its celebrated restaurant offers a mix of traditional and nouvelle dishes, particularly fish dishes that go splendidly with champagne, as well as such specialities as veal *grenadin* and chicken fricassée. There is a nice selection of local cheeses and an extensive wine list from which a competent and friendly sommelier will help you select a champagne or local still wine not normally found outside France. Expect to see producers entertaining their guests in the comfortable and tastefully decorated dining room with a lovely view of the vine-covered hills. Restaurant closed for three weeks in January. Reservations advised. Major credit cards accepted. On N51, Champillon (phone: 26-52-87-11; fax: 26-52-89-69). Expensive.

Hautvillers

This tiny hilltop village has old houses with arched doorways and interesting wrought-iron signs depicting the various tasks of the *vigneron*, but it is the Abbaye de St Pierre d'Hautvillers that always has been the focus for travellers. Of all the medieval abbeys in Champagne – and the abbeys of the Middle Ages were powerful, both as intellectual centres and as the owners of vast properties, including vineyards – none was better known than Hautvillers, which for nearly twelve centuries (from the time of its founding in 660) was one of the most famous in France. The continuing fame of the abbey (though not much of it remains) is due to the Benedictine monk Pierre Perignon, its cellar master from the late 1660s to the end of his life, in 1715. Dom Perignon revolutionized local wine making by developing the technique of the second fermentation in the bottle that gives champagne its sparkle, by creating the *cuvée* (blend) that in part is champagne's guarantee of quality and consistency, and by making other innovations. Dom Perignon is said to have exclaimed to his fellow monks, 'Come quickly! I am drinking stars!' on the occasion of the world's first champagne tasting.

The abbey site, above the village, is now owned by Moët et Chandon, whose attractive *Musée Dom Perignon*, filled with historical documents and artifacts relating to champagne making, is open only to guests of the company. Open to the general public (and not to be missed) is the spectacular view from the abbey's broad stone terrace – the same spot is sometimes used for celebrations and fêtes relating to champagne. Then visit the little church, with its fine woodcarvings and organ, where Dom Perignon and his uncle and friend, Dom Thierry Ruinart, are buried.

En route from Hautvillers

Return to D1 and turn right to reach Cumières, a village known for its delicate red wine. The picturesque road continues along the right bank of the Marne through Damery, which has a fine twelfth- to sixteenth-century church, and then through Venteuil, Reuil, and Binson, which has an old priory with a restored twelfth-century chapel. A little farther west and just off D1 is Châtillon-sur-Marne, with a large statue of Pope Urban II, the remains of a castle, and a good view of the Marne. Go through Verneuil and Vincelles – the limit of the Marne *département* – and cross the river to Dormans, a picturesque old town considerably damaged by the war, but still endowed with a beautiful church dating from the thirteenth century and a seventeenth-century château. From the Chapelle de la Reconnaissance (Chapel of Gratitude), built in the middle of a large park to commemorate the battles of the Marne (1914 and 1918), there is a fine view over the valley.

Dormans is the turnaround point for the stretch of the Champagne route leading through the vineyards of the Marne Valley. Return to Epernay along the southern side of the river by staying on N3 the whole way, or for a better view from a higher road, by going part of the way on D222 (reached by taking D226 uphill out of Port-à-Binson) and passing through Oeuilly, Boursault, and Vauciennes before dropping down again to N3.

The vineyards of the Côte des Blancs, where the aristocratic white chardonnary grapes grow, are traversed by D10 and D9 south of Epernay. The excusion – as far as Bergères-les-Vertus – is a peaceful and leisurely morning or afternoon drive begun by leaving Epernay on N51 and turning left on to D10 at Pierry.

Eating Out
La Brigueterie: A quiet place surrounded by gardens and vineyards, this hotel is in one of the area's nicest spots. Since it is only about 4 miles (6 km) from Epernay (off N51 beyond Pierry), it can be a convenient base for touring. Its 42 rooms and public areas recently underwent extensive renovation, and brought the comfort level in line with the French government's four-star rating. A swimming pool, sauna, workout room, conference facilities, and a new restaurant were added. Pleasant and inviting, the one-star (Michelin) restaurant is the sort of place where French families take their midday meal on Sundays. The continental breakfast is wonderful. During the summer, have a drink outside on the lovely terrace. Open daily. Major credit cards accepted. 4 Rte de Sezanne, Vinay (phone: 26-59-99-99; fax: 26-59-92-10). Expensive.

En route from Vinay

Heading south on D10, you come to the boundary of the black grape area at Cuis, where a twelfth-century Romanesque church built on a terrace dominating the village affords a pretty view. The next town, Cramant, is one of the most renowned in the region for the quality of its grapes, which are white only. Cramant is a charming village, and if you detour up through its vineyards you'll see the elegant and finely maintained Château Saran, set imposingly on the hillside. South of Cramant, Avize, in the heart of the Côte des Blancs, has an interesting church, mostly twelfth-century Romanesque, but with a fifteenth-century Gothic transept and choir. Next comes Oger, also with an early church, and then Le Mesnil-sur-Oger, another village producing famous *blanc de blancs*, with another interesting church. Note particularly the seventeenth-century panelling inside and the Renaissance door.

Vertus lies on D9 after it merges with D10. This quiet little town with irregular streets and charming squares was once a fortified city. A medieval gate remains as does the church of St Martin, a remarkable example of the transition from Romanesque to Gothic style. Walk around the church to see 'the wells of St Martin', where springs form a mirrorlike pond.

Eating Out
La Commedia: This restaurant (guest rooms are no longer available) provides a chance to meet

the people and try the local food – veal kidney and fish with champagne sauce are good choices. Three very inexpensive *prix fixe* menus are offered. Major credit cards accepted. 4 Rue de Châlons, Vertus (phone: 26-52-12-20). Inexpensive.

Hostellerie de la Reine Blanche: Looking something like a streamlined Alpine ski lodge, this 23-room hotel is well equipped and comfortable, and includes a restaurant. Closed two weeks in February. Major credit cards accepted. 18 Av. Louis Lenoir, Vertus (phone: 26-52-20-76; fax: 26-52-16-59). Hotel, inexpensive; restaurant, moderate to inexpensive.

En route from Vertus

Between Vertus and Bergères-les-Vertus, the Côte des Blancs ends and black grapes are seen again. Beyond Bergères, Mont-Aime, the site of prehistoric, Roman, and feudal remains, offers a splendid view back over the Côte des Blancs vineyards and forward towards Châlons-sur-Marne, 18 miles (29 km) northeast on N33.

Châlons-sur-Marne

Built on both sides of the Marne, this ancient crossroads town of 54,300 is an administrative centre for the Marne *département*. Attila the Hun was defeated on the plain of Châlons in AD 451, and the town has played a significant role in military history ever since, especially under Napoleon III and during the two world wars. It is still the home of an important military school. Châlons has, in part, a bourgeois look, with seventeenth- and eighteenth-century townhouses, tree-lined riverbanks, and sixteenth-century bridges (Pont de l'Arche Mauvillan, Pont des Viviers, Pont des Mariniers) crossing canals formed by Marne tributaries. A tourist office is at 3 Quai des Arts (phone: 26-65-17-89).

Two of Châlons's many churches stand out. The Cathédrale St Etienne is known for the pure Gothic style of its northern façade and for its beautiful stained-glass windows, which span the twelfth to the sixteenth century – a vertitable survey of the development of the art. Its seventeenth-century western portal is massive and impressive, and there is also superb artwork in various other sections – in the chapels, the northern transept, and in the treasury. The Eglise Notre Dame en Vaux shows characteristics of the Romanesque–Gothic transition period and is a masterpiece of twelfth-century *champenoise* architecture. The interior is harmoniously proportioned and illuminated by beautiful sixteenth-century stained-glass windows, and its carillon of 56 bells chimes out ancient melodies. Just north is the *Musée du Cloître* (Rue Nicolas Durand; phone: 26-64-03-87), which contains some 50 recently excavated carved columns, marvels of twelfth-century art. (Open daily except Tuesdays from 10 a.m. to noon and from 2 to 6 p.m.)

Two other medieval churches in Châlons – St Jean and St Alpin – also are noteworthy, particularly for their stained-glass windows. The eighteenth-century Préfecture (County Hall) is of architectural interest, and the *Musée Municipal*, containing artifacts from the Stone Age to the Gallo-Roman era, is of archaeological interest (Rue Carnot; phone: 26-64-38-42; open from 2 to 6 p.m. daily except Tuesdays and holidays). The Bibliothèque Municipale (Town Library), in an eighteenth-century residence (Passage Vendel; phone: 26-68-54-44), has a rich collection of antiquarian books and illuminated manuscripts, including *The Confessions of St Augustine*, the *Romance of the Rose*, and the *Book of Hours*. (Open from 9 a.m. to noon and 2 to 6 p.m. except Sundays, Mondays, and holidays.)

Eating Out
Angleterre: In the centre of town, this charming hotel has 18 rooms and a garden where

you may lunch or dine. Named after its chef, Jacky Michel, the restaurant offers three attractive *prix fixe* menus, a wine list that changes monthly, and good value – especially on champagne. Considered by many to be the best in town; Michelin has awarded it one star. Closed Saturdays at lunch, Sundays, and from late December to early January and the first half of July. Reservations advised. Major credit cards accepted. 19 Pl. Monseigneur-Tissier, Châlons-sur-Marne (phone: 26-68-21-51). En route from Chalons: Take N77 directly to Troyes, 48 miles (77 km) away.

Troyes

The southern part of Champagne is all too often ignored by visitors, especially Troyes, the region's former capital. This was not so in the Middle Ages, when the city was a centre of international commerce and one of the sites of the annual champagne trade fairs (troy weight, one of the standards of measurement set by the fairs, persists today). Troyes was an equally famous centre of the arts in medieval times and remained so even after its commercial importance had begun to decline. As the Renaissance replaced the Gothic age, the influence of a uniquely Troyen school of architecture spread over the entire region and into Burgundy, Troyen sculptors approached their finest hour, and Troyen stained-glass craftsmen were well on their way to filling the city's churches with kaleidoscopic light. Today, Troyes remains at once one of the great art towns of France, with a delightful old section of narrow streets and half-timbered houses, and a modern, bustling, prosperous town of 64,800 inhabitants, many employed in the manufacture of textiles – as their ancestors were since the sixteenth century. There's an Office du Tourisme near the station (16 Bd. Carnot; phone: 25-73-00-36), and another one near the cathedral (24 Quai Dampierre; phone: 25-72-34-30) that is open only from early June to mid-September.

Troyes's churches were the main beneficiaries of its artists' outpouring of sculpture and stained glass, and the Cathédrale St Pierre et St Paul is endowed with a wealth of it. Built from the thirteenth to the seventeenth century, the church has a richly decorated sixteenth-century Flamboyant Gothic façade with a rose window above the central portal (carvings and statues missing from the tympana of the doors were destroyed during the French Revolution). Walk around to the doorway of the north transept – the thirteenth-century *Beau Portail* – for another rose window and four rosettes. Inside, the stained glass is stunning, from the earlier, thirteenth-century windows of the choir to the mainly sixteenth-century windows of the nave, including the Tree of Jesse window. The treasury of the church has a collection of beautiful sixteenth-century enamels, and the church tower provides a fine view of the town. Friday and Saturday evenings from early June through September, a spectacular *Cathédrale de Lumière* show featuring laser images and sound is performed here, as in the cathedrals of nearby Reims and L'Epine. At press time, it was uncertain whether the show would continue. For information, call the tourist office (phone numbers listed above).

The Basilique St Urbain, built in the thirteenth century by Pope Urban IV on the spot where his father had a cobbler's shop, is also known for its splendid stained-glass windows – which here occupy so much wall space, you'll wonder how the edifice stays upright. It is also known for its many noteworthy statues, especially the *Vierge au raisin*, a beautiful example of local sixteenth-century sculpture. A third church, Eglise Ste Madeliene, dates from the twelfth century. Though it is Troyes's oldest church, the marvellous stained glass in its choir is from the sixteenth century, as are its sculptured masterpieces: the intricately Flamboyant rood screen and the statue of St Martha.

You'll see the picturesque old section of town, full of restored sixteenth-century houses, if you wander around in the vicinity of the Eglise St Jean. Do walk along Rue Champeaux, and don't miss Rue des Chats, where the cantilevered gables of the houses almost touch each other across the narrow street. Troyes also has several interesting small museums. The *Musée des Beaux-Arts et d'Histoire Naturelle* (1 Rue Chrétien de Troyes), in the eighteenth-century Abbaye St Loup, has a varied collection of art and artifacts including a nice collection of fifteenth- to sixteenth-century paintings. (Open from 10 a.m. to noon and 2 to 6 p.m. daily except Tuesdays.) The *Musée Historique de Troyes et de Champagne*, with good sculptures, drawings, and paintings from the region, and the *Musée de la Bonneterie*, which traces the history of the region's textile industry, are both in the Hôtel de Vauluisant (4 Rue de Vauluisant with an interesting façade; its hours are the same as those of the *Musée des Beaux-Arts*, with which there is a reciprocal entry arrangement). There also is the *Maison de l'Outil et de la Pensée Ouvrière* (7 Rue de la Trinité; phone: 25-73-28-26), which has tools and craftsmen's implements. (Open daily except Tuesdays from 9 a.m. to noon and 2 to 7 p.m., the *Musée des Beaux-Arts* closes an hour earlier in winter.) The *Musée de Pharmacie* (Hôtel Dieu le Comte, Quai des Comtes de Champagne) is a beautiful old pharmacy that remains as it was at the beginning of the eighteenth century. It includes collections of tools, faïence, and other objects used in the original pharmacy. For information about this and other museums in Troyes, call 25-80-49-84. But to many, the city's most interesting museum is the *Musée d'Art Moderne* (Pl. St Pierre; phone: 25-80-57-30). Located to the right of the cathedral in the former episcopal palace, this collection featuring some 1,500 works by Braque, Bonnard, Cézanne, Gauguin, Matisse, Picasso, and other artists is one of Europe's most important gatherings of contemporary art. (Open from 11 a.m. to 6 p.m., except Tuesdays and holidays.)

Eating Out

Valentino: The city's finest place to eat, and its prettiest, is in the old part of town. The emphasis is on fish; the sea bass preparations are remarkable. And don't skip dessert. Closed Sunday evenings, Mondays, mid-August to 6 September, and early February. Major credit cards accepted. Cour de la Rencontre, Troyes (phone: 25-73-14-14). Expensive.

Le Chanoine Gourmand: A tiny dollhouse of an eatery located just behind the cathedral where the bright young chef-owner Heriot Christian turns out inventive and delicate dishes such as langoustine with hot lime vinaigrette and *coq rouge* (a rare fish) in red wine sauce. In summer, a pleasant garden behind the restaurant expands the seating capacity. Closed Sunday evenings and Mondays, one week in mid-March, one week in mid-August, and Christmas to mid-January. Major credit cards accepted. 32 Rue de la Cité, Troyes (phone: 25-80-42-06). Expensive to moderate.

Bourgogne: This is a safe address in Troyes, meaning that the dishes are well prepared (one Michelin star) but not very innovative, and that the wine list is nice but limited. The service, however, is impeccable. Closed Sundays, Monday evenings, and August. Reservations advised. Major credit cards accepted. 40 Rue Général de Gaulle, Troyes (phone: 25-73-02-67). Moderate.

7
MINI-GUIDE TO PARIS

With the site of the Euro Disney Resort set so close to Paris, it is inevitable that visitors to Euro Disneyland will spend significant amounts of time in the City of Light. For that reason, we are including this qualitative guide to Paris, hoping that the data that follows will make a visit to the French capital more enjoyable and illuminating.

Like a magnet, Paris has always attracted visitors from every corner of the earth. But despite this constant wave of new inhabitants, the city has remained fiercely French – some would say provincial – with its own argot, neighbourhood sovereignty, and a sense that it is still a collection of 20 separate villages.

As the quintessentially beautiful centre of intellectual life and the home of the arts of every sort, Paris has earned its City of Light title. Even though it is more and more affected by the blights that mar other municipalities around the globe, its pervasive beauty and romantic atmosphere remain, and its supreme talent for civilized living has made the city beloved by French and non-French alike.

After all, this is the place where food preparation became fine art, where fashion standards – for men and women – are set, and where new trends for all of Europe are embraced or discarded. Yet despite its willingness to review innovative ideas, Parisians are determined that their city should remain as it has always been. They love their remarkable heritage with unshakable passion, and perhaps it is this love – together with the irrepressible local sense of good living – that has made Paris so irresistibly attractive to others.

Paris At-a-Glance

Seeing the City

It's impossible to single out just one perfect Paris panorama; they exist in profusion. The most popular is the bird's-eye view from the top of the Eiffel Tower on the Left Bank; there are several places to have snacks and drinks and enjoy a view (on a clear day) of more than 50 miles. (There also are three restaurants where you can enjoy fine dining.) The tower is open daily, 10 a.m. to 11 p.m.; admission charge (Champ-de-Mars; phone: 45-55-91-11). From the top of the towers of Notre-Dame, eager spectators enjoy close-ups of the cathedral's Gothic spires and flying buttresses, along with a magnificent view of the Ile de la Cité and the rest of Paris. Start climbing the steps at the foot of the north tower; admission charge (Rue du Cloître Notre-Dame, 4e; phone 43-25-42-92). On the Right Bank there's a stunning view from the terrace of Sacré-Coeur. The observatory on Tour Montparnasse also offers a striking panorama, as does the landing at the top of the escalator at the Centre Georges Pompidou, and the observation deck of Samaritaine, the ten-floor department store at the foot of the Pont-Neuf. The most satisfying view, if not the highest, is from the top of the Arc de Triomphe. The arch is the centre of Place Charles-de-Gaulle, once Place de l'Etoile (Square of the Star), so called because it is the centre of a 'star' whose radiating points are the twelve broad avenues,

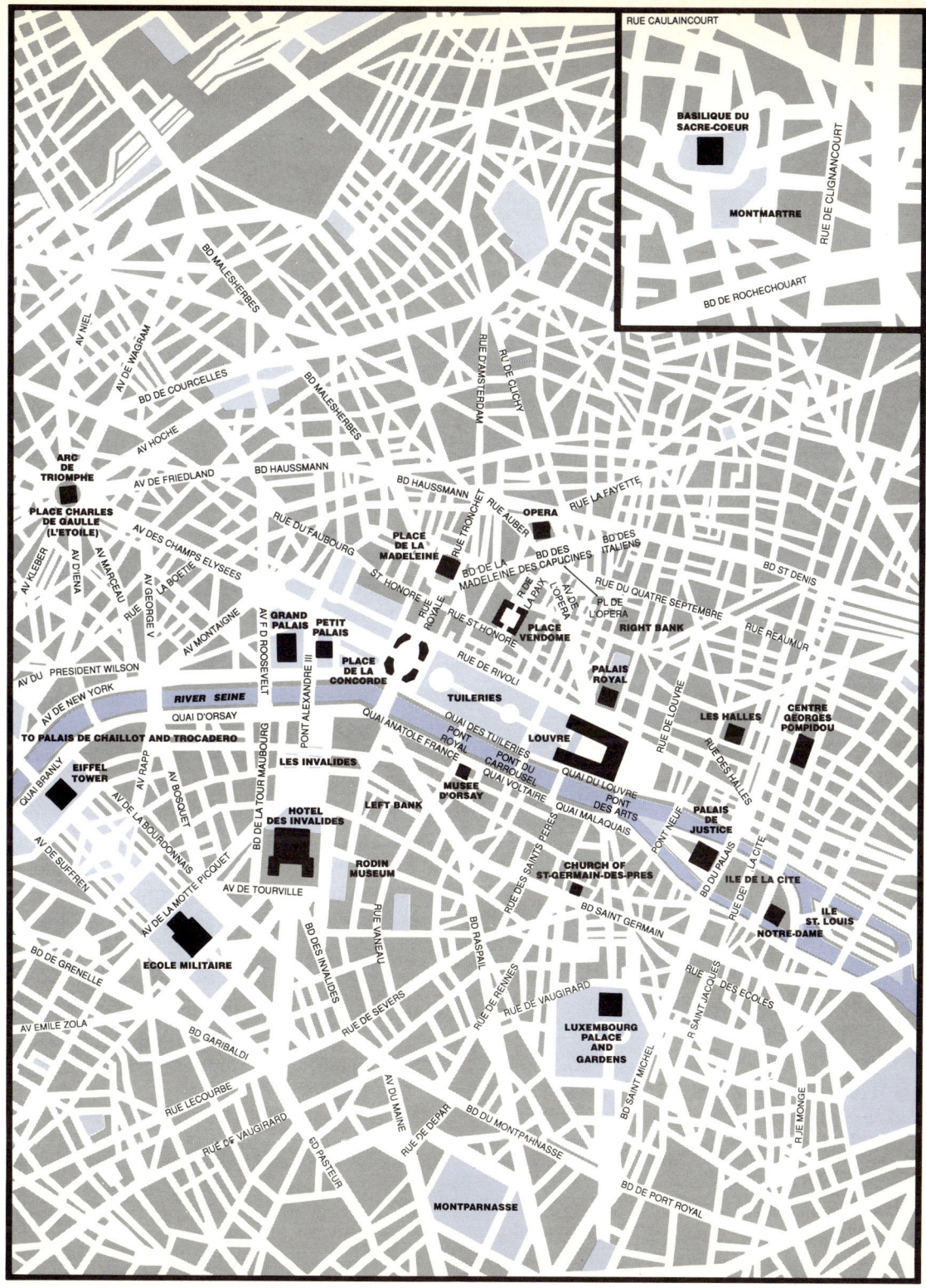

Paris: map of the city

including the Champs-Elysées, planned and built by Baron Haussmann in the mid-nineteenth century. Open daily, 10 a.m. to 5.30 p.m.; admission charge (phone: 43-80-31-31).

Special Places

Getting around this sprawling metropolis isn't difficult once you understand the layout of the 20 *arrondissements*. We suggest that visitors orient themselves by taking one of the many excellent sightseeing tours offered by Cityrama (4 Pl. des Pyramides, 1er; phone: 42-60-30-14) or Paris Vision (214 Rue de Rivoli, 1er; phone: 42-60-31-25). Their bubble-top, double-decker buses are equipped with earphones for simultaneous commentary in English and several other languages. Reserve through any travel agent or your hotel's concierge. Once you have a better idea of the basic layout of the city, buy a copy of *Paris Indispensable* or *Plan de Paris par Arrondissement* at any bookshop or newsstand. These little lifesavers list streets alphabetically and indicate the nearest métro station on individual maps and an overall plan. Now you're ready to set out by foot (the most rewarding) or by métro (the fastest and surest) to discover Paris for yourself.

Street addresses of the places mentioned throughout the chapter are followed by their *arrondissement* number.

La Rive Droite (The Right Bank)

Arc de Triomphe and Place Charles-de-Gaulle: This monumental arch (165 feet high, 148 feet wide) was built between 1806 and 1836 to commemorate Napoleon's victories. It underwent a major clean-up and restoration for the bicentennial of the French Revolution. Note the frieze and its six-foot-high figures, the ten impressive sculptures (especially Rude's 'La Marseillaise' on the right as you face the Champs-Elysées), and the arches inscribed with the names of Bonaparte's victories, as well as those of Empire heroes. Beneath the arch is the French Tomb of the Unknown Soldier and its Eternal Flame, which is rekindled each day at 6.30 p.m. An elevator (or 284 steps) takes visitors to the top for a great view of the city and the twelve avenues radiating from l'Etoile. Admission charge. Pl. Charles-de-Gaulle (phone: 43-80-31-31).

Champs-Elysées: Paris's legendary promenade, the 'Elysian Fields', was swampland until 1616. It has come to be synonymous with everything glamorous in the city, though the 'Golden Arches' and shlocky shops recently have replaced much of the old glamour (a commission was formed in 1990 to try to restore some of the old elegance). The Champs-Elysées stretches for more than two miles between the Place de la Concorde and the Place Charles-de-Gaulle (l'Etoile). The very broad avenue, lined with rows of plane and horse chestnut trees, shops, cafés, and cinemas, is perfect for strolling, window shopping, and people watching.

The area from the Place de la Concorde to the Rond-Poit des Champs-Elysées is a charming park, where Parisians often bring their children. On the north side of the gardens is the Palais de l'Elysée, the official home of the President of the French Republic. Ceremonial events, such as the Bastille Day Parade (14 July), frequently take place along the Champs-Elysées.

Grand Palais: Off the Champs-Elysées, on opposite sides of Avenue Winston Churchill, are the elaborate turn-of-the-century Grand Palais and Petit Palais (Large Palace and Small Palace), built of glass and stone for the 1900 World Exposition. With its stone columns, mosaic frieze, and flat glass dome, the Grand Palais contains a large area devoted to temporary exhibits, as well as the Palais de la

Découverte (the Paris science museum and the planetarium). Closed Tuesdays; open Wednesdays until 9.45 p.m. Av. Franklin-Roosevelt, 8e (phone: 42-89-54-10).

Petit Palais: Built contemporaneously with the Grand Palais, it has exhibits of the city's history, as well as a variety of fine and applied arts and special shows. Closed Mondays. Admission charge. Av. Winston-Churchill, 8e (phone: 42-65-12-73).

Place de la Concorde: This square, surely one of the most magnificent in the world, is grandly situated in the midst of equally grand landmarks: the Louvre and the Tuileries on one side, the Champs-Elysées and the Arc de Triomphe on another, the Seine and the Napoleonic Palais Bourbon on a third, and the pillared façade of the Madeleine on the fourth. Designed by Gabriel for Louis XV, the elegant square was where his unfortunate successor, Lous XVI, lost his head to the guillotine, as did Marie Antoinette, Danton, Robespierre, Charlotte Corday, and others. It was first named for Louis XV, then called Place de la Révolution by the triumphant revolutionaries. Ornamenting the square, the eight colossal statues representing important French provincial capitals were polished and blasted clean for the bicentennial celebration in 1989. The 3,300-year-old, 75-foot-high obelisk was a gift from Egypt in 1829.

Jardin des Tuileries: Carefully laid out in patterned geometric shapes, with clipped shrubbery and formal flower beds, statues, and fountains, this is one of the finest examples of French garden design (in contrast to an informal English garden, exemplified by the Bois de Boulogne). Along the Seine, between the Place de la Concorde and the Louvre.

Orangerie: A museum on the edge of the Tuileries gardens, it displays a series of large paintings of water lilies by Monet called the Nympheas and the collection of Jean Walter and Paul Guillaume, with works by Cézanne, Renoir, Matisse, Picasso, and others. Open 10 a.m. to 5.15 p.m.; closed Tuesdays. Admission charge. Pl. de la Concorde and Quai des Tuileries, 1er (phone: 42-97-48-16).

Rue de Rivoli This charming old street has perfume shops, souvenir stores, boutiques, bookstores, cafés, and such hotels as the Maurice and the Inter-Continental under its nineteenth-century arcades. The section facing the Tuileries, from the Place de la Concorde to the Louvre, is an especially good place to explore on rainy days.

Louvre: Built on the site of a medieval fortress on the banks of the Seine, this palace was the home of the French kings during the sixteenth and seventeenth centuries, until Louis XIV moved the court to Versailles in 1682. In 1793 it became a museum, and now is one of the world's greatest art repositories. It's easy to spend a couple of days here, savouring treasures like the Venus de Milo, Winged Victory, the Mona Lisa and the French crown jewels – just a few of the 297,000 pieces in six different collections. Nor is the outside of this huge edifice to be overlooked. Note especially the Cour Carrée (the courtyard of the old Louvre), the southwest corner of which, dating from the mid-1550s, is the oldest part of the palace and a beautiful example of the Renaissance style that François I had so recently introduced from Italy. Note, too, the Colonnade, which forms the eastern front of the Cour Carrée, facing the Place du Louvre; fully classical in style, it dates from the late 1660s, not too long before the Sun King left for Versailles. Newer wings of the Louvre embrace the palace gardens, in the midst of which stands the Arc de Triomphe du Carrousel, erected by Napoleon. From here, the vista across the Tuileries and the Place de la Concorde and on up the Champs-Elysées to the Arc de Triomphe is one of the most beautiful in Paris – which says a lot. The glass pyramids – designed by I. M. Pei and opened in 1989 – sit centre stage in the Louvre's grand interior courtyard, and the largest of the intrusive trio now is the museum's main entrance. The controversial structure is the first step of a major expansion; when completed (the target date is 1993), the Louvre's underground galleries, shops, and exhibit space will connect the North and South wings, increasing museum exhibition space by almost 80%.

Good guided tours in English, covering the highlights of the Louvre, are frequently available, although not every day, so be sure to check in advance. Open from 9.45 a.m. to 6.30 p.m.; Wednesdays and Mondays from 9.45 a.m. to 9.45 p.m.; closed Tuesdays. Admission charge. Pl. du Louvre, 1er (phone: 40-20-51-51 for recorded information in French and English, or 40-20-50-50 for more detailed information).

Place Vendôme: Just north of the Tuileries is an aristocrat of a square, one of the loveliest in Paris, the octagonal Place Vendôme, designed by Mansart in the seventeenth century. Its arcades contain world-famous jewellers, perfumers, and banks, the Ritz hotel, and the Ministry of Justice. The 144-foot column in the centre is covered with bronze from the 1,200 cannon captured at Austerlitz by Napoleon in 1805. Just off Place Vendôme is the famous Rue du Faubourg-St-Honoré, one of the oldest streets in Paris, which now holds elegant shops selling the world's most expensive made-to-order items. To the north is the Rue de la Paix, noted for its jewellers.

Opéra: Charles Garnier's imposing rococo edifice stands in its own busy square, its façade decorated with sculpture, including a copy of Carpeaux's 'The Dance' (the original is now in the Musée d'Orsay). The ornate interior has an impressive grand staircase, a beautiful foyer, lavish marble from every quarry in France, and Chagall's controversially decorated dome. Until a few years ago, the opera house could be seen only by attending a performance (held September–June); now, however, visitors may explore its magnificent interior and enjoy its special exhibitions daily from 11 a.m. to 4.30 p.m., except on the days when there are special performances. Pl. de l'Opéra, 9e (phone: 47-42-57-50).

Opéra de La Bastille: In sharp contrast to Garnier's Opéra is the curved glass façade of modern architect Carlos Ott's new Paris opera house. Set against the historic landscape of the Bastille quarter, this austere, futuristic structure houses over 30 acres of theatres, shops, and urban promenade. Inaugurated for the bicentennial of the Revolution on 14 July 1989, the opera house opened in March 1990 with a production of Berlioz's *Les Troyens*. It looks a lot like the prison-fortress that started the French Revolution. Pl. de la Bastille, Ile (phone: 40-01-17-89).

La Madeleine: Starting in 1764, the Church of St Mary Magdalene was built and razed twice before the present structure was commissioned by Napoleon in 1806 to honour his armies. The church is based on a Greek temple design, with 65-foot-high Corinthian columns supporting the sculptured frieze. From its portals, the view extends down Rue Royale to Place de la Concorde and over to the dome of Les Invalides. Nearby are some of Paris's most tantalizing food shops. Open from 7.30 a.m. to 7 p.m. for concerts (held 4 p.m. Sundays) and other frequent musical events. Pl. de la Madeleine, 8e (phone: 42-65-52-17).

Sacré-Coeur and Montmartre: Built on the highest of Paris's seven hills, the white-domed Basilica of Sacré-Coeur provides an extraordinary view from its steps, especially at dawn or sunset. The area around the church was the artists' quarter of late-nineteenth- and early twentieth-century Paris. The more garish aspects of Montmartre's notoriously frivolous 1890s nightlife, particularly the dancers and personalities at the Moulin Rouge, were immortalized by the paintings of Toulouse-Lautrec. And if the streets look familiar, chances are you've seen them in the paintings of Utrillo; they still look the same. The Place du Tertre is still charming, though often filled with tourists and overly eager, mostly undertalented artists. Go early in the day to see it as it was when Braque, Dufy, Modigliani, Picasso, and Utrillo lived here. Montmartre has the last of Paris's vineyards – and still contains old houses, narrow alleys, steep stairways, and carefree cafés enough to provide a full day's entertainment; at night, this is one of the centres of Paris life. Spare yourself most of the climb to Sacré-Coeur by taking the funicular (as we went to press, it was being replaced by a more modern, glass contraption – bringing the Louvre's main pyramid to mind) or the Montmartre bus (marked with an icon of Sacré-Coeur on the front instead of the usual number) from Place St-Pierre. Butte Montmartre, 18e.

Les Halles: Just northeast of the Louvre, this 80-acre area, formerly the Central Market, 'the Belly of Paris', was razed in 1969. Gone are most of the picturesque early-morning fruit-and-vegetable vendors, butchers in blood-spattered aprons, truckers bringing the freshest produce from all over France. Their places have been usurped by trendy shops and galleries of youthful entrepreneurs and artisans, small restaurants with lots of charm, the world's largest subway station, acres of trellised gardens and playgrounds, and Le Forum des Halles, a vast complex of boutiques, ranging from the superchic designer ready-to-wear to more ordinary shops, as well as concert space and movie theatres. Touch-sensitive locator devices, which help visitors find products and services, are placed strategically. A few echoes of the earthy past remain, however, and you can still dine at Au Pied de Cochon, Le Pharamond, and L'Escargot Montorgueil, or have a drink with the few remaining workmen (before noon) at one of the old brasseries.

Le Centre National d'Art et de Culture Georges-Pompidou (Le Centre Georges-Pompidou): Better known as 'the Beaubourg', after the plateau on which it is built, this stark, six-level creation of steel and glass, with its exterior escalators and blue, white, and red pipes, created a stir the moment its construction began. Outside, a computerized digital clock ticks off the seconds remaining until the twenty-first century. This wildly popular museum brings together all the contemporary art forms – painting, sculpture the plastic arts, industrial design, music, literature, cinema, and theatre – under one roof, and that roof offers one of the most exciting views of Paris. The old houses and cobbled, tree-shaded streets and squares vie for attention with galleries, boutiques, and the spectacle provided by jugglers, mimes, acrobats, and magicians in the plaza out front. The scene in the courtyard often rivals the exhibits inside. Open weekdays from noon to 10 p.m.; 10 a.m. to 10 p.m. weekends. Closed Tuesdays; no admission charge on Sundays except for special exhibitions. Rue Rambuteau, at the corner of Rue St-Martin, 4e (phone: 42-77-12-33).

Le Marais: Northeast of the Louvre, a marshland until the sixteenth century, this district became the height of residential fashion during the seventeenth century. But as the aristocracy moved on, it fell into disrepair. Recently, after a long period of neglect, the Marais has been enjoying a complete face-lift. Spurred on by the opening of the Picasso Museum in the Hôtel du Sale, preservationists have lovingly restored more than a hundred of the magnificent old mansions to their former grandeur. They now are museums of exquisite beauty, with muralled walls and ceilings, and their courtyards are the sites of dramatic and musical presentations during the summer Festival du Marais. Among the houses to note are the Palais de Soubise, now the National Archives, and the Hôtels d'Aumont, de Clisson, de Rohan, de Sens, and de Sully (hôtel in this sense means private residence or townhouse). The Caisse Nationale des Monuments, housed in the last one, can provide maps of the area, as well as fascinating and detailed tours. It also offers lectures on Saturdays and Sundays. 62 Rue St-Antoine, 4e (phone: 42-74-22-22).

Place des Vosges: In the Marais district, the oldest square in Paris – and also one of the most beautiful – was completed in 1612 by order of Henri IV, with its houses elegantly 'built to a like symmetry'. Though many of the houses have been rebuilt inside, their original façades remain, and the recently restored square is one of Paris's enduring delights. Corneille, Racine, and Mme de Sévigné lived here. At No. 6 is the Maison de Victor-Hugo, once the writer's home and now a museum. Closed Mondays; admission charge (4e; phone: 42-72-10-16).

Musée Carnavalet: Also in the Marais, this once was the home of Mme de Sévigné, a noted seventeenth-century letter writer, and now its beautifully arranged exhibits cover the history of the city of Paris from the days of Henri IV to the present. Its recent expansion through the next door and into the neighbouring Le Peletier hotel doubled the exhibition space, making it the largest museum in the world devoted to the history of a single capital city. The expansion, housing a permanent major exhibit on the French Revolution, was part of Paris's celebration of the Revolution's bicentennial. Watch for special exhibitions here. The museum also rents out its concert hall to various music groups. Closed Mondays; no admission charge on Sundays. 23 Rue de Sévigné, 3e (phone: 42-72-21-13).

Musée Picasso: This long-awaited museum, which contains a large part of the artist's private collection, is at the Hôtel du Sale. To tell the truth, the building is at least as interesting as the artworks it houses – too many recent works, too few early ones – but a visit is worthwhile just to see Picasso's collection of works by other artists (the Cézannes are best). Open Mondays and Thursdays through Saturdays from 9.15 a.m. to 5 p.m., Wednesdays from 9.15 a.m. to 10 p.m. 5 Rue de Thorigny, 3e (phone: 42-71-25-21).

Cimetière Pere-Lachaise: For those who like cemeteries, this one is a beauty. In a wooded park, it's the final resting place of many illustrious personalities. A map is available at the gate to help you find the tombs of Balzac, Sarah Bernhardt, Chopin, Colette, Corot, Delacroix, Héloïse and Abélard, La Fontaine, Modigliani, Musset, Edith Piaf, Rossini, Oscar Wilde, and even Jim Morrison (of the Doors rock group), among others. Note, too, the legions of resident cats. Open daily from 8 a.m. to 5.30 p.m. Bd. de Ménilmontant at Rue de la Roquette, 20e (phone: 43-70-70-33).

La Villette: The City of Sciences and Industry, a celebration of technology, stands in its own park on the northeastern edge of the capital and houses a planetarium, the spherical Geode cinema, lots of hands-on displays, and a half-dozen exhibitions at any given time. Restaurants and snack bars. Open 10 a.m. to 6 p.m. Closed Mondays. 30 Av. Cotentin Cariou, 20e (phone: 40-05-70-00).

Bois de Boulogne: Once part of the Forest of Rouvre, on the western edge of Paris, this 2,140-acre park was planned along English lines by Napoleon. Ride a horse or a bike, row a boat, shoot skeet, go bowling, smell roses, picnic on the grass, see horse races at Auteuil and Longchamp, visit a children's amusement park (Jardin d'Acclimatation) and a zoo, see a play, walk to a waterfall – and there's lots more.

Bois de Vincennes: As a counterpart to the Bois de Boulogne, a park, a palace, and a zoological garden were laid out on 2,300 acres during Napoleon III's time. Visit the fourteenth-century château and its lovely chapel; the large floral garden; and the zoo, with animals in their natural habitat. It's at the southeast edge of Paris (métro: Château de Vincennes).

Palais de Chaillot: Built just off the Seine, near the Arc de Triomphe, for the Paris Exposition of 1937 – on the site of the old Palais du Trocadéro left over from the Exposition of 1878 – its terraces have excellent views across gardens and fountains to the Eiffel Tower on the Left Bank. Two wings house a theatre, Cinémathèque, and four museums – du Cinéma (phone: 45-53-74-39), de l'Homme (anthropology; phone: 45-53-70-60), de la Marine (maritime; phone: 45-53-31-70), and des Monuments Français (monument reproductions; phone: 47-27-97-27). Closed Tuesdays and major holidays. Pl. du Trocadéro, 16e.

La Rive Gauche (The Left Bank)

Tour Eiffel: It is impossible to imagine the Paris skyline without this mighty symbol, yet what has been called Gustave Eiffel's folly was never meant to be permanent. Originally built for the Universal Exposition of 1889, it was due to be torn down in 1909, but it was saved because of the development of the wireless – the first transatlantic wireless telephones were operated from the tower in 1916. Its centennial was celebrated with great fanfare in 1989. Extensive renovations have taken place, and a post office, three restaurants (Jules Verne is the best), and a few boutiques have opened up. On a really clear day, it's possible to see for 50 miles. Open daily from 10 a.m. to 11 p.m.; in the summer from 10 a.m. to midnight. Admission charge. Champ-de-Mars, 7e (phone: 45-55-91-11).

Chaillot to UNESCO: From the Eiffel Tower, it is possible to look out over a group of Paris's twentieth-century buildings and gardens on both sides of the Seine, including the Palais de Chaillot, the Trocadéro and Champ-de-Mars gardens, and the UNESCO buildings. Also part of the area (but not of the same century) is the huge Ecole Militaire, an impressive example of eighteenth-century French architecture on Avenue de la Motte-Picquet. The Y-shaped building just beyond it, facing Place de Fontenoy, is the main UNESCO building, dating from 1958. It has frescoes by Picasso, Henry Moore's 'Reclining silhouette', a mobile by Calder, murals by Miro, and Japanese gardens by Noguchi.

Les Invalides: Built by Louis XIV as a refuge for disabled soldiers, this vast classical building has more than ten miles of corridors and a golden dome by Mansart. For yet another splendid Parisian view, approach the building from the Alexandre III bridge. Besides being a masterpiece of the age of Louis XIV (seventeenth century), the royal Church of the Dome, part of the complex, contains the impressive red-and-green granite Tomb of Napoleon (admission charge). Also at Les Invalides is the Musée de l'Armée, one of the world's richest museums, displaying arms and armour together with mementoes of French military history. Open daily from 10 a.m. to 5 p.m. Av. de Tourville, Pl. Vauban, 7e (phone: 45-51-92-84).

Musée d'Orsay: This imposing former railway station has been transformed (by the Milanese architect Gae Aulenti, among others) into one of the shining examples of modern museum curating. Its eclectic collection includes not only the Impressionist paintings decanted from the once-cramped quarters in the Jeu de Paume, but also less consecrated academic work and a panorama of the nineteenth century's achievements in sculpture, photography, and the applied arts. Closed Mondays. Admission charge; reduced on Sundays. 1 Rue de Bellechasse, 7e (phone: 40-49-48-14).

Musée Rodin: The famous statue 'The Thinker' is in the garden of this splendid eighteenth-century residence. The chapel and the mansion also contain Rodin sculptures. Open daily except Mondays from 10 a.m. to 4.30 p.m. Admission charge. 77 Rue de Varenne, 7e (phone: 47-05-01-34).

Montparnasse: Just south of the Luxembourg Gardens, in the early twentieth century there arose an artist's colony of avant-garde painters, writers, and Russian political exiles. Here Hemingway, Picasso, and Scott and Zelda sipped and supped in places like La Closerie des Lilas, La Coupole, Le Dôme, Le Sélect, and La Rotonde. The cafés, small restaurants, and winding streets still exist in the shadow of a new shopping centre.

Tour Montparnasse: This giant complex dominates Montparnasse. The fastest elevator in Europe whisks Parisians and tourists alike (for a fee) up 59 storeys for a view down at the Eiffel Tower, from 9.30 a.m. to 9.30 p.m. daily; Fridays and Saturdays until 10.30 p.m. The shopping centre here boasts all the famous names, and the surrounding office buildings are the headquarters of some of France's largest companies. 33 Av. du Maine, 15e, and Bd. de Vaugirard, 14e (phone: 45-38-52-56).

Palais et Jardin du Luxembourg: In what once were the southern suburbs, the Luxembourg Palace and Garden were built for Marie de Medicis in 1612. A prison during the Revolution, the Renaissance palace now houses the French Senate. The classic, formal gardens, with lovely statues and the famous Medicis fountain, are popular with students meeting under the chestnut trees and with neighbourhood children playing around the artifical lake. 15 Rue de Vaugirard, 6e.

Mosquée de Paris: One of the most beautiful structures of its kind in the non-Muslim – or even in the Muslim – world, it is dominated by a 130-foot-high minaret in gleaming white marble. Shoes are taken off before entering the pebble-lined gardens full of flowers and dwarf trees. Inside, the Hall of Prayer, with its lush Oriental carpets, may be visited daily except Fridays, from 9.30 to noon and 2 to 6 p.m. Admission charge. Next door is a restaurant and a patio for sipping Turkish coffee and tasting oriental sweets. Pl. du Puits-de-l'Ermite, 5e (phone: 45-35-97-33).

Panthéon: This eighteenth-century 'non-religious Temple of Fame dedicated to all the gods' has an impressive interior, with murals depicting the life of Ste Geneviève, patron saint of Paris. It contains the tombs of Victor Hugo, the Resistance leader Jean Moulin, Rousseau, Voltaire, and Emile Zola. Open daily from 10 a.m. to 12.30 p.m. and 2 to 5.30 p.m. Admission charge. Pl. du Panthéon, 5e (phone: 43-54-34-51).

Quartier Latin: Extending from the Luxembourg Gardens and the Panthéon to the Seine, this famous neighbourhood still maintains an "atmosphere". A focal point for Sorbonne students since the Middle Ages, it's a jumble of narrow streets, old churches, and academic buildings. Boulevard St-Michel and Boulevard St-Germain are its main arteries, both lined with cafés, bookstores, and boutiques of every kind. There are some charming old side streets, such as the Rue de la Huchette, near Place St-Michel. And don't miss the famous *bouguinistes* (bookstalls) along the Seine, around the Place St-Michel on the Quai des Grands-Augustins and the Quai St-Michel.

Eglise St-Germain-des-Prés: Probably the oldest church in Paris, it once belonged to an abbey of the same name. The original basilica (AD 558) was destroyed and rebuilt many times. The Romanesque steeple and its massive tower date from 1014. Inside, the choir and sanctuary are as they were in the twelfth century, and the marble shafts used in the slender columns are fourteen centuries old. Pl. St-Germain-des-Prés, 6e (phone: 43-25-41-71).

Surrounding the church is the quarter of Paris's 'fashionable' intellectuals and artists, with art galleries, boutiques, and renowned cafés for people watching such as the Flore (Sartre's favourite) and Les Deux-Magots (once a Hemingway haunt).

Musée de Cluny: One of the last remaining examples of medieval domestic architecture in Paris. The fifteenth-century residence of the abbots of Cluny later became the home of Mary Tudor and now is a museum of medieval arts and crafts, including the celebrated Lady and the Unicorn tapestry. Open daily, except Tuesdays, from 9.30 a.m. to 5.15 p.m. Admission charge. 6 Pl. Paul-Painlevé, 5e (phone: 43-25-62-00).

Eglise St-Severin: This church still retains its beautiful Flamboyant Gothic ambulatory, considered a masterpiece of its kind, and lovely old stained-glass windows dating from the fifteenth and sixteenth centuries. The small garden and the restored charnel house are also of interest. 3 Rue des Prêtres, 5e (phone: 43-25-96-63).

Eglise St-Julien-le-Pauvre: One of the smallest and oldest churches (twelfth to thirteenth century) in Paris offers a superb view of Notre-Dame from its charming Place René-Viviani. 1 Rue Eglise St-Julien-le-Pauvre, 5e (no phone).

The Islands

Ile de la Cité: The birthplace of Paris, settled by Gallic fishermen about 250 BC, this island in the Seine is so rich in historical monuments that an entire day could be spent here and on the neighbouring Ile St-Louis. A walk all around the islands, along the lovely, tree-shaded quays on both banks of the Seine, opens up one breathtaking view of Notre-Dame Cathedral after another.

Cathédrale de Notre-Dame de Paris: It is said that the Druids once worshipped on this consecrated ground. The Romans built their temple, and many Christian churches followed. In 1163, the foundations were laid for the present cathedral, one of the world's finest examples of Gothic architecture, grand in size and proportion. Henry VI and Napoleon were crowned here. Take a guided tour (offered in English at noon Tuesdays and Wednesdays and in French at noon other weekdays, 2.30 Saturdays, and 2 p.m. Sundays) or quietly explore on your own, but be sure to climb the 225-foot towers for a marvellous view of the city and try to see the splendid stained-glass rose windows at sunset. Pl. du Parvis, 4e (phone: 43-26-07-39).

Palais de Justice and Sainte Chapelle: This complex recalls centuries of history; it was the first seat of the Roman military government, then the headquarters of the early kings, and finally the law courts. In the thirteenth century, St Louis (Louis IX) built a new palace and added Sainte Chapelle to house the Sacred Crown of Thorns and other holy relics. Built in less than three years, the chapel, with its 15 splendid stained-glass windows and 247-foot spire, is one of the jewels of Paris. Open daily from 10 a.m. to 4.30 p.m. Admission charge. 4 Bd. du Palais, 1er (phone: 43-54-30-09).

Conciergerie: This remnant of the Old Royal Palace was used as a prison during the Revolution. Here Marie Antoinette, the Duke of Orleans, Mme du Barry, and many others of lesser fame awaited the guillotine. It was restored extensively for the celebration of the bicentennial of the French Revolution, and the great arch-filled hall is especially striking. Open daily. Admission charge. 4 Bd. du Palais, 1er (phone: 43-54-30-06).

Ile St-Louis: Walk across the footbridge at the back of Notre-Dame and you're in a charming, tranquil village. This 'enchanted isle' has managed to keep its provincial charm despite its central location. Follow the main street Rue St-Louis-en-l'Ile, down the middle of the island, past courtyards, balconies, curious stairways, the Eglise St-Louis, and discreet plaques bearing the names of illustrious former residents (Mme Curie, Voltaire, Baudelaire, Gautier, and Daumier, for example); then take the quay back along the edge.

Local Sources and Resources

Tourist Information

The Office du Tourisme de Paris (127 Champs-Elysées, 8e; phone: 47-23-61-72), open daily from 9 a.m. to 8 p.m., is the place to go for information, brochures, maps, or hotel reservations. If you call the office, be prepared for a 4- to 5-minute wait before someone answers. Other offices are found at major train stations, such as the Gare du Nord (phone: 45-26-94-82) and the Gare de Lyon (phone: 43-43-33-24).

Local Coverage

Paris Selection is the official tourist office magazine in French and English. It lists events, sights, 'Paris by Night' tours, places to hear jazz, some hotels, restaurants, shopping, and other information. Far more complete are three weekly guides, *L'Officiel des Spectacles*, *Paris 7*, and *Pariscope*. All are in simple French and are available at newsstands. For insights on eating out and finding the best of French food and wine, consult *The Food Lover's Guide to Paris* (Workman) by American-in-Paris Patricia Wells.

Telephone

All French telephone numbers have 8 digits. The procedure for calling most areas of France from abroad is as follows: dial the international access code PLUS the country code PLUS the local 8-digit number (which includes the city code). The only exception to this rule is when calling the Paris/Ile-de-France area: you must add a 1 (the city code) before the local 8-digit number.

France is essentially divided into two zones: Paris/Ile-de-France and all the rest, that is, the provinces. The procedure for dialling within France is as follows:

To call within Paris and the Ile-de-France area: dial the local 8-digit number (begining with 4, 3, or 6).

To call from the Paris/Ile-de-France area to the provinces: dial 16 (wait for a dial tone) + the local 8-digit number.

To call from the provinces to the Paris/Ile-de-France area: dial 16 (wait for a dial tone) + 1 + the local 8-digit number.

To call between provinces: dial the local 8-digit number.

Getting Around

Boat

See Paris from the Seine by day and by night for about 30–35 ff. Modern, glass-enclosed river ramblers provide a constantly changing picture of the city. Contact *Bateaux-Mouches* (Pont d'Alma, 7e; phone: 42-25-96-10), *Les Bateaux Parisiens* (Pont d'Iéna, 7e; phone: 47-05-50-00), or *Vedettes Pont-Neuf* (Square du Vert-Galant, 1er; phone: 46-33-98-38). For 90 ff, *Paris Canal* (phone: 42-40-96-97) offers a 3-hour barge trip starting on the Seine, then navigating through some of the city's old canals, locks, and a subterranean water route under the Bastille. An interesting commentary is given in both English and French. There are two trips daily between the Musée d'Orsay and the Parc de la Villette – one leaves from the Musée d'Orsay at 9.30 a.m. and the other departs from the Parc de la Villette at 2.30 p.m. Reservations are required.

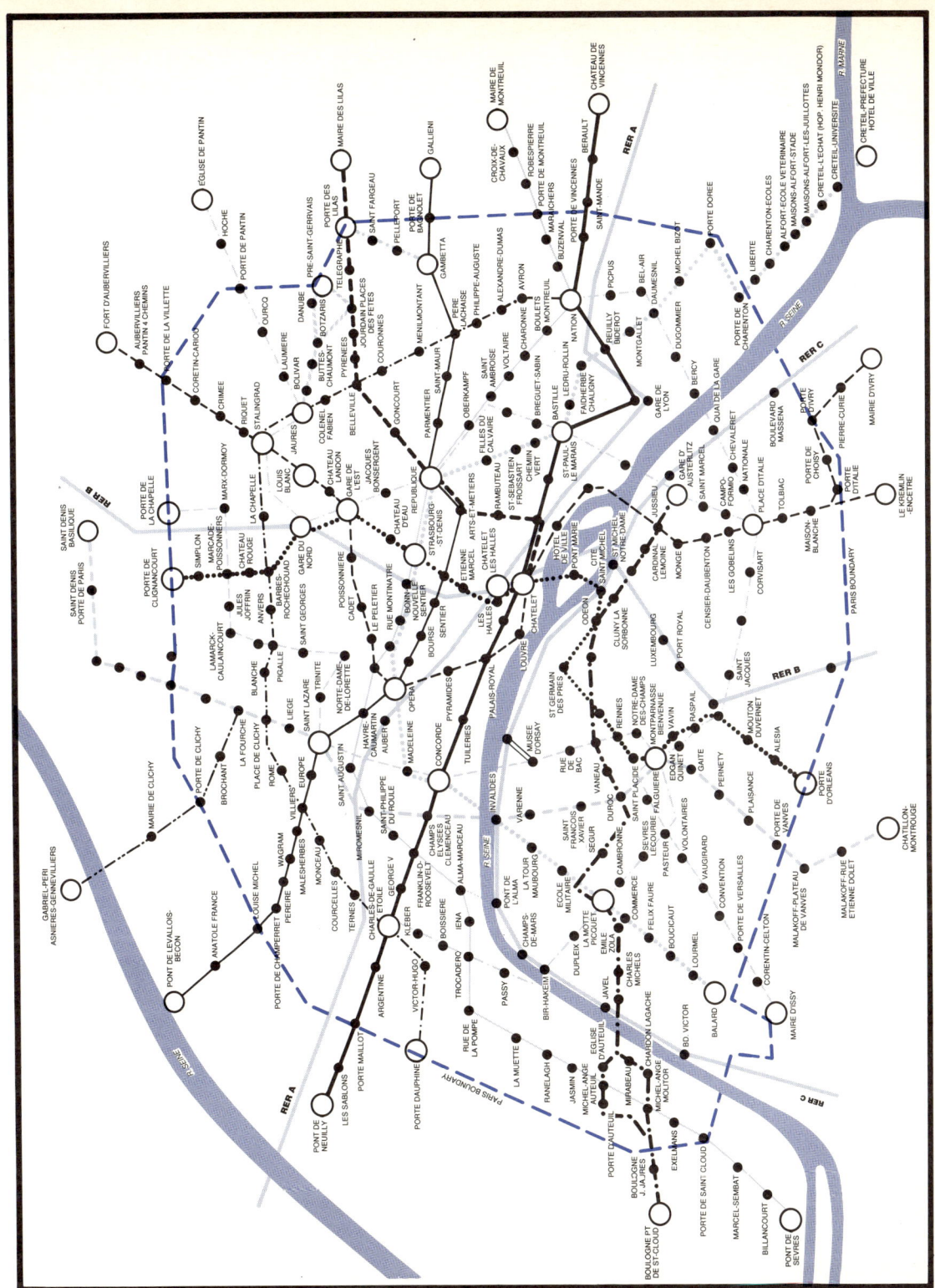

The Paris metro system

Metro

Operating from 5.30 a.m. to about 1 a.m., it is safe, clean, quiet, easy to use, and, since the Paris regional rapid transit authority (RATP) began to sponsor cultural events and art exhibits in some subway stops in an effort to cut down on crime and make commuting more enjoyable, entertaining as well. The events have been so popular that so far they've been offered in about 200 of Paris's 368 métro stations. The different lines are identified by the names of their terminals at either end. Every station has clear directional maps, some with push-button devices that light up the proper route after a destination button is pushed. Keep your ticket (you may need to show it to one of the controllers who regularly patrol the métro) and don't cheat; there are spot checks. As we went to press, the RATP had abandoned the two-class system. A 10-ticket book (*carnet*) is available at a reduced rate. The Paris–Visite card, a tourist ticket that entitles the bearer to 1, 3, or 5 consecutive days of unlimited travel on the métro and on city-run buses, may be purchased in France upon presentation of your passport at 44 subway stations and 4 regional express stations, or at any of the 6 French Railway stations.

Bus

They generally operate from 6.30 a.m. to 9.30 p.m., although some run later. Slow, but good for sightseeing. Métro tickets are valid on all city-run buses. Lines are numbered, and both stops and buses have signs indicating routes. One or two tickets may be required, depending on the distance travelled. The RATP, which operates both the métro and bus system, also has designated certain lines as being of particular interest to tourists. A panel on the front of the bus indicates in English and German 'This bus is good for sightseeing.' RATP has a tourist office at Place de la Madeleine, next to the flower market (phone: 43-46-14-14), which organizes bus trips in Paris and the region.

Car Rental

Book when making your plane reservation, or contact *Avis* (phone: 45-50-32-31), *Budget* (phone: 46-86-65-65), *Europcar* (phone: 45-00-08-06), or *Hertz* (phone: 47-88-51-51).

SITU

Handy streetside bus and subway directions are now available in some métro stations from SITU (Système d'Information des trajets Urbains), a computer that prints out the fastest routeing on to a wallet-size piece of paper, complete with the estimated length of the trip. The RATP service is free and augments the lighted wall maps that guide métro riders. High-traffic spots such as the Chatelet métro station, outside the Gare Montparnasse, and on the Boulevard St-Germain, now sport SITU machines.

Taxi

Found at stands at main intersections, outside railway stations and official buildings, and in the streets. A taxi is available if the entire 'TAXI' sign is illuminated (with a white light); the small light beside the roof light signifies availability after dark. Be aware that Parisian cab drivers are notoriously selective about whom they will pick up, and how many passengers they will allow in their cab – a foursome inevitably has trouble. You also can call Taxi Bleu (phone: 49-36-10-10) or Radio Taxi (phone: 47-39-33-33). The meter starts running from the time the cab is dispatched, and a tip of about 15% is customary. Fares increase at night and on Sundays and holidays.

Train

Paris has six main train stations, each one serving a different area of the country. The general information number is 45-82-50-50; for telephone reservations, 45-65-60-60. North: Gare du Nord (18 Rue de Dunkerque; phone: 42-80-63-63); East: Gare de l'Est (P. du 11-Novembre; phone: 42-03-96-31); Southeast: Gare de Lyon (20 Bd. Diderot; phone: 40-19-60-00); Southwest: Gare d'Austerlitz (51 Quai d'Austerlitz; phone: 45-84-14-19); West: Gare Montparnasse (17 Bd. de Vaugirard; phone: 40-48-10-00); West and Northwest: Gare St-Lazare (20 Rue de Rome; phone: 42-85-88-00). The TGV (*train à grande vitesse*), the world's fastest train, has cut 2 hours off the usual 4-hour ride between Paris and Lyon; it similarly shortens travelling time to Marseilles, the Côte d'Azur, the Atlantic Coast, and Switzerland. It leaves from the Gare de Lyon, except for the Atlantic Coast run, which departs from the Gare d'Austerlitz; reservations are necessary.

Special Events

After the Christmas season, Paris prepares for the January *fashion shows*, when press and buyers come to town to pass judgment on the spring and summer haute couture collections. (The general public can see what the designers have wrought after the professionals leave.) More buyers come to town in February and March for the ready-to-wear shows (autumn and winter clothes), open to the trade only. March is the month of the first *Foire Nationale à la Brocante et aux Jambons* of the year. This fair of regional food products held concurrently with an antiques flea market (not items of the best quality, but not junk, either) is repeated in September. The running of the *Prix du Président de la République*, the first big horse race of the year, takes place at Auteuil in April. From late April to early May is the *Foire de Paris*, the capital's big international trade fair. In late April or May there's the *Paris Marathon*; in late May (through early June), the *French Open Tennis Championships*. Odd years only, the *Paris International Air Show* is an early June attraction at Le Bourget Airport. Horse races crowd the calendar in June – there's not only the *Prix de Diane* at Chantilly, but also the *Grande Semaine* of Longchamp, Auteuil, and St-Cloud. And in the middle of June, the *Festival du Marais* begins a month's worth of music and dance performances in the courtyards of the Marais district's old townhouses. *Bastille Day*, 14 July, is celebrated with music and fireworks, parades, and dancing till dawn in every neighbourhood. Meanwhile, the *Tour de France* is under way; the cyclists arrive in Paris for the finish of the 3-week race later in July. Also in July, press and buyers arrive to view the autumn and winter haute couture collections, but the ready-to-wear shows (spring and summer clothes) wait until September and October, because August for Parisians is vacation time. Practically the whole country takes a holiday then, and in the capital the classical concerts of the *Festival Estival* (in July and August) are among the few distractions. When they finish, the *Festival d'Automne*, a celebration of the contemporary in music, dance, and theatre, takes over (from mid-September through December). The Foire Nationale à la Brocante et aux Jambons returns in September, but in even-numbered years it's eclipsed by the *Biennale des Antiquaires*, a major antiques event from late September to early October. Also in even years, usually in November, is the *Paris Motor Show*. Every year on the first Sunday of October, the last big horse race of the season, the *Prix de l'Arc de Triomphe*, is run at Longchamp; and every year in early October, Paris holds the *Fête des Vendanges à Montmartre* to celebrate the harvest of the city's last remaining vineyard. On 11 November, ceremonies at the Arc de Triomphe and a parade mark *Armistice Day*. An *International Cat Show* and a *Horse and Pony Show* come in early December; then comes Christmas, which is celebrated most movingly with a Christmas Eve midnight mass at Notre-Dame. At midnight a week later, the New Year bows in to spontaneous street revelry in the Latin Quarter and along the Champs-Elysées.

Museums

Some Paris museums (*musées*) are free or offer reduced admission fees on Sundays. 'La Carte', a pass that can be used at over 60 museums and monuments in the city, is available at métro stations and at major museums. Prices are the equivalent of 90 ff for a 1-day pass, 150 ff for a 3-day pass, and 210 ff for a 5-day pass. Note that 'La Carte' is not valid for certain special exhibits. Museums of interest not described in 'Special Places' include the following:

Archaeological Crypt of Notre-Dame: Under the square in front of the cathedral are walls and floor plans from all periods. Open daily from 10 a.m. to 4.30 p.m. Parvis de Notre-Dame, 4e (phone: 43-29-83-51).

Catacombs: Dating from the Gallo-Roman era and also containing the remains of Danton, Robespierre, and many others. Bring a flashlight. Closed Mondays. 1 Pl. Denfert-Rochereau, 14e (phone: 43-22-47-63).

Egouts (Sewers of Paris): Underground city of tunnels, a very popular afternoon tour, daily except Thursdays and Fridays, and on holidays and the days preceding and following them. Pl. de la Résistance, in front of 93 Quai d'Orsay, 7e (phone: 47-05-10-29).

Galerie Nationale de Jeu de Paume: Inaugurated in June 1991, this museum is devoted to contemporary art from 1960 on and includes paintings, sculpture, photographs, and videos, all installed in what was formerly the temple of Impressionism – the Jeu de Paume, at one end of the Tuileries. The interior has been redone to provide more and better exhibition space. Open Wednesdays, Thursdays, and Fridays from noon to 7 p.m.; Tuesdays from noon to 9.30 p.m.; and Saturdays and Sundays from 10 a.m. to 7 p.m. Corner of the Tuileries gardens at the Place de la Concorde.

Maison de Balzac: The house where the writer lived, with a garden leading to one of the prettiest little alleys in Paris. Closed Mondays. 47 Rue Raynouard, 16e (phone: 42-24-56-38).

Manufacture des Gobelins: The famous tapestry factory, in operation since the fifteenth century. Guided tours of the workshops take place Tuesdays, Wednesdays, and Thursdays from 2.15 to 3.15 p.m. 42 Av. des Gobelins, 13e (phone: 42-74-44-50).

Mémorial de la Déportation: Set in a tranquil garden in the shadow of Notre-Dame at the tip of Ile de la Cité, this monument is dedicated to 200,000 French women and men of all religions and races who died in Nazi concentration camps during World War II. Square de l'Ile de France, 4e.

Mémorial du Martyr Juif Inconnu: A moving tribute to Jews killed during the Holocaust, this 35-year-old, newly renovated memorial includes World War II documents and photographs. Open daily, except Friday afternoons and Saturdays, from 10 a.m. to noon and 2 to 5.30 p.m. 17 Rue Geoffroy L'Asniers, 4e (phone: 42-77-44-72). The French Government Tourist Office has published a booklet, *France for the Jewish Traveller*, that describes these two memorials, as well as other places of interest to Jews visiting France.

Musée des Antiquités Nationales: Archaeological specimens from prehistoric through Merovingian times, including an impressive Gallo-Roman collection. Open daily, except Tuesdays, from 9.30 a.m. to noon and 1.30 to 5.15 p.m. Pl. du Château, St-Germain-en-Laye, 14e (phone: 34-51-53-65).

Musée des Arts Africains et Océaniens: One of the world's finest collections of African and Oceanic art. Closed Tuesdays. 293 Av. Daumesnil, 12e (phone: 43-43-14-54).

Musée des Arts Décoratifs: Furniture and applied arts from the Middle Ages to the present, Oriental carpets, and Dubuffet paintings and drawings. *Galerie Art Nouveau-Art Déco* features Jeanne Lanvin's bedroom and bath. It also houses three centuries of French posters. Closed Mondays and Tuesdays. 107 Rue de Rivoli, 1er (phone: 42-60-32-14).

Musée Cernuschi: Art of China. Closed Mondays and holidays. 7 Av. Velasquez, 8e (phone: 45-63-50-75).

Musée de la Chasse et de la Nature: Art, weapons, and tapestries relating to the hunt. Note the courtyard where horses once were kept – it is decorated with sculpture. Open daily except Tuesdays from 10 a.m. to 12.30 p.m. and 1.30 to 5.30 p.m. Admission charge. 60 Rue des Archives, 3e (phone: 42-72-86-43).

Musée Cognacq-Jay: Art, snuffboxes, and watches from the seventeenth and eighteenth centuries. Closed Mondays. 8 Rue Elzevir, 3e (phone: 40-27-07-21).

Musée des Collections Historiques de la Préfecture de Police: On the second floor of the modern police precinct, in the 5th *arrondissement*, are historic arrest orders (for Charlotte Corday, among others), collections of contemporary engravings, and guillotine blades. Open Mondays through Saturdays from 9 a.m. to 5 p.m. 1 bis Rue des Carmes, 5e (phone: 43-29-21-57).

Musée Eugèbe-Delacroix: Studio and garden of the great painter; exhibits change yearly. Closed Tuesdays. 6 Rue de Furstenberg, 6e (phone: 43-54-04-87).

Musée Grévin: Waxworks of French history from Charlemagne to the present day. 10 Bd. Montmartre, 9e (phone: 47-70-85-05). A branch devoted to La Belle Epoque is in the Forum des Halles shopping complex. Open daily. Pl. Carrée, 1er (phone: 40-26-28-50).

Musée Guimet: The Louvre's Far East collection. Closed Tuesdays. 6 Pl. d'Iéna, 16e (phone: 47-23-61-65).

Musée Gustave-Moreau: A collection of the works of the early symbolist. Closed Mondays and Tuesdays. 14 Rue de la Rochefoucauld, 9e (phone: 48-74-38-50).

Musée Jacquemart-Andre: Eighteenth-century French decorative art and European Renaissance treasures, as well as frequent special exhibitions. Closed Mondays and Tuesdays. 158 Bd. Haussmann, 8e (phone: 42-89-04-91).

Musée Marmottan: Superb Monets, including the nine masterpieces that were stolen in a daring 1985 robbery. Happily, however, all were recovered in a villa in Corsica and have been cleaned – some for the first time – before being rehung. Closed Mondays. 2 Rue Louis-Boilly, 16e (phone: 42-24-07-02).

Musée de la Mode et du Costume: A panorama of French contributions to fashion in the elegant Palais Calliera. Closed Mondays. 10 Av. Pierre-1er de Serbie, 16e (phone: 47-20-85-23).

Musée de la Monnaie: More than 2,000 coins and 450 medallions, plus historic coinage machines. Open daily, except Mondays, from 1 to 6 p.m. Admission charge. 11 Quai de Conti, 6e (phone: 40-46-56-66).

Musée Montmartre: A rich collection of paintings, drawings, and documents depicting life in this quarter. Open Mondays through Saturdays from 2.30 to 6 p.m., Sundays from 11 a.m. to 6 p.m. 12 Rue Corlot, 18e (phone: 46-06-61-11).

Musée Nissim de Camondo: A former manor house filled with beautiful furnishings and art objects from the eighteenth century. Closed Mondays, Tuesdays, and holidays. 63 Rue de Monceau, 8e (phone: 45-63-26-32).

Musée de Sèvres: Just outside Paris, next door to the Sèvres factory, is one of the world's finest collections of porcelain. Closed Tuesdays. 4 Grande Rue, Sèvres (phone: 45-39-99-99).

Musée du Vin: Housed in a thirteenth-century abbey that was destroyed during the Revolution, the museum was restored in 1981. The history and making of wine is traced through displays, artifacts, and a series of wax figure tableaux. Open daily, except Mondays, from noon to 6 p.m. Saturdays, and Sundays to 5.30 p.m. Admission charge includes a glass of wine. 5–7 Sq. Charles-Dickens, 16e (phone: 45-25-63-26).

Parc Océanique Cousteau: Based on the work of the French oceanographer, this museum houses ocean exhibits and interactive displays. Open Mondays, Tuesdays, and Thursdays from noon to 7 p.m.; Wednesdays, Saturdays, Sundays, and holidays from 10 to 7.30 p.m. Admission charge. Forum des Halles, Pl. Carrée, 1er (phone: 40-28-98-98).

Pavillon des Arts: Exhibition space in the mushroom-shaped buildings overlooking the Forum des Halles complex. Presentations range from ancient to modern, paintings to sculpture. Closed Mondays and holidays. 101 Rue Rambuteau, 1et (phone: 42-33-82-50).

Galleries

Few artists live in Montparnasse nowadays, as the centre of the Paris art scene has shifted from the narrow streets of the Latin Quarter, which set the pace in the 1950s, to the Right Bank around the Centre Georges-Pompidou. Here are some galleries of note:

Agathe Gaillard: Contemporary photography, including Cartier-Bresson and the like. 3 Rue du Pont-Louis-Philippe, 4e (phone: 42-77-38-24).

Artcurial: Early moderns, such as Braque and Sonia Delaunay, as well as sculpture and prints, with a fine art bookshop. Av. Matignon, 8e (phone: 42-99-16-16).

Beaubourg: Well-known names in the Paris art scene, including Niki de Saint-Phalle, César, Tinguely, Klossowski. 23 Rue du Renard, 4e (phone: 42-71-20-50).

Caroline Corré: Exhibitions by contemporary artists, specializing in unique artists' books. 14 Rue Guenegaud, 6e (phone: 43-54-57-67).

Claude Bernard: Francis Bacon, David Hockney, and Raymond Mason are among the artists exhibited here. 5 Rue des Beaux-Arts, 6e (phone: 43-26-97-07).

Daniel Malingue: Works by the Impressionists, as well as notable Parisian artists from the 1930s to the 1950s – Foujita, Fautrier, and so forth. 26 Av. Matignon, 8e (phone: 42-66-60-33).

Darthea Speyer: Run by a former American Embassy attaché, now an art dealer. Contemporary painting. 6 Rue Jacques-Callot, 6e (phone: 43-54-78-41).

Hervé Odermatt Cazeau: Early moderns – among them Picasso, Léger, Pissarro – and antiques. 85 bis Rue du Faubourg-St-Honoré, 8e (phone: 42-66-92-58).

Isy Brachot: Master surrealists, American hyper-realists, and new realists. 35 Rue Guenegaud, 6e (phone: 43-54-22-40).

Maeght-Lelong: The great moderns on display include Chagall, Tapies, Bacon, Moore, Miro. 13–14 Rue de Teheran, 8e (phone: 45-63-13-19).

Nikki Diana Marquardt: Spacious gallery of contemporary work opened by an enterprising dealer from the Bronx. 9 Pl. des Vosges, 4e (phone: 42-78-21-00).

Virginia Zabriskie: Early and contemporary

photography by Atget, Brassaï, Diane Arbus. Also painting and, occasionally, sculpture. 37 Rue Quincampoix, 4e (phone: 42-72-35-47).

Shopping

From new wave fashions to classic haute couture, Paris starts the trends and sets the styles the world copies. Prices are generally high, but more than a few people are willing to pay for the quality of the products, not to mention the cachet of a Paris label, which enhances the appeal of many things besides clothing. Perfume, cosmetics, jewellery, leather goods and accessories, wine and liqueurs, porcelain, and art are among the many other things for which Paris is famous.

The big department stores are excellent places to get an idea of what's available. They include *Galeries Lafayette* (40 Bd. Haussmann, 9e; phone: 42-82-34-56; and other locations); *Au Printemps* (64 Bd. Haussmann, 9e; phone: 42-85-80-00); *Aux Trois Quartiers-Madelios* (17 Bd. de la Madeleine, 1er; phone: 42-60-39-30); *La Samaritaine* (19 Rue de la Monnaie, 1er; phone: 40-41-20-20); *Le Bazar de l'Hôtel de Ville* (52 Rue de Rivoli, 4e; phone: 42-74-90-00); and *Au Bon Marché* (22 Rue de Sèvres, 7e; phone: 45-49-21-22). Two major shopping centres – *Porte Maillot* (Pl. de la Porte Maillot) and *Maine Montparnasse* (at the intersection of Bd. Montparnasse and Rue de Rennes) – also are worth a visit.

There are several shopping neighbourhoods, and they tend to be specialized. Haute couture can be found in the streets around the Champs-Elysées: Av. George-V, Av. Montaigne, Rue François 1er, and Rue du Faubourg-St-Honoré; famous designers are also represented in department stores. Boutiques are especially numerous on Av. Victor-Hugo, Rue de Passy, Bd. des Capucines, in the St-Germain-des-Prés area, in the neighbourhood of the Opéra, in the Forum des Halles shopping centre, and around the Place des Victoires. The Rue d'Alesia has several blocks devoted solely to discount fashion shops.

The Rue de Paradis is lined with crystal and china shops, and St-Germain-des-Prés has more than its share of art galleries. The best and most expensive antique dealers are along the Faubourg-St-Honoré on the Right Bank. On the Left Bank there's Le Carré Rive Gauche, an association of more than 100 antique shops in the area bordered by Quai Voltaire, Rue de l'Université, Rue des Sts-Pères, and Rue du Bac. Antique and curio collectors should explore Paris's several flea markets, which include the Montreuil, near the Porte de Montreuil; Vanves, near the Porte de Vanves; and the largest and best known, Puces de St-Ouen, near the Porte de Clignancourt.

A few more tips: Sales take place during the first weeks in January and in late June and July. Any shop labelled *degriffe* (the word means, literally, 'without the label') offers discounts on brand name clothing, often last season's styles. Discount shops also are known as 'stock' shops.

Here is a sampling of the wealth of shops in Paris, many of which have more than one location in the city:

Agnes B.: Supremely wearable, trendy, casual clothes. 3 and 6 Rue du Jour, 1er (phone: 40-26-36-87 or 45-08-56-56); 13 Rue Michelet, 6e (phone: 46-33-70-20); 25 Av. Pierre-1er de Serbie, 16e (phone: 47-20-22-44); and 81 Rue d'Assas, 6e (phone: 43-54-69-21). The latter store is for chidren only.

Alfred Dunhill: Menswear, toiletries, and the luggage articles from the celebrated English tobacconist. 15 Rue de la Paix, 2e (phone: 42-67-57-58).

Arnys: Conservative and elegant men's clothing. 14 Rue de Sèvres, 6e (phone: 45-48-76-99).

Azzedine Alaia: The Tunisian designer who brought the body back. 14 Rue de la Verrerie, 4e (phone: 48-04-03-60).

Baccarat: High-quality porcelain and crystal. 30 bis Rue de Paradis, 10e (phone: 47-70-64-30); and 11 Pl. de la Madeleine, 8e (phone: 42-65-36-26).

La Bagagerie: Perhaps the best bag and belt boutique in the world. 12 Rue Tronchet, 8e (phone: 42-65-03-40), and other locations.

Au Bain Marie: The most beautiful kitchenware and tabletop accessories, with emphasis on Art Deco designs. 10 Rue Boissy d'Anglas, 8e (phone: 42-66-59-74).

Balenciaga: Ready-to-wear and designer haute couture. 10 Av. George-V, 8e (phone: 47-20-21-11).

Bazar de l'Hotel de Ville: Perhaps the world's most celebrated hardware store – from nuts and bolts to a French bistro sign or a washing machine. Some people travel to Paris just to visit BHV's grim, cavernous expanse. 52 Rue de Rivoli, 3e (phone: 42-74-90-00).

Beauté Divine: Antique perfume bottles, Art Deco bathroom accessories, glove stretchers, nail buffers, and moustache cups. 40 Rue St-Sulpice, 6e (phone: 43-26-25-31).

Boucheron: One of several fine jewellers clustered around the elegant Place Vendôme. 26 Pl. Vendôme, 1er (phone: 42-61-58-16).

Brentano's: British and American novels, critiques on the American arts, and a variety of books on technical and business subjects – in English. 37 Av. de l'Opéra, 2e (phone: 42-61-52-50).

Cacherel: Fashionable ready-to-wear in great prints. 34 Rue Tronchet, 8e (phone: 47-42-12-61), and other locations.

Cadolle: Founded in 1889 by the woman credited with inventing the brassiere, it still sells corsets as well as other items of frilly, pretty lingerie. 14 Rue Cambon, 1er (phone: 42-60-94-94).

Carel: Beautiful shoes. 12 Rond-Point des Champs-Elysées, 8e (phone: 45-62-30-62), and other locations.

Carita: Paris's most extensive – and friendliest – beauty/hair salon. 11 Rue du Faubourg-St-Honoré, 8e (phone: 42-68-13-40).

Cartier: Fabulous jewellery. 11–13 Rue de la Paix, 2e (phone: 42-61-58-56), and other locations.

Castorama: One of 86 stores throughout France, this department store sells 45,000 European-designed housewares – from flowerpots to home security systems. 1–3 Rue Caulaincourt, 18e (phone: 45-22-07-11).

Céline: A popular women's boutique for clothing and accessories. 24 Rue François 1er, 8e (phone: 47-20-22-83); 3 Av. Victor-Hugo, 16e (phone: 45-01-70-48).

Cerruti: For women's clothing, 9 Pl. de la Madeleine, 8e (phone: 40-17-03-16); for men's, 27 Rue Royale, 8e (phone: 42-65-68-72).

Chanel: Classic women's fashions, inspired by the late, legendary Coco Chanel, now under the direction of Karl Lagerfeld. 42 Av. Montaigne, 8e (phone: 47-20-84-45); and 29–31 Rue Cambon, 1er (phone: 42-86-28-00).

Chantal Thomas: Ultra-feminine fashions, 5 Rue du Vieux-Colombier, 6e (phone: 45-44-07-52); sexy lingerie, 12–14 Galerie du Rond-Point, 8e (phone: 43-59-87-34), and other locations.

Charles Jourdan: Sleek, high-fashion shoes. 86 Av. des Champs-Elysées, 8e (phone: 45-62-29-28); 5 Bd. de la Madeleine, 1er (phone: 42-61-50-07); and other locations.

Charley: Excellent selection of lingerie at fairly low prices. 14 Rue du Faubourg-St-Honoré, 8e (phone: 47-42-17-70).

MINI-GUIDE TO PARIS

Charvet: Paris's answer to Savile Row. An all-in-one men's shop, where shirts are the house speciality – they stock more than 4,000. Ties, too. 28 Pl. Vendôme, 1er (phone: 42-60-30-70).

Chaumet: Crownmakers for most of Europe's royalty. Expensive jewels, including antique watches covered with semi-precious stones. 12 Pl. Vendôme, 1er (phone: 42-60-32-82); and 46 Av. George-V (phone: 49-52-08-25).

Chloe: Designs for women. 3 Rue de Gribeauval and 60 Rue du Faubourg-St-Honoré, 8e (phone: 42-66-01-39).

Christian Dior: One of the most famous couture names in the world. 28–30 Av. Montaigne, 8e; Miss Dior and Baby Dior for children are also at this location (phone: 40-73-54-44).

Christian Lacroix: The first major new fashion house to open in Paris in two decades. Offers the 'hautest' of haute couture. 73 Rue du Faubourg-St-Honoré, 8e (phone: 42-65-79-08).

Christofle: The internationally famous silversmith. 9 Rue Royale, 8e (phone: 49-33-43-00).

Claude Montana: Ready-to-wear and haute couture from this *au courant* designer. 31 Rue de Grenelle, 7e (phone: 42-22-69-56).

Comme des Garçons. 40–42 Rue Etienne-Marcel, 1er (phone: 42-33-05-21).

Courrèges: Another bastion of haute couture, with its own boutique. 40 Rue François 1er, 8e, and 46 Rue du Faubourg-St-Honoré, 8e (phone: 47-23-00-73).

Daniel Hechter: Sportswear and casual clothing for men and women. 146 Bd St-Germain, 6e (phone: 43-26-96-36), and other locations.

Destination Paris: Glittering selection of knickknacks, hand-painted T-shirts, scarves, picture frames, and souvenirs. 9 Rue du 29 Juillet, 1er (phone: 49-27-98-90).

Dorothée Bis: Definitely a trendsetter in women's wear. 33 Rue de Sèvres, 6e (phone: 42-22-02-90).

Les Drugstores Publics: A uniquely French version of the American drugstore, with an amazing variety of goods – perfume, books, records, foreign newspapers, magazines, film, cigarettes, food, and more, all wildly overpriced. 149 Bd. St-Germain, 6e (phone: 42-22-92-50); 133 Av. des Champs-Elysées, 8e (phone: 47-23-54-34); and 1 Av. Matignon, 8e (phone: 43-59-38-70).

E. Dehillerin: An enormous selection of professional cookware. 18–20 Rue Coquillière, 1er (phone: 42-36-53-13).

Emmanuel Ungaro: Couturier boutique for women. 2 Av. Montaigne, 8e (phone: 47-23-61-94).

Eres: Avant-garde sportswear for men and women. 2 Rue Tronchet, 8e (phone: 47-42-24-55).

Fabrice: Trendy costume jewellery. 22 and 54 Rue Bonaparte, 6e (phone: 43-26-57-95).

Fauchon: The place to buy fine food and wine of every variety, from *ouefs en gelée* to condiments and sweets. 26–30 Pl. de la Madeleine, 8e (phone: 47-42-60-11).

Fouguet: Beautiful displays of chocolates, fresh fruit candies, herbs, condiments, and jams. 22 Rue François 1er, 8e (phone: 47-23-30-46), and other locations.

France Faver: Top-quality and comfortable shoes for women. 79 Rue des Sts-Pères, 6e (phone: 42-22-04-29).

Fratelli Rossetti: All kinds of shoes, made from buttery-soft leather, for men and women. 54 Rue du Faubourg-St-Honoré, 8e (phone: 42-65-26-60).

Freddy: A popular shop for gifts, perfume, gloves, ties, scarves, and other items at good prices. 10 Rue Auber, 9e (phone: 47-42-63-41).

Galignani: Recently renovated, this shop sells books in English and French. It has been run by the same family since the beginning of the nineteenth century. 224 Rue de Rivoli, 1er (phone: 46-60-76-07).

La Gaminerie: Reasonably priced, good sportswear; outstanding window displays. 137 Bd. St-Germain, 6e (phone: 43-26-27-98).

Gianni Versace: women's clothing. 11 Rue du Faubourg-St-Honoré, 8e (phone: 42-65-27-04); and 67 Rue des Sts-Pères, 7e (phone: 42-84-00-40).

Givenchy: Beautifully tailored clothing by the master couturier. 3 Av. George-V, 8e (phone: 47-23-81-36).

Le Gourmet: The Galeries Lafayette's chic, new grocery featuring exotic, high-priced food, wine, and confections from around the world. 40 Bd. Haussmann, 9e (phone: 48-74-37-13).

Guerlain: For fine perfume and cosmetics. 2 Pl. Vendôme, 1er; 68 Champs-Elysées, 8e (phone: 45-62-52-57); 39 Rue de Sèvres, 6e; and 93 Rue de Passy, 16e.

Guy Laroche: Classic and conservative couture. 30 Rue du Faubourg-St-Honoré, 8e (phone: 42-65-62-74); and 29 Av. Montaigne, 8e (phone: 40-69-69-50).

Hanae Mori: The grande dame of Japanese designers in Paris. 17 Av. Montaigne, 8e (phone: 47-23-52-03); and 9 Rue du Faubourg-St-Honoré, 8e.

Hediard: Pricey but choice food shop, notable for its assortment of coffees and teas. Chic tearoom upstairs. 21 Pl. de la Madeleine, 8e (phone: 42-66-44-36).

Hermès: For very high quality ties, scarves, handbags, shoes, saddles, and accessories, though the prices may send you into cardiac arrest. 24 Rue du Faubourg-St-Honoré, 8e (phone: 42-65-30-74).

Karl Lagerfeld: Women's clothing. 17 Rue du Faubourg-St-Honoré, 8e (phone: 42-66-64-64).

Lanvin: Another fabulous designer, with several spacious, colourful boutiques under one roof. 15 and 22 Rue du Faubourg-St-Honoré, 8e (phone: 42-65-14-40); and 2 Rue Cambon, 1er (phone: 42-60-38-83).

Laura Ashley: The English designer's familiar Victorian styles. 94 Rue des Rennes, 6e (phone: 42-22-77-80); and 261 Rue St-Honoré, 1er (phone: 42-86-84-13).

Loewe: Classic leather goods in elegant quarters. One of Spain's oldest and highest-quality names in leather, and owned by Louis Vuitton since 1985. 57 Av. Montaigne, 8e (phone: 45-63-73-38).

Louis Feraud: Couturier fashions for women at 88 Rue du Faubourg-St-Honoré, and men at No. 62, 8e (phone: 40-07-01-16); and other locations.

Louis Vuitton: High-quality luggage and handbags. 78 bis Av. Marceau, 8e (phone: 47-20-47-00); and 54 Av. Montaigne, 8e (phone: 45-62-47-00).

Maison de la Truffe: The world's largest truffles retailer. (They're fresh, not preserved, from November to March.) 19 Pl. de la Madeleine (phone: 42-65-53-22).

Marché aux Puces: Paris's famous Flea Market, with 3,000 dealers in antiques and secondhand items. Open Saturdays, Sundays, and Mondays. Bargaining is a must. Porte de Clignancourt, 18e.

Marie Papier: Handsome marbled stationery and writing accessories. 26 Rue Vavin, 6e (phone: 43-26-46-44).

Marithe & François Girbaud: Not just jeans at this shop for men and women. 33 Rue Etienne-Marcel, 2e (phone: 42-33-54-69).

Maud Frizon: Sophisticated, imaginative shoes and handbags. 83 Rue des Sts-Pères, 6e (phone: 42-22-06-93 or 42-22-19-86).

Miss Maud: Shoes aimed at a young market, but classy and fashionable enough for all ages. No longer connected with Maud Frizon, above. Several locations, including 90 Rue du Faubourg-St-Honoré, 8e (phone: 42-65-27-96).

Missoni: Innovative, original Italian knitwear. 43 Rue du Bac, 7e (phone: 45-48-38-02).

Monique Germain: Unique hand-painted silk clothing at affordable prices: cocktail dresses, bridal wear, padded patchwork jackets. 59 Bd. Raspail, 6e (phone: 45-48-22-63).

M.O.R.A.: One of Paris's 'professional' cookware shops, though it sells to individuals as well. Just about any piece of equipment you can imagine, and an interesting selection of cookbooks – in French. 13 Rue Montmartre, 1er (phone: 45-08-19-24).

Morabito: Magnificent handbags and luggage at steep prices. 1 Pl. Vendôme, 1er (phone: 42-60-30-76).

Le Must de Cartier: Actually two boutiques, on either side of the Ritz hotel, offering such Cartier items as lighters and watches at prices that, though not low, are almost bearable when you deduct the 25% VAT tax. 7 23 Pl. Vendôme, 1er (phone: 42-61-55-55).

Au Nain Bleu: The city's greatest toy store. 408 Rue St-Honoré, 8e (phone: 42-60-30-01).

Nina Ricci: Women's fashions, as well as the famous perfume. 17 Rue François 1er, 8e (phone: 47-23-78-88); and 39 Av. Montaigne, 8e (phone: 47-23-78-88).

Les Olivades: Provençal printed goods, a little less pricey than Souleiado (see below). Shops throughout France, including 25 Rue de l'Annonciation, 16e (phone: 45-27-07-76).

Paloma Picasso: Perfume, clothing, and jewellery from one of France's pre-eminent designers and you-know-who's daughter. 5 Rue de la Paix, 2e (phone: 42-86-02-21).

Per Spook: One of Paris's best young designers. 18 Av. George-V, 8e (phone: 47-23-00-19), and elsewhere.

Le Petit Faune: A marvellous place to buy children's things. 33 Rue Jacob, 6e (phone: 42-60-80-72), and other locations.

Au Petit Matelot: Classic sportswear, outdoor togs, and nautical accessories for men, women, and children. Especially terrific are their Tyrolean-style olive, beige, or navy loden coats. 27 Av. de la Grande-Armée, 16e (phone: 45-00-15-51).

Pierre Balmain: Couturier boutique for women's fashions. 44 Rue François 1er, 8e (phone: 47-20-35-34), and other locations.

Pierre Cardin: A famous designer's own boutique. 83 Rue du Faubourg-St-Honoré, 8e (phone: 42-66-62-94); 27 Av. Victor-Hugo, 16e (phone: 45-01-88-13); 14 Pl. François 1er, 8e (phone: 45-63-29-13); and other locations.

Pixi & Cie: Terrific collection of dolls, toy soldiers, and antique windup cars. 95 Rue de Seine, 6e (phone: 43-25-10-12).

Porthault: Terribly expensive, but elegantly exquisite bed and table linen. 18 Av. Montaigne, 8e (phone: 47-20-75-25).

Puiforçat: Art Deco tableware in a beautiful setting. 22 Rue François 1er, 8e (phone: 47-20-74-27).

Raymond: Charming and fairly inexpensive Porcelaine de Paris items. 100 Rue du Faubourg-St-Honoré, 8e (phone: 42-66-69-49).

Romeo Gigli: Men's and women's arty ready-to-wear and haute couture. 46 Rue de Sévigné, 3e (phone: 42-71-08-40).

Sabbia Rosa: Simple, chic, and sexy lingerie is sold in this tiny shop on the Left Bank. 73 Rue des Sts-Pères, 6e (phone: 45-48-88-37).

Shakespeare and Company: This legendary English-language bookstore, opposite Notre-Dame, is something of a tourist attraction in itself. 37 Rue de la Blacherie, 5e (no phone).

Simon: A wide range of professional cookware, and a dazzling, but confusing, array of bistroware, flatware, cheese trays, snail holders, and tiny terrines. 36 Rue Etienne-Marcel, 2e (phone: 42-33-71-65).

Sonia Rykiel: Stunning sportswear and knits. 6 Rue de Grenelle, 15e; and 70 Rue du Faubourg-St-Honoré, 8e (phone: 42-65-20-81).

Souleiado: Vibrant, traditioal Provençal fabrics made into scarves, shawls, bags, and tableware. 78 Rue de Seine, 6e (phone: 43-54-62-25); and 83 Av. Paul-Doumer, 16e (phone: 42-24-99-34).

Stephane Kelain: High-fashion, high-quality, and high-priced men's and women's shoes, in several locations, including 4 Pl. des Victoires, 1er (phone: 42-36-31-84).

Tartine et Chocolat: Clothing for children, from infancy to twelve years old, and dresses for mums-to-be. Their trademark item: striped unisex overalls. 90 Rue de Rennes, 6e (phone: 42-22-67-34).

Ted Lapidus: A compromise between haute couture and excellent ready-to-wear. 23 Rue du Faubourg-St-Honoré, 8e (phone: 44-60-89-91); 35 Rue François 1er, 8e (phone: 47-20-56-14); and other locations.

Thierry Mugler: Dramatic ready-to-wear for women. 49 Av. Montaigne, 8e (phone: 47-23-37-62).

Torrente: Women's fashions. 60 Av. Montaigne, 8e (phone: 42-56-14-14).

Trussardi: Italian ready-to-wear from a designer whose leather goods and canvas carryalls are much appreciated by the French and Japanese. 21 Rue du Faubourg-St-Honoré, 8e (phone: 42-65-11-40).

Upla: Sporty handbags, scarves, and casual clothing. 17 Rue des halles, 1er (phone: 40-26-49-96).

Valentino: Ready-to-wear and haute couture fashions for men and women from the Italian designer. 17–29 Av. Montaigne, 8e (phone: 47-23-64-61).

Van Cleef & Arpels: One of the world's great jewellers. 22 Pl. Vendôme, 1er (phone: 42-61-58-58).

Vicky Tiel: Strapless evening gowns decorated with beads and bows, as well as contemporary sweaters and baseball-style jackets. 21 Rue Bonaparte, 6e (phone: 46-33-53-58).

Victoire: Ready-to-wear, with attractive accessories. 12 Pl. des Victoires, 2e (phone: 47-04-49-87), and other locations.

Walter Stiger: Some of the capital's most expensive and exclusive footwear for men and women. The flagship shop displays satin slippers like precious jewels – and with prices to match. 83 Rue du Faubourg-St-Honoré, 8e (42-66-65-08).

W. H. Smith and Sons: The largest (and best) Parisian bookstore for reading material in English. It sells the Sunday *New York Times*, in addition to many British and American magazines and books. 248 Rue de Rivoli, 1er (phone: 42-60-37-97).

Yves Saint Laurent: The world-renowned designer, considered one of the most prestigious names in high fashion. 38 Rue du Faubourg-St-Honoré, 8e (phone: 42-65-74-59); 5 Av. Marceau, 8e (phone: 47-23-72-71); 6 Pl. St-Sulpice, 6e (phone: 43-29-43-00); and other locations.

Discount Shops

If you're one of those – like us – who believes that the eighth deadly sin is buying retail, you'll treasure these inexpensive outlets.

Anna Lowe: Saint Laurent's styling, among others, at a discount. 35 Av. Matignon, 8e (phone: 45-63-45-57).

Bab's: High fashion at low – or at least reasonable – prices. 29 Av. Marceau, 16e (phone: 47-20-84-74); and 89 bis Av. des Ternes, 17e.

Biderman: Menswear from Yves Saint Laurent, Kenzo, and Courrèges, in a warehouse of a store in the Marais. 11 Rue de Turenne, 3e (phone: 44-61-17-14).

Boetie 104: Good buys on men's and women's shoes. 104 Rue La Boetie, 8e (phone: 43-59-72-38).

Boutique Stock: A vast selection of big-name knits at less than wholesale. 26, 30, and 51 Rue St-Placide, 6e (phone: 45-48-83-66).

Cacharel Stock: Surprisingly current Cacharel fashions at about a 40% discount. 114 Rue d'Alesia, 14e (phone: 45-42-53-04).

Catherine: One of the most hospitable of the perfume and cosmetics shops. A 40% discount (including VAT) is given on purchases totalling 1,500 ff or more. 6 Rue Castiglione, 1er (phone: 42-60-81-49).

Catherine Baril: Women's ready-to-wear by designers such as Yves Saint Laurent and Jean-Louis Scherrer. 14–15 Rue de la Tour, 16e (phone: 45-20-95-21).

Dépôt des Grandes Marques: A third-floor shop near the stock market, featuring up to 50% markdowns on Louis Feraud, Cerruti, Renoma, and similar labels. 15 Rue de la Banque, 2e (phone: 42-96-99-04).

Dorothée Bis Stock: Ms Bis's well-known designs at about 40% off. 74 Rue d'Alesia, 14e (phone: 45-42-17-11).

Drôles des Choses pour Drôles des Gens: Half-price clothes by Marithe and François Girbaud. 33 Rue Etienne-Marcel, 1er (phone: 43-72-15-23).

Emmanuelle Khanh: The designer's clothes at a substantial discount. 6 Rue Pierre-Lescot, 1er (no phone).

Georges Rech: Currently one of the most popular makers of classy, very Parisian styles, and at more affordable prices than other manufacturers of similarly styled goods. 273 Rue St Honoré, 1er (phone: 42-61-41-14); and 23 Av. Victor-Hugo, 16e (phone: 45-00-83-19).

Griff 'Mod: Names like Laroche and Lapidus at sale prices. 20 Rue des Petits-Champs, 2e (phone: 42-97-47-45).

Halle Bys: High fashions at discount prices. 60 Rue de Richelieu, 2e (phone: 42-96-65-42).

Jean-Louis Scherrer: Haute couture labels by Scherrer and others at about half their original prices. 29 Av. Ledru-Rollin, 12e (phone: 46-28-39-27).

Lady Soldes: Prime fashion labels at less than normal prices. 221 Rue du Faubourg-St-Honoré, 8e (phone: 45-61-09-14).

Lanvin Soldes Trois: Lanvin fashions at about half their normal retails cost. 3 Rue de Vienne, 8e (no phone).

Max Mara: Italian ready-to-wear for many different moods. High quality, yet affordable. 37 Rue du Four, 6e (phone: 43-29-91-10); 265 Rue St-Honoré, 1er (phone: 40-20-04-58); and other locations.

Mendes: Less-than-wholesale prices on haute couture, especially Saint Laurent and Lanvin. 65 Rue Montmartre, 2e (phone: 45-08-52-62 or 42-36-83-32).

Miss Griffes: The very best of haute couture in small sizes (up to size 10) at small prices. Alterations. 19 Rue de Penthièvre, 8e (phone: 42-65-10-00).

Mouton à Cinq Pattes: Ready-to-wear clothing for men, women, and children at 50% off original prices. 8, 10, and 14 Rue St-Placide, 6e (phone: 45-48-86-26).

Pierre Cardin Stock: Terrific buys on the famed designer's men's clothing. 72 Rue St-Honoré, 1er (phone: 40-26-74-73).

Réciproque: Billed as the largest 'dépôt-vent' in Paris, this outlet features names like Chanel, Alaia, Lanvin, and Scherrer. Several hundred square yards of display area are arranged by designer and by size. 95 Rue de la Pompe, 16e (phone: 47-04-82-24); men's clothing and accessories next door at No. 101. New boutiques are at Nos. 89, 91, and 123 Rue de la Pompe.

Stéphane: Men's designer suits by Pierre Balmain, Ted Lapidus, and André Courrèges at 25% to 45% discount. 130 Bd. St-Germain, 6e (phone: 46-33-94-55).

Stock Coupons: Features discounted Daniel Hechter for men, women, and children. 92 Rue d'Alesia, 14e (phone: 45-42-82-66).

Stock Griffes: Women's ready-to-wear apparel at 40% off their original prices. 17 Rue Vieille-du-Temple, 4e (phone: 48-04-82-34); and 1 Rue des Trois-Frères, 18e (phone: 42-55-42-49).

Stock System: Prêt-à-porter clothing for men and women at a 30% discount. 112 Rue d'Alesia, 14e (phone: 45-42-80-86).

Note: For a modest price (80 ff and up), you can also take home a bit of the Louvre. The museum's 200-year-old Department of Chalcography houses a collection of 16,000 engraved copper plates – renderings of monuments, battles, coronations, Egyptian pyramids, and portraits – dating from the seventeenth century. Prints made from these engravings come reproduced on thick vellum, embossed with the Louvre's imprint. The Chalcography Department (open daily, except Tuesdays, from 2 to 5 p.m.) is one flight up from the Porte Barbet de Jouy entrance on the Seine side of the Louvre.

Also, Rue de Paradis (10e) is the best area to shop for crystal and porcelain – Baccarat, Saint-Louis, Haviland, Bernardaud, and Villeroy & Boch – at amazing prices. Try *Cristallerie de Paris* at No. 10; *Boutique Paradis,* 1 bis; *L'Art et La Table,* 3; *Limoges-Unio,* Nos. 8 and 12; *Porcelain Savary,* 9; *Arts Céramiques,* 15; and *Cristallerie Paradis,* at No. 17.

Nightclubs and Nightlife

Organized 'Paris by Night' group tours (Cityrama, Paris Vision, and other operators offer them; see *Special Places*) include at least one 'Spectacle' – beautiful girls in minimal, yet elaborate, costumes, with lavish sets and effects and sophisticated striptease. Most music halls offer a package (starting as high as 670 ff per person), with dinner, dancing, and a half bottle of champagne. It is possible to go to these places on your own, save money by skipping dinner and the champagne (both usually way below par), and take a seat at the bar to see the show. The most famous extravaganzas occur nightly at *Crazy Horse* (12 Av. George-V, 8e; phone: 47-23-32-32), *Folies-Bergère* (32 Rue Richer, 9e; phone: 42-46-77-81), *Lido* (116 bis Champs-Elysées, 8e; phone: 40-76-56-10), *Moulin Rouge* (Pl. Blanche, 18e; phone: 46-06-00-19), and *Paradis Latin* (28 Rue du Cardinal-Lemoine, 5e; phone: 43-29-07-07). An amusing evening can also be spent at smaller cabaret shows like René Cousinier (*La Branlette*; 4 Impasse Marie-Blanche, 18e; phone: 46-06-49-46), *Au Lapin Agile* (22 Rue des Saules, 18e; phone: 46-06-85-87), and *Michou* (80 Rue des Martyrs, 18e; phone: 46-06-16-04). Reserve all a few days in advance.

There's one big difference between discotheques and private clubs. Fashionable 'in' spots like *Le Palace* (8 Rue Faubourg-Montmartre, 9e; phone: 42-46-10-87), *Régine's* (49 Rue de Ponthieu, 8e; phone: 43-59-21-60),

Chez Castel (15 Rue Princesse, 6e, members only; phone: 43-26-90-22), *Olivia Valère* (40 Rue de Colisée, 8e, members only; phone: 42-25-11-68), *Les Bains* (7 Rue du Bourg-l'Abbé, 3e; phone: 48-87-01-80), and *Elysées Matignon* (48 Av. Gabriel, 8e; phone: 42-25-73-13) super-screen potential guests. No reason is given for accepting some and turning others away; go here with a regular or look as if you'd fit in with the crowd. Go early and on a weeknight – when your chances of getting past the gatekeeper are at least 50–50. Don't despair if you're refused; the following places are just as much fun and usually more hospitable: *La Scala* (188 bis Rue de Rivoli, 1er; phone: 42-61-64-00), *L'Aventure* (122 Rue d'Assas, 6e; phone: 46-34-22-60), an *L'Ecume des Nuits* (Hôtel Méridien, 81 Bd. Gouvion-St-Cyr, 17e; phone: 40-68-30-89).

Some pleasant, popular bars for a nightcap include *Bar de la Closerie des Lilas* (171 Bd. Montparnasse, 6e; phone: 42-26-70-50), *Harry's New York Bar* (5 Rue Daunou, 2e; phone: 42-61-71-14), *Fouquet's* (99 Champs-Elysées, 8e; phone: 47-23-70-60), *Ascot Bar* (66 Rue Pierre-Charron, 8e; phone: 43-59-28-15), *Bar Anglais* (Plaza-Athenée Hôtel, 25 Av. Montaigne, 8e; phone: 47-23-78-33), and *Pub Winston Churchill* (5 Rue de Presbourg, 16e; phone: 45-00-75-35).

Jazz buffs have a large choice including *Caveau de la Huchette* (5 Rue de la Huchette, 5e; phone: 43-26-65-05), *Le Bilboquet* (13 Rue St-Benoît, 6e; phone: 45-48-81-84), *New Morning* (7–9 Rue des Petites Ecuries, 10e; phone: 45-23-51-41), and *Le Petit Journal* (71 Bd. St-Michel, 6e; phone: 43-26-28-59).

Enghien-les-Bains, 8 miles (13 km) away, is the only casino in the Paris vicinity (3 Av. de Ceinture, Enghien-les-Bains; phone: 34-12-90-00). Open 3 p.m. to about 4 a.m., it easily can be reached by train from the Gare du Nord.

Eating Out

Paris considers itself the culinary capital of the world, and you will never forget food for long here. Whether you grab just a freshly baked croissant and café au lait for breakfast or splurge on an epicurean fantasy for dinner, this is the city in which to indulge all your gastronomic dreams.

Remember, too, that there is no such thing as 'French' food; rather, Paris provides the perfect mosaic in which to try regional delights from Provence, Alsace, Normandy, Brittany, and many other delicious places.

Restaurants classed as very expensive charge 1390ff and way up for two; expensive is 830 ff to 1100 ff; moderate, 560 ff to 830 ff; inexpensive, less than 560 ff; and very inexpensive, 280 ff or less. A service charge of 15% is added to the bill, but most people leave a small additional tip for good service; wine is not included in the price. Street addresses of the restaurants below are followed by their arrondissement number.

Note: To save frustration and embarrassment, always reconfirm dinner reservations before noon on the appointed day. Also remember that some of the better restaurants do not accept credit cards; it's a good idea to check when making reservations. It may come as a surprise to discover that many of the elite Paris restaurants close over the weekend; also note that many Paris restaurants are closed for all of July or August. So check ahead in order to avoid disappointment at the restaurant of your choice, and it's worth remembering that many offer special lunch menus at considerably lower prices. Below is a sampling of the best restaurants that Paris has to offer.

L'Ambroisie Quietly elegant, beneath the arcade of historic Place des Vosges, this is the showcase for chef Bernard Pacaud's equally elegant cuisine. The menu is limited to only a few entrées, such as duck with foie gras, skate and sliced green cabbage in sherry vinegar sauce, veal sweetbreads with shallots and parsley on ultra-fresh pasta, and oxtail in a savoury sauce, but the quality has earned the place three Michelin stars. Closed Sundays, Monday lunch, August, and holidays. Reservations necessary. Major credit cards accepted. 9 Pl. des Vosges, 4e (phone: 42-78-51-45). Very expensive.

Beauvilliers Deliciously flirtatious and festive, this restaurant on the northern slope of the Butte of Montmartre is one of the most romantic spots in Paris. Proust or Balzac might have felt at home in its intimate dining rooms or on hydrangea-rimmed summer terraces in the shadow of a white-stone cathedral. The food – a rich, generous cuisine prepared in the best bourgeois tradition – complements the surroundings. Try the sweetbreads with foie gras, guinea hen with spices and mussels, or the turbot *au jus de jarret*. Closed the first two weeks in September, Monday lunch, and Sundays. Reservations necessary. Major credit cards accepted. 52 Rue Lamarck, 18e (Phone: 42-54-54-42). Very expensive.

Le Grand Vefour Founded in 1760, this sedately elegant Empire-style establishment – with paintings on the mirrors – is known for refined menus (two Michelin stars) and perfect service. It's famous for toast Rothschild (shrimp in crayfish sauce set in a brioche) and pigeon Aristide Briand (boned roast pigeon stuffed with foie gras and truffles). Closed Saturdays at lunch, Sundays, and August. Reservations necessary. Major credit cards accepted. 17 Rue Beaujolais, 1er (phone: 42-96-56-27). Very expensive.

Jamin Due to the culinary talents of owner-chef Joel Robuchon, this is one of the city's finest restaurants – with a three-star ranking by Michelin – and one of the most difficult to get into. Robuchon calls his cuisine 'moderne', similar to but not always as light as nouvelle. The dining room is very small, so reserve far in advance. Waiting time is almost eight weeks. Closed weekends and July. Reservations necessary. Major credit cards accepted. 32 Rue de Longchamp, 16e (phone: 47-27-12-27). Very expensive.

Lasserre The ultimate in luxury, with a magical ceiling that opens periodically during dinner to reveal the night-time sky. Equally sublime is the food, served in the style Lasserre – vermeil dessert settings, plates rimmed in gold, and extravagant garnishes with each dish. The classic menu is heavy on foie gras, caviar, truffles, and rich sauces. Michelin downgraded the food to two stars a few years ago, but we think it's still topnotch. Closed Sundays, Monday lunch, and August. Reservations necessary. Major credit cards accepted. 17 Av. Franklin-D.-Roosevelt, 8e (phone: 43-59-53-43). Very expensive.

Lucas-Carton Once proprietor of the Michelin three-star restaurant called L'Archestrate, chef Alain Senderens dropped that name (but not his triple-star rating) in 1985 when he moved to larger, more elegant quarters in a historic building that boasts a gorgeous Belle Epoque interior. Senderens enjoys the reputation of being one of France's most innovative culinary talents, combining many tenets of nouvelle cuisine with Oriental and African influences. Closed Saturdays, Sundays, and most of August. Reservations necessary. Major credit cards accepted. 9 Pl. de la Madeleine, 8e (phone: 42-65-22-90). Very expensive.

Maxim's A legend for its Belle Epoque decor and atmosphere. It's good for celebrations, but though the service is impeccable, it's hard to feel comfortable if you aren't known here. Owned by fashion designer Pierre Cardin, this is one of the few places in Paris where you are expected to dress formally – on Friday evenings. There's an orchestra for dancing from 9.30 p.m. until 2 a.m. Closed Sundays in July and August. Reservations necessary. Major credit cards accepted. 3 Rue Royale, 8e (phone: 42-65-27-94). Very expensive.

Le Taillevent Full of tradition, Louis XVI furnishings, eighteenth-century porcelain dinner service – all in a nineteenth-century mansion – this epicurean haven offers no-nonsense cuisine classique, which currently is the best in Paris. Try terrine of truffled sweetbreads, seafood sausage, duck in cider, and especially chef Claude Deligne's soufflés in original flavours like Alsatian pear and cinnamon chocolate. Three stars in the Guide Michelin. Closed weekends, part of February, and most of August. Reservations necessary. Americans often have difficulty reserving here (although it's a bit easier if there are four in your party), and it's best to try at least 60 days ahead. No credit cards accepted. 15 Rue Lamennais, 8e (phone: 45-61-12-90). Very expensive.

La Tour d'Argent Another of the five Parisian restaurants to be awarded three stars by the Guide Michelin and probably the best known – though recent visits have not been up to the standards of years past. The spectacular view of Notre-Dame and the Ile St-Louis competes with the food for the attention of a very touristy clientele. Pressed duck – prepared before you – is the speciality, but the fifteen other varieties of duck are equally interesting. A single main dish here can cost 560 ff, and to be quite frank, it just ain't worth it. Closed Mondays. Reservations necessary. Major credit cards accepted. 15 Quai de la Tournelle, 5e (phone: 43-54-23-31). Very expensive.

L'Ami Louis This is the archetypal Parisian bistro, unattractive physically but with huge portions of food that we rate as marvellous. Though the original Louis is gone, his heirs have maintained the rough welcome and informal ambience. Specialities include foie gras, roast chicken, spring lamb, ham, and burgundy wines. A favourite among Americans, this is the place to sample authentic French fries. Closed Mondays, Tuesdays, and most of July and August. Reservations necessary. Major credit cards accepted. 32 Rue de Vertbois, 3e (phone: 48-87-77-48). Expensive.

Amphycles Since it opened in May 1989, Philippe Groult's tiny restaurant near the Arc de Triomphe has won praise and in 1991, a second Michelin star. A former student of star-chef Joel Robuchon of Jamin, Groult prepares wonderful dishes, including *crème de morilles au chou nouveau* (cream of mushroom soup flavoured with new cabbage). Reservations necessary. Major credit cards accepted. 78 Av. des Ternes, 17e (phone: 40-68-01-01). Expensive.

Apicius Jean-Pierre Vigato's highly original recipes have won him a reputation as one of Paris's finest chefs (and earned him two Michelin stars). Favourites include such delicacies as sweet-and-sour foie gras, rougets (a Mediterranean fish) with olive oil and potato purse, and a panache of five mouth-watering chocolate desserts. Closed weekends and August. Reservations necessary. Major credit cards accepted. 122 Av. de Villiers, 17e (phone: 43-80-19-66). Expensive.

L'Arpège Paris's current rage is two-star chef Alain Passard, who prepares specialities such as *ris de veau à la truffes* (sweetbreads with truffles and chestnuts) and *lotte aux épices* (spicy monkfish). The *prix fixe* lunch at this eatery near the Musée Rodin is easily the best bargain around. Closed Saturdays and Sunday lunch and August. Reservations necessary. Major credit cards accepted. 84 Rue de Varenne, 7e (phone: 45-51-20-02). Expensive.

La Carré des Feuillants Alain Dutournier of Le Trou Gascon has set up shop right in midtown. The cuisine is still Gascon-inspired, but Dutournier is allowing his imagination more licence with, for example, such creations as frogs' legs with watercress sauce and salmon served with braised cabbage and bacon. Michelin has awarded him two stars. Closed Saturdays for lunch and Sundays. Reservations necessary. Major credit cards accepted. 14 Rue de Castiglione, 1er (phone: 42-86-82-82). Expensive.

Castel You might be able to get a reservtion at this, one of the few private clubs in Paris, if you ask for help from the concierge at one of the town's grand hotels. The Belle Epoque interior is breathtaking, the cooking fine, and there's a disco in the basement. Specialities include lobster and chicken with cucumbers. Closed Sundays. Reservations necessary. Major credit cards accepted. 15 Rue Princesse, 6e (phone: 42-26-90-22). Expensive.

Chiberta Elegant and modern, and boasting the acclaimed (two Michelin stars) nouvelle cuisine of Jean-Michel Bodier. Try *bavarois de saumon au coulis de tomates frais* (salmon mousse with fresh tomato sauce) and *marbre de rouget au fenouil* (red mullet with fennel). Closed weekends and August. Reservations necessary. Major credit cards accepted. 3 Rue Arsène-Houssaye, 8e (phone: 45-63-77-90). Expensive.

Le Divellec This bright and airy place serves some exquisitely fresh seafood. Try the sea bass, the rouget, and the sautéed turbot. The latter is served with 'black pasta' – thick strips of pasta flavoured with squid ink. Closed Sundays, Mondays, and August. Reservations necessary. Major credit cards accepted. 107 Rue de l'Université, 7e (phone: 45-51-91-96). Expensive.

Dodin-Bouffant Popular because it was set up by the gifted, imaginative, and long-gone Jacques Manière, it still offers excellent seafood and inventive dishes (it has been awarded one Michelin star). Open late. Closed Sundays, two weeks at Christmas time, and August. Reservations necessary. Major credit cards accepted. 25 Rue Frédéric-Sauton, 5e (phone: 43-25-25-14). Expensive.

Drouant Founded in 1880, this classic favourite reopened after an extensive face-lift, with an ambitious chef and menu. Michelin has awarded it one star. Open daily. Reservations necessary. Major credit cards accepted. 18 Rue Gaillon, 2e (phone: 42-65-15-16). Expensive.

Duquesnoy Jean-Paul Duquesnoy, one of Paris's most promising young chefs, is in his element in nifty quarters. Warm carved woods and tasteful decor set the stage for specialities that include a new potato and caviar salad, terrine of leeks and langoustine, and a chocolate mousse and pistachio-filled mille-feuille. Two Michelin stars. Closed Saturday lunch and Sundays. Reservations necessary. Major credit cards accepted. 6 Av. Bosquet, 7e (phone: 47-05-96-78). Expensive.

Faugeron Among the finest nouvelle restaurants, awarded two stars by Michelin, it rates even higher with us. Superb food, lovely service, and one of Paris's prettiest table settings in what once was an old school. Closed weekends and August. Reservations necessary. Major credit cards accepted. 52 Rue de Longchamp, 16e (phone: 47-04-24-53). Expensive.

Fouquet's Bastille Sister restaurant to the Champs-Elysées institution (see *Wine Bars and Cafés*), this post-modern location next to Paris's new Opéra Bastille offers traditional fare with a modern touch. Closed Saturday lunch and Sundays. Reservations advised. Major credit cards accepted. 130 Rue de Lyon, 12e (phone: 43-42-18-18). Expensive.

Gérard Besson Michelin has given this small and formal eatery two stars. The service is impeccable and the classic menu includes specialities such as fricassée of lobster. Closed Saturdays and Sundays 13 to 30 July, and from 22 December to 7 January. Reservations necessary. Major credit cards accepted. 5 Rue Coq-Héron, 1er (phone: 42-33-14-74). Expensive.

Jacques Cagna The talented eponymous chef always provides an interesting menu at these charming premises on the Left Bank, very near the Seine. Guide Michelin has awarded it two stars. Closed August, Christmas week, Saturdays, and Sundays. Reservations necessary. Major credit cards accepted. 14 Rue des Grands-Augustins, 6e (phone: 43-26-49-39). Expensive.

Lamazère Truffle heaven. The menu is a triumph of rich products from the southwest of France. The owner is a magician in the real sense of the word, as well as with food. The elegant bar and salons are open late. Closed Sundays and August. Reservations necessary. Major credit cards accepted. 23 Rue de Ponthieu, 8e (phone: 43-59-66-66). Expensive.

Ledoyen This grand dowager of Paris dining places received a major face-lift in 1988 when Régine, the capital's nightlife queen, took it over. Its look, and menus ordained by consulting chef Jacques Maximin, have received generally favourable reviews (one star from Michelin), particularly from high-powered business people. Closed Sundays. Reservations necessary. Major credit cards accepted. Carré des Champ-Elysées, 8e (phone: 47-42-23-23). Expensive.

Miravile Gilles Epie, one of Paris's promising young chefs, recently moved across the river into larger quarters. He brought with him his customers, his Michelin star, and memorable dishes such as a lobster and potato cake. Closed Saturday lunch and Sundays. Reservations necessary. Major credit cards accepted. 72 Quai de l'Hôtel-de-Ville, 4e (phone: 42-74-72-22). Expensive.

Olympe Owner and chef Dominique Nahmias is the first female chef to be awarded three toques – very high honours – by Gault Millau. Her nouvelle cuisine is painstakingly prepared and simply glorious; an excellent wine list adds to the meal's enjoyment. Closed Saturday and Sunday lunch, Mondays, and August. Reservations necessary. Major credit cards accepted. 8 Rue Nicolas-Charlet, 15e (phone: 47-34-86-08). Expensive.

Le Petit Montmorency In his location near the Champs-Elysées, chef Daniel Bouche presents one of the most exciting and unusual menus in Paris. Very, very popular. Closed weekends and August. Reservations necessary. Major credit cards accepted. 5 Rue Rabelais, 8e (phone: 42-25-11-19). Expensive.

Pre Catelan It's the large restaurant right in the middle of the Bois de Boulogne, and believe it or not, the food here is very good. Ingredients are fresh and sauces are light. Specialities include four or five new dishes daily. Michelin has awarded it one star. Closed Sunday evenings, Mondays, and two weeks in February. Reservations necessary. Major credit cards accepted. Rte de Suresnes, Bois de Boulogne, 16e (phone: 45-24-55-58). Expensive.

Régine's The food actually is good in this beautifully decorated nightclub, which is frequented by Parisians as well as the chic international set. Ask your hotel manager to get you in, because it's nominally a private club. Try the foie gras (made on the premises) and the goose. Closed Sundays. Reservations advised. Major credit cards accepted. 49 Rue de Ponthieu, 8e (phone: 43-59-21-60). Expensive.

Relais Louis XIII Old-style decor and new cuisine in one of Paris's prettiest houses. The Guide Michelin has given it two stars. Closed Sundays, Monday lunch, and August. Reservations advised. Major credit cards accepted. 1 Rue Pont de Lodi, 6e (phone: 43-26-75-96). Expensive.

Tan-Dinh The perfect pause from a constant diet of French specialities. Despite the loss of its Michelin star, its Vietnamese specialities are simply superb. Shrimp rolls, Vietnamese ravioli, and minced fillet of beef are only three examples of the marvellous menu (ask for the version in English). Remarkable wine list. Closed Sundays and August. Reservations advised. Major credit cards accepted. 60 Rue de Verneuil, 7e (phone: 45-44-04-84). Expensive.

Le Toit de Passy The food here is good (Michelin has awarded chef Yann Jacquot one star), and the rooftop view in one of Paris's more exclusive districts is spectacular. Try specialities such as *pigeonneau en croûte de sel* (squab in a salt crust) while dining outdoors. Closed Saturdays (except for September through mid-December), Sundays, and holidays, one week in May, one week in September and Christmas week. Reservations necessary. Major credit cards accepted. 94 Av. Paul-Doumer, 16e (phone: 45-24-55-37). Expensive.

Vivarois Claude Peyrot is one of France's finest chefs. Specialities in his small, elegant eating place include curried oysters au gratin, turbot, and assortments of desserts. Michelin has awarded it two stars. Closed weekends and August. Reservations necessary. Major credit cards accepted. 192 Av. Victor-Hugo, 16e (phone: 45-04-04-31). Expensive.

Auberge des Deux Signes This place was once the cellars of the priory of St-Julien-le-Pauvre; try to get an upstairs table overlooking the gardens. Auvergnat cooking à la nouvelle cuisine. Closed Sundays. Reservations necessary. Major credit cards accepted. 46 Rue Galande, 5e (phone: 43-25-46-56). Expensive to moderate.

Le Bistrot d'a Cote Flaubert Michelin two-star chef Michel Rostang offers cuisine de terroir (uncomplicated, back-to-basic regional fare) in a turn-of-the-century bistro. Closed Saturday lunch, Sundays, and holidays. Reservations advised. Major credit cards accepted. 10 Rue Gustave-Flaubert, 17e (phone: 42-67-05-81). Expensive to moderate.

Brasserie Lorraine Bustling and convivial until late at night, this place pulls in the neighbourhood's bourgeoisie for animated evenings over the foie gras salads. Open daily from noon to 2 a.m. Reservations unnecessary. Major credit cards accepted. Pl. des Ternes, 8e (phone: 42-27-80-04). Expensive to moderate.

La Cantine des Gourmets This restaurant specializes in light, inventive creations of high quality (one Michelin star). Closed Sundays. Reservations advised. Major credit cards accepted. 113 Av. Bourdonnais, 7e (phone: 47-05-47-96). Expensive to moderate.

La Coquille A classic bistro, where the service is unpretentious and warm, and the food consistently good. From October to May, the house speciality is coquilles St-Jacques, a version that consists of scallops roasted with butter, shallots, and parsley. Closed Sundays, Mondays, holidays, and August. Reservations advised. Major credit cards accepted. 6 Rue du Débarcadère, 17e (phone: 45-74-25-95). Expensive to moderate.

Le Duc The atmosphere is warm and comfortable, and Paul Minchelli is incomparably inventive with fish and shellfish (cooked and raw). Quality and variety are the rule here, with such specialities as curried oysters, tuna tartar, coquilles St-Jacques cru, and an extraordinary seafood platter. Closed Saturdays, Sundays, and Mondays. Reservations necessary. No credit cards accepted. 243 Bd Raspail, 14e (phone: 43-22-59-59 or 43-20-96-30). Expensive to moderate.

Faucher Rising star Gérard Faucher opened this elegant restaurant two years ago and has drawn praise for his light touch with fish dishes and desserts. Michelin awarded him a star this year. Closed Saturday lunch and Sundays. Reservations necessary. Major credit cards accepted. 123 Av. Wagram, 17e (phone: 42-27-61-50). Expensive to moderate.

Morot-Gaudry On the top floor of a 1920s building with a great view of the Eiffel Tower, especially from the flowered terrace. Among the inventive dishes are calf's liver with raspberry vinegar, compote of chicken with leeks, and rice cake with ginger. One Michelin star. Closed weekends. Reservations necessary. Major credit cards accepted. 6 Rue de la Cavalerie, 15e (phone: 45-67-06-85). Expensive to moderate.

Pavillon des Princes Under the direction of Pascal Bonichon, it serves delicious duck sausage salad with avocado, coquilles St-Jacques with fresh pasta, and lamb nuggets with cabbage and tomatoes. On the edge of the Bois de Boulogne. Open daily. Reservations advised. Major credit cards accepted. 69 Av. de la Porte d'Auteuil, 16e (phone: 47-43-15-15). Expensive to moderate.

Au Quai d'Orsay Sophisticated, very French, and very intimate. Traditional copious bourgeois cooking and good beaujolais. Closed Sundays. Reservations advised. Major credit cards accepted. 49 Quai d'Orsay, 7e (phone: 45-51-58-58). Expensive to moderate.

Timonerie Be sure to reserve three or four days in advance in order to dine at this one-Michelin-star restaurant. Specialities include *sandre rôti au chou et pommes de terre* (perched pike with cabbage and potatoes) and the chocolate tart. Especially recommended is the very affordable *prix fixe* lunch. Closed Mondays from March to August, Saturdays from September to February, Sundays, and mid-February to mid-March. Visa and MasterCard accepted. 35 Quai de la Tournelle, 5e (phone: 43-25-44-42). Expensive to moderate.

Le Trou Gascon Alain Dutournier created the inspired and unusual cooking that features southwestern French specialities and a vast choice of regional wines and armagnacs. He has moved on to a more elegant neighbourhood, but his wife holds down the fort at this one-Michelin-star restaurant. Closed weekends. Reservations advised. Major credit cards accepted. 40 Rue Taine, 12e (phone: 43-44-34-26). Expensive to moderate.

Allard A very popular bistro with hearty country cooking and excellent burgundy wines. Snails, turbot, and beef bourguignon are the prime lures. Spring, when white asparagus and the new turnips arrive, is a special time here. Don't miss the chocolate charlotte for dessert. Closed weekends and August and for 10 days at Christmas. Reservations advised. Major credit cards accepted. 41 Rue St-André-des-Arts, 6e (phone: 43-36-48-23). Moderate.

L'Amanguier This series of garden restaurants serves an appetizing brand of nouvelle cuisine. Stick to a main course, which comes with a choice of appetizers, and the price is surprisingly low. The desserts are tempting. Open daily for lunch and dinner. Reservations advised. Major credit cards accepted. 51 Rue du Théâtre, 15e (phone: 45-77-04-01); 110 Rue de Richelieu, 2e (phone: 42-96-37-79); 43 Av. des Ternes, 17e (phone: 43-80-19-28); and 12 Av. de Madrid, Neuilly (phone: 47-45-79-73). Moderate.

Ambassade d'Auvergne Its young chef creates delicious, unusual, classic Auvergnat dishes with a modern touch (try the lentil salad and the sliced ham). Also known for seasonal specialities and wonderful cakes. Open daily for lunch and dinner. Reservations advised. Major credit cards accepted. 22 Rue du Grenier-St-Lazare, 3e (phone: 42-72-31-22). Moderate.

Astier An honest-to-goodness neighbourhood hangout that always is packed, because the clientele know they can rely on it for the staples of bourgeois cooking, lovingly prepared. Closed Saturdays, Sundays, and August. Reservations advised. Major credit cards accepted. 44 Rue Jean-Pierre-Timbaud, 11e (phone 42-57-16-35). Moderate.

Balzar Perhaps because of its location right next to the Sorbonne, this mirrored brasserie has always attracted intellectuals. The steaks and pommes frites also are worth a visit. Open daily for lunch and dinner; closed Christmas week and August. Reservations necessary. Major credit cards accepted. 49 Rue des Ecoles, 5e (phone: 43-54-13-67). Moderate.

La Barrière Poquelin The excellent cooking à la nouvelle cuisine includes a splendid foie gras salad. Closed Saturdays for lunch, Sundays, and three weeks in August. Reservations advised. Major credit cards accepted. 17 Rue Molière, 1er (phone: 42-96-22-19). Moderate.

Bistro 121 A hearty menu and excellent wines are offered in a modern setting that's always chic and crowded. Try *poisson cru marine au citron vert* (seafood marinated in lime juice) and chocolate charlotte for dessert. One Michelin star. Closed Sundays, Mondays, and mid-July to mid-August. Reservations advised. Major credit cards accepted. 121 Rue de la Convention, 15e (phone: 45-57-52-90). Moderate.

Le Bistrot de Paris Michel Oliver offers informality, original and classic bistro fare, and a good wine list. Closed Saturdays for lunch and Sundays. Reservations advised. Major credit cards accepted. 33 Rue de Lille, 7e (phone: 42-61-16-83). Moderate.

Le Boeuf sur le Toit In the building that once housed a restaurant of the same name, a haunt of Jean Cocteau and other Paris artists in the 1940s, this eatery off the Champs-Elysées is managed by the Flo group, well known for good value. Piano bar until 2 a.m. Reservations advised. Major credit cards accepted. 34 Rue de Colisée, 8e (phone: 43-59-83-80). Moderate.

Bofinger For magnificent Belle Epoque decor, this is the place; it's one of Paris's oldest brasseries and it is beautiful, even if the food is occasionally disappointing. Order onion soup and choucroute and you won't be unhappy. Open daily. Reservations advised. Major credit cards accepted. 3 Rue de la Bastille, 4e (phone: 42-72-87-82). Moderate.

Café de la Jatte Only those in the know venture this far down the Seine for dinner. This leafy island, l'Ile de la Jatte, was ripe for a smart renovation, and this huge, high-ceilinged dining room, with half-moon-shaped windows and a pink floor, is now full of the choicest local clientele. The fare is healthy and simple: generous salads and roast chicken along with more nouvelle items. Open daily for lunch and dinner. Reservations advised. Major credit cards accepted. 60 Av. Vital Bouhot, Neuilly, 15 minutes by car from central Paris (phone: 47-45-04-20). Moderate.

Chez André A classic, bustling bistro near the chic shopping of Avenue Montaigne. Although a bit too noisy and crowded, it is quite popular with the well-heeled crowd, perhaps because it offers impeccably prepared sole meunière, blanquette de veau, gigot d'agneau, and other traditional dishes. Reservations advised. Major credit cards accepted. 12 Rue Marbeuf, 8e (phone: 47-20-59-57). Moderate.

Chez Benoît A pretty but unpretentious bistro with fine old-fashioned Lyonnaise cooking and exquisite wines. Just about at the top of the bistro list, it's rated one Michelin star. Closed weekends and August. Reservations necessary. No credit cards accepted. 20 Rue St-Martin, 4e (phone: 42-72-25-76). Moderate.

Chez Georges This narrow, old-fashioned bistro – with a whole platoon of matronly waitresses in starched aprons – is a bastion of traditional French cooking. Closed Sundays and holidays. Reservations advised. Major credit cards accepted. 1 Rue du Mail, 2e (phone: 42-60-07-11). Moderate.

Chez Josephine and *La Rôtisserie Chez Dumonet* Two restaurants share the same building and the same management. Josephine is an old-time bistro with traditional cuisine and an excellent wine cellar; the Rôtisserie is lively and more modern, with steaks and grills over an open fire. Josephine is closed weekends and July; the Rôtisserie, Mondays, Tuesdays, and August. Reservations advised. Major credit cards accepted. 117 Rue du Cherche-Midi, 6e (phone: 45-48-52-40). Moderate.

Chez Maître Paul The cooking of the Franche-Comté region is the speciality of this recently expanded restaurant with an auberge ambience. Try the *saucisse Montbeliard* (smoked garlic sausage), the *poulet au vin jaune* (chicken cooked in Jura wine), and the *gâteau aux noix* (nut cake). Closed Saturday lunch and Sunday. Reservations advised. Major credit cards accepted. The *prix fixe* menu is good value. 12 Rue Monsieur-le-Prince, 6e (phone: 43-54-74-59). Moderate.

Chez Pauline The perfect bistro. The tiny, wood-panelled downstairs room (ask to be seated there) is brightened by large mirrors and fresh flowers; the place settings look like Florentine marbelling. Try the oysters in a watercress sauce or the assortment of seafood with a saffron sauce, and save room for dessert – mille-feuille of orange with raspberry sauce is sublime. Closed Saturdays, Sundays, July, and from 24 December to 2 January. Reservations advised. Major credit cards accepted. 5 Rue Villedo, 1er (phone: 42-96-20-70). Moderate.

Chez René A neighbourhood bistro on the Left Bank offers hearty helpings of regional fare. Closed Saturdays, Sundays, August, and Christmas week. Reservations advised. Major credit cards accepted. 14 Blvd. St-Germain, 5e (phone: 43-54-30-23). Moderate.

Chez Toutoune This modest place specializing in Provençal dishes has become very popular for two good reasons: the food is tasty and the prices are fairly reasonable. The five-course, *prix fixe* menu features a rather short but very interesting selection of appetizers, entrées, and desserts. Closed Sundays, Monday lunch, and mid-August to mid-September. Reservations advised. Major credit cards accepted. 5 Rue de Pontoise, 5e (phone: 43-26-56-81). Moderate.

La Coupole A big, brassy brasserie, once the haunt of Hemingway, Josephine Baker, and Picasso, it is owned by the Flo group. The atmosphere is still great, the food still mediocre. Open daily until 2 a.m. Closed August. Reservations advised. Major credit cards accepted. 102 Bd. du Montparnasse, 14e (phone: 43-20-14-20). Moderate.

Le Domarais This used to be the Crédit Municipal, or state pawnshop, and its elegant cupola now houses a sophisticated restaurant serving such inventions as Camembert fondue, grilled Bayonne ham, and a *petit salé* of duck. Closed Saturdays for lunch and Mondays. Reservations advised. Major credit cards accepted. 53 bis Rue des Francs-Bourgeois, 4e (phone: 42-74-54-17). Moderate.

L'Escargot Montorgueil The polished wood panelling, the brass fittings, and the spiral staircase at this beautiful place, which dates from 1830, only add to the pleasure of a meal that might include snails in any of half a dozen styles or duck with orange sauce. Closed Monday lunch. Reservations advised. Major credit cards accepted. 38 Rue Montorgueil, 1er (phone: 42-36-83-51). Moderate.

La Ferme St-Simon Among our favourites for wholesome cuisine d'autrefois (old-fashioned cooking). Nothing very chichi here, just well-prepared, authentic dishes – the kinds you'd expect from a traditional Left Bank restaurant. Leave room for dessert; the owner once was a top assistant to Gaston Lenotre. A perfect place for lunch. Michelin has awarded it one star. Closed Saturday lunch, Sundays, and August. Reservations advised. Major credit cards accepted. 6 Rue de St-Simon, 7e (phone: 45-48-35-74). Moderate.

Au Gamin de Paris Combines the cosiness of a classic bistro with the chic of a historic Marais building and serves well-prepared, imaginative food. Open daily. No reservations after 8 p.m. Major credit cards accepted. 51 Rue Vieille-du-Temple, 4e (phone: 42-78-97-24). Moderate.

Le Grand Colbert Bright and brassy, with delightful polychrome, Belle Epoque motifs, and traditional offerings such as *boeuf gros sel* (boiled beef with coarse salt) and *merlan Colbert* (lightly breaded, pan-fried whiting), this renovated nineteenth-century brasserie is next to the Bibliothèque Nationale. Open daily. Reservations advised. Major credit cards accepted. In the Galerie Colbert, 2 Rue Vivienne, 2e (phone: 42-86-87-88). Moderate.

Jo Goldenberg The best-known eating house in the Marais's quaint Jewish quarter, with good chopped liver and cheesecake and a range of Eastern European Jewish specialities. It's also a fine place to sip mint tea at the counter in the middle of a busy day. Open daily. Reservations unnecessary. Major credit cards accepted. 7 Rue des Rosiers, 4e (phone: 48-87-20-16 or 48-87-70-39). Moderate.

Julien Belle Epoque decor with all the flourishes. Reliable, if uninspired, meals are served in a bustling atmosphere until 1.30 a.m. Open daily. Reservations advised. Major credit cards accepted. 16 Rue du Faubourg-St-Denis, 10e (phone: 47-70-12-06). Moderate.

Le Manufacture The second eatery of two-star chef Jean-Pierre Vigato (of Apicius), this modern place in an old cigar factory at the southern edge of Paris offers an excellent quality/price ratio. Closed Saturday afternoons and Sundays. Reservations advised. Visa accepted. 30 Rue Ernest-Renan, Issy-les-Moulineaux, 15e (phone: 40-93-08-98). Moderate.

La Marée Unobtrusive on the outside, there is great comfort within – also the freshest of fish, the best restaurant wine values in Paris, and fabulous desserts. Michelin has awarded it one star. Closed weekends, holidays, and August. Reservations advised. Major credit cards accepted. 1 Rue Raru, 8e (phone: 47-63-52-42). Moderate.

Le Moulin du Village Light and airy, especially in summer, when tables are put out on the cobbles of Cité Berryer, a tiny pedestrian alley very near the Madeleine, just off the Rue Royale. Cuisine is nouvelle and wines good. Closed Sundays. Reservations advised. Visa accepted. 25 Rue Royale, 8e (phone: 42-65-08-47). Moderate.

Le Muniche St-Germain's best brasserie is a bustling place with a rather extensive menu, and it's popular until 3 a.m. Open daily. Reservations advised. Major credit cards accepted. 27 Rue de Buci, 6e (phone: 46-33-62-09). Moderate.

La Petite Chaise Founded in 1680, it occupies two storeys of a seventeenth-century stone house on the Left Bank. The intimate (and slightly run-down) atmosphere of the home of an ancient aunt characterizes this place, with brocaded walls, brass chandeliers, and antique oils contributing to the period decor. The trout you see swimming in a tank also are on the menu, as are specialities like shellfish crêpes and veal Pojarsky, in which the meat is combined with minced chicken. Always open. Reservations advised. Major credit cards accepted. 36 Rue de Grenelle, 7e (phone: 42-22-13-35). Moderate.

Au Pied de Cochon No more choucroute on the menu (sob!). Crowded and colourful 24 hours a day, and its customers enjoy shellfish, pigs' feet, and crocks of onion soup, all in the old Les Halles area. The food and service aren't what they used to be, and a garish redecoration has mangled most of the old atmosphere. But it still has appeal. Reservations advised. Major credit cards accepted. 6 Rue Coquillière, 1er (phone: 42-36-11-75). Moderate.

Pierre au Palais Royal Delightful, with admirable bourgeois cooking (one Michelin star) and lovely chinon and saumur wines. Closed weekends and August. Reservations necessary. Major credit cards accepted. 10 Rue de Richelieu, 1er (phone: 42-96-27-17). Moderate.

Le Recamier The so-called garden is actually a courtyard between a couple of high-rise buildings, but as the sun goes down, it's a very congenial place to dine in good weather. Martin Cantegrit is a perfect host, and the menu features first-rate (and one-Michelin-star) fish dishes (try the turbot, if possible). The apple tart for dessert is special (order it warm), and the wine list is one of the most fairly priced on the Left Bank. Closed Sundays. Reservations necessary. Major credit cards accepted. 4 Rue Recamier, 7e (phone: 45-48-86-58). Moderate.

Restaurant du Marche Cuisine Landaise, which means solid, country-style cooking – foie gras, confits d'oie, and fine wines from the Landes region in the southwest of France, near Bordeaux. An amazing choice of herb teas, and a pretty terrace for summer dining. Open daily for lunch and dinner. Reservations advised. Major credit cards accepted. 59 Rue de Dantzig, 15e (phone: 45-32-26-88 or 45-33-23-72). Moderate.

La Rôtisserie du Beaujolais A *de rigueur* spot for Paris's 'in set' is Claude Terrail's casual canteen on the quay in the shadow of his three-star gastronomic temple, La Tour d'Argent. Most of the meat, produce, and cheese served come from Lyon. Closed Monday and Tuesday afternoons. No reservations. Major credit cards accepted. 19 Quai de la Tournelle, 5e (phone: 43-54-17-47). Moderate.

Le Soufflé On the street just behind the Rue Rivoli, not far from Place Vendôme, this is the place to enjoy an orgy of soufflés. We suggest crayfish soufflé for an appetizer, cheese soufflé as a main course, and chocolate soufflé for dessert – then head directly to your cardiologist! Closed Sundays. Reservations advised. Major credit cards accepted. 36 Rue du Mont-Thabor, 1er (phone: 42-60-27-19). Moderate.

Le Télégraphe This former dormitory for female employees of the French post office attracts a trendy crowd, including Princess Stephanie of Monaco. The food is simple – saumon unilateral (salmon fillet cooked on one side with olive oil and herbs), and a good crème brûlée. Open daily. Reservations advised. Major credit cards accepted. 41 Rue de Lille, 7e (phone: 40-15-06-65). Moderate.

Le Train Bleu Fine food, good wine, and baroque decor so gorgeous it's been made a national monument. And it's in a train station. Open daily for lunch and dinner. Reservations usually unnecessary. Major credit cards accepted. Gare de Lyon, 20 Bd. Diderot, 12e (phone: 43-43-09-06). Moderate.

Ty-Coz Breton cuisine features fish, cider, and crêpes; no meat, no cheese. Closed Sundays and Mondays. Reservations advised. Major credit cards accepted. 35 Rue St-Georges, 9e (phone: 48-78-34-61). Moderate.

Le Zeyer After a hard morning discount shopping on the nearby Rue d'Alesia, here's a good neighbourhood place for mussels marinière, grilled lotte with sorrel, or platters of shellfish.

Open daily. Reservations unnecessary. Major credit cards accepted. 234 Av. du Maine, 14e (phone: 45-40-43-88). Moderate.

Androuet There's a great cheese emporium on the main floor and, upstairs, a unique restaurant where cheese is the base of every dish. The quality has slipped somewhat, but it still is a unique experience. Closed Sundays. Reservations advised. Major credit cards accepted. 41 Rue Amsterdam, 8e (phone: 48-74-26-90). Moderate to inexpensive.

Brasserie Lipp This famous café is fashionable for a late supper of choucroute and Alsatian beer and for people watching inside and out. The food's just as good there, however. Closed fifteen days at Christmas. Reservations advised. Major credit cards accepted. 151 Bd. St-Germain, 6e (phone: 45-48-53-91). Moderate to inexpensive.

Chez La Vieille Adrienne's cooking is simple, savoury, and very popular. For lunch only. Closed weekends. Reservations necessary. No credit cards accepted. 28 Rue de l'Arbre-Sec, 1er (phone: 42-60-15-78). Moderate to inexpensive.

Clos de la Tour This popular restaurant has 'bistro moderne' decor. Closed Saturdays at lunch, Sundays, and August. Reservations advised. Major credit cards accepted. 22 Rue Faiguière, 15e (phone: 43-22-34-73). Moderate to inexpensive.

Coup de Coeura With a 2-level design, this place features inventive cooking, eager waiters, and an interesting wine list. Closed Saturday lunch and Sundays. Reservations advised. Major credit cards accepted. 19 Rue St-Augustin, 2e (phone: 47-03-45-70). Moderate to inexpensive.

Les Grandes Marches Formerly the Tour d'Argent Bastille, though never related to Claude Terrail's three-star temple overlooking the Seine, it is a bustling, turn-of-the-century-style brasserie serving oysters, seafood and grilled meats. Located next to the new Opéra de la Bastille. Reservations advised. Major credit cards accepted. 6 Pl. de la Bastille, 11e (phone: 43-42-90-32). Moderate to inexpensive.

Joe Allen's Just like the original on West 46th Street in New York City, it has good T-bone steaks, hamburgers, chili, and apple pie. Open daily till 1 a.m. Reservations advised after 8 p.m. Major credit cards accepted. 30 Rue Pierre-Lescot, 1er (phone: 42-36-70-13). Moderate to inexpensive.

Les Noces de Jeanette Under new management, this place now offers inventive cuisine at reasonable prices. Closed Sunday evenings. Reservations advised. Major credit cards accepted. 14 Rue Favart, 2e (phone: 42-96-36-89). Moderate to inexpensive.

Le Petit Nicois This tiny bistro, serving delicious bouillabaisse, is a favourite of French TV news crews who broadcast from a nearby building. A few good specials vary from night to night. Closed Sundays and Monday lunch. Reservations advised. Major credit cards accepted. 10 Rue Amélie, 7e (phone: 45-51-83-65). Moderate to inexpensive.

Au Petit Riche Genuine 1900s decor, Touraine cooking, and inexpensive vouvray, chinon, and bourgueil wines. Closed Sundays and August. Reservations advised. Major credit cards accepted. 25 Rue Le Peletier, 9e (phone: 47-70-68-68). Moderate to inexpensive.

Le Pharamond Serves only the best Norman food in a beautiful Belle Epoque, timbered townhouse that has been declared a historic monument by the French government. Famous for tripes à la mode de Caen and pommes soufflés since 1862. Closed Sundays, Monday lunch, and July. Reservations advised. Major credit cards accepted. 24 Rue de la Grande-Truanderie, 1er (phone: 42-33-06-72). Moderate to inexpensive.

Atelier Maître Albert Unlike most other eateries on the Left Bank, this one is pleasantly roomy, with a log fire in winter and an honest *prix fixe* menu year-round. Notre-Dame looms up in front of you as you walk out the door and on to the quay. Open daily except Sundays for dinner. Reservations advised. Major credit cards accepted. 1 Rue Maître-Albert, 5e (phone: 46-33-13-78). Inexpensive.

Aux Bigorneaux A souvenir of the old Les Halles, this place is frequented by arty types and journalists. Especially recommended are the foie gras frais maison, the chicory salad, the steak au poivre, the Reserve Maison wine, and the sumptuous desserts. Closed Sundays, Mondays, and for dinner in winter. Reservations advised. Major credit cards accepted. 12 Rue Mondetour, 1er (phone: 45-08-49-33). Inexpensive.

Brasserie Flo One of the last of the brasseries of the 1900s, owned by the enterprising Flo group. Hidden in a hard-to-find courtyard, it's excellent for oysters, foie gras, wild boar, and Alsatian specialities. Open daily and late. Reservations advised. Major credit cards accepted. 7 Cour des Petites-Ecuries, 10e (phone: 47-70-13-59). Inexpensive.

Brissemoret Popular with Parisians, this eatery serves basic quality food at bargain prices. The tasteful ambience is a perfect setting for excellent foie gras, raw salmon marinated in fresh herbs, and great sauces (try the breast of duck in wine sauce). Closed Saturdays and Sundays. Reservations necessary. Major credit cards accepted. 5 Rue St-Marc, 2e (phone: 43-36-91-72). Inexpensive.

Chez Fernand A nondescript hole in the wall that produces surprisingly tasty dishes. Pot au feu, steak with shallots, and fish pâté all are first-rate, but the real lure is the huge tub of chocolate mousse served for dessert – a chocoholic's fantasy come true. Open evenings only. Reservations advised. Visa accepted. 13 Rue Guirsade, 6e (phone: 43-54-61-47). Inexpensive.

Chez Jenny A roisterous Alsatian brasserie, where the waitresses still wear white lace collars and dirndls. There are oysters year-round, though perhaps more in keeping with the place's character are the huge platters of choucroute (sauerkraut and assorted pork meats) accompanied by good Riesling wine. Open daily. No reservations. Major credit cards accepted. 39 Bd. du Temple, 3e (phone: 42-74-75-75). Inexpensive.

Chez Marianne A friendly Jewish delicatessen/restaurant; the falafels make nourishing fuel for any exploration of the Marais. Closed Fridays. Reservations unnecessary. Major credit cards accepted. 2 Rue des Hospitalières-St-Gervais, 4e (phone: 42-72-18-86). Inexpensive.

Chez Yvette This excellent, small, bourgeois restaurant has good home cooking, lots of choices, and great desserts. Closed weekends and August. Reservations advised. Major credit cards accepted. 46 bis Bd. Montparnasse, 6e (phone: 42-22-45-54). Inexpensive.

Chicago Meatpackers Head here for hamburgers or chili; finish your American food fix with apple pie or chocolate chip cheesecake. Open daily. Reservations unnecessary. Major credit cards accepted. 8 Rue Coquillière, 1er (phone: 40-28-02-33). Inexpensive.

Gérard A hearty pot-au-feu and other country favourites are served at this bistro. Closed Saturday lunch and Sundays. Reservations unnecessary. No credit cards accepted. 4 Rue du Mail, 2e (phone: 42-96-24-36). Inexpensive.

Le Jardin de la Mouffe A choice of hors d'oeuvres, entrées, and desserts, plus a cheese course, half a carafe of wine, and a garden view. Closed Mondays. Reservations unnecessary. Visa accepted. 75 Rue Mouffetard, 5e (phone: 47-07-19-29). Inexpensive.

Lunchtime One of the few eateries in Paris that satisfies the desire for a light lunch, serving crispy mixed salads made with the freshest greens and a wide range of sandwiches, including blue cheese with cream, curried chicken with currants, and American standbys such as roast beef. The desserts are homemade and delicious. Lunch only. Closed Saturdays, Sundays, holidays, and August. Reservations unnecessary. No credit cards accepted. Two locations: 156 bis Av. Charles-de-Gaulle, Neuilly (phone: 46-24-08-99), and 255 Rue St-Honoré, 1er (phone: 42-60-80-40). Inexpensive.

Moulin à Vent (Chez Henri) Located across the street from what was once Paris's wine market warehouses, this bistro's decor has remained intact for over 40 years. The bar is adorned with half barrels and small lights that are inscribed with the names of different wines and growers. Try the frogs' legs and the steak with shallots. Closed Sundays, Mondays, and August. Reservations necessary. Major credit cards accepted. 20 Rue des Foses St-Bernard, 5e (phone: 43-54-99-37). Inexpensive.

Paul Once a secret, it is now known by the whole world. There's good solid fare here, and the premises always are packed. Closed Mondays, Tuesdays, and August. Reservations advised. No credit cards accepted. 15 Pl. Dauphine, 1er (phone: 43-54-21-48). Inexpensive.

Petit Zinc A popular late (3 a.m.) spot for fish, oysters, foie gras, and an ample, reasonably priced wine list. Open daily. Reservations advised. Major credit cards accepted. 25 Rue de Buci, 6e (phone: 36-33-51-66). Inexpensive.

Polidor Regulars here keep their napkins in numbered pigeonholes, and the place's history includes frequent patronage by such starving artists as Paul Verlaine, James Joyce, Ernest Hemingway, and, more recently, Jean-Paul Belmondo. The College de Pataphysique, founded by Raymond Queneau and Ionesco, still meets here regularly for the good family-style food. Ask to see the house scrapbook. Closed in August. Reservations unnecessary. No credit cards accepted. 412 Rue Monsieur-le-Prince, 6e (phone: 43-26-95-34). Inexpensive.

Le Procope One of Paris's oldest restaurants, where the food is reasonably good and the atmosphere couldn't be more Parisian; the service leaves a lot to be desired. Open daily. Reservations advised. Major credit cards accepted. 13 Rue de l'Ancienne-Comédie, 6e (phone: 43-26-99-20). Inexpensive.

Relais de Venise Always a crowd waiting outside this place near the Porte Maillot, better known as 'L'Entrecôte'. The *prix fixe* menu includes free second helpings of steaks with pepper sauce and French fries. Fancy strawberry desserts cost extra. Open daily. No reservations. Major credit cards accepted. 271 Bd. Pereire, 17e (phone: 45-74-27-97). Inexpensive.

Robert et Louise Family bistro, with warm panelled decor and a very high standard for ingredients and cooking. Try the boeuf bourguignon or the open-fire grilled côte de boeuf. Also good are the fromage blanc and the vin en pichet. Closed Sundays, holidays, and August. Reservations unnecessary. No credit cards accepted. 64 Rue Vieille-du-Temple, 3e (phone: 42-78-55-89). Inexpensive.

Le Roi du Pot-au-Fe A very good place to sample this delicious peasant dish. Closed Sundays. Reservations advised. Major credit cards accepted. 34 Rue Vignon, 9e (phone: 47-42-37-10). Inexpensive.

La Route du Beaujolais It's a barn-like workers' bistro on the Left Bank, serving Lyonnaise specialities and beaujolais wines. Don't miss the charcuterie and the fresh bread here, and try the tarte tatin (caramellized apple tart) for dessert. Closed Saturday lunch and Sundays. Reservations unnecessary. Visa accepted. 17 Rue de Lourmel, 15e (phone: 45-79-31-63). Inexpensive.

Le Trumilou The formidable proprietress sets the tone of this robust establishment, which serves huge, steaming portions of boar, pheasant, and venison in season under a frieze of some excruciatingly bad rustic oils. Closed Mondays. Reservations unnecessary. Major credit cards accepted. 84 Quai de l'Hôtel-de-Ville, 5e (phone: 42-77-63-98). Inexpensive.

Vagenende An Art Nouveau spot with fantasy decor that has changed little since it opened in 1898. It features adequate, filling meals at low prices. Open daily until 1 a.m. Reservations unnecessary. Major credit cards accepted. 142 Bd. St-Germain, 6e (phone: 42-36-68-18). Inexpensive.

Assiette au Boeuf Steaks, salad, and pommes frites, with music in the evening. Open daily until 1 a.m. No reservations. Major credit cards accepted. 123 Champs-Elysées, 8e (phone: 47-20-01-13). Very inexpensive.

Bistro de la Gare Michel Oliver offers a choice of three appetizers and three main courses with pommes frites. Excellent for a quick lunch. Open daily. No reservations. Major credit cards accepted. Ten locations, including 73 Champs-Elysées, 8e (phone: 43-59-67-83); 59 Bd. Montparnasse, 6e (phone: 45-48-38-01); 38 Bd. des Italiens, 9e (phone: 48-24-49-61). Very inexpensive.

Chartier Huge, turn-of-the-century place with lots of down-to-earth food for the money. No reservations. No credit cards accepted. 7 Rue du Faubourg-Montmartre, 9e (phone: 47-70-86-29). Very inexpensive.

Drouot The younger member of the Chartier family, but less known, and with more berets and fewer tourists. The waiters and waitresses, clad in black and white, look as if they emerged from a Renoir painting, although the decor is 1920s, with brass hat stands. The simple food is a bargain. To avoid a long wait for a table, arrive before 9 p.m. No reservations. No credit cards accepted. 103 Rue de Richelieu, 2e (phone: 42-96-68-23). Very inexpensive.

L'Etoile Verte Not much to look at, but always full, it serves fresh and generous helpings of standard French classics – quenelles, seafood timbales, and so forth – at rock-bottom prices. Open daily. Reservations unnecessary. Major credit cards accepted. 13 Rue Brey, 17e (phone: 43-80-69-34). Very inexpensive.

L'Olympic Bar Crowded at all hours, this popular hangout is open for meals at lunch only. Blue-collar workers, students, executives, fashionable women, and others eat and drink with pinball noise as a background. The decor is nothing to speak of, but the food is good, the portions are huge, and the price is right. Closed Sundays and sometimes for Saturday lunch. Reservations unnecessary. No credit cards accepted. 77 Rue St-Dominique, 7e (phone: 45-51-75-87). Very inexpensive.

Le Petit Gavroche A hole-in-the-wall bistro-cum-restaurant with a lively clientele, an inexpensive and classic menu, and the feeling that nothing has changed in years. Closed Sundays. Reservations unnecessary. No credit cards accepted. 15 Rue Ste-Croix-de-la-Bretonnerie, 4e (phone: 48-87-74-26). Very inexpensive.

Le Petit St Benoît French cooking at its simplest, in a plain little place with tiled floors and curlicued hat stands. Open weekdays. Reservations unnecessary. No credit cards accepted. 4 Rue St-Benoît, 6e (phone: 42-60-27-92). Very inexpensive.

Au Pied de Fouet This former coach house has had its habitués, including celebrities as diverse as Graham Greene, Le Corbusier, and

Georges Pompidou. Service is fast and friendly, and it's a place to order the daily special. Desserts, such as charlotte au chocolat, are marvellous. Arrive early; it closes at 9 p.m. Closed Saturday evenings, Sundays, two weeks at Christmas and Easter, and August. No reservations. No credit cards accepted. 45 Rue de Babylone, 7e (phone: 47-05-12-27). Very inexpensive.

Extra Special

Although we've noted the existence of *Fauchon* (under *Shopping*) we would be remiss in omitting it from the restaurant listings. Actually three spectacular stores stocking elegant edibles (at 26, 28, and 30 Pl. de la Madeleine, 8e), Fauchon is considered so much a bastion of the privileged that one of its stores was bombed by radicals back in 1978. But the shops thankfully have long been back in full working order, which is a blessing for every abdomen in town.

One Fauchon shop specializes in the most beautiful fruits and vegetables available anywhere, plus pâtés, terrines, and as many other incomparable carryout items as even the most jaded gourmet's palate could conceive. If you're planning any sort of picnic, and are looking for something out of the ordinary, this is the place to pack your hamper. There also is a new grocery and sweetshop on the street level.

For chocoholics: The very best hot chocolate in Paris (if not the universe) is served at *Angelina's* on the Rue de Rivoli, 1er, and at its other location in the Palais de Congrès, near the Porte Maillot métro. The best chocolate ice cream in the City of Light is at *Berthillon* on the Ile St-Louis (31 Rue St-Louis-en-l'Ile, 4e). The best (and most generous) services of chocolate mousse are offered at *Chez Fernand* (13 Rue Guirsade, 6e, on the Left Bank).

But it's across the narrow street in the far corner of the Place de la Madeleine that all of Paris congregates for nonpareil pastries, coffee, and an occasional snack or drink. Chocolate opera cakes and macaroons in many hues, as well as mille-feuilles and other custardy concoctions, are sold by the slice and can be sampled downstairs. Two years ago, the two original shops were joined by a Fauchon cafeteria/bar in the basement of the building located at 30 Place de la Madeleine and by a first class restaurant on the second floor. Breakfasts, lunches, snacks, and coffee are served downstairs throughout the day, while the restaurant upstairs is open for lunch and dinner. If you need a sugar surge during the course of your Paris meanderings, these are the places to take your high-caloric breaks.

8
EN ROUTE

Introduction

Getting to or from the Euro Disney Resort can be a significant part of the fun of a visit to this unique destination. Rather than suggest routes that are no more than six lanes of unattractive rapid roadway, we've recommended routes that have a variety of interesting sights and sites along the way.

We've already suggested the highlights of the city of Paris that should be part of any Euro Disneyland visit, as well as day-trips from the park site itself – to add some special spice to your stay. We think that three days is plenty of time to spend at the Euro Disneyland enclave to see and do all that's best thereabouts. So in addition to our basic guide to the City of Light and our day-trip drives, we're adding these recommended routings to make sure that your Euro Disneyland visit is memorable from start to finish.

England

Having journeyed underwater for 31 miles, via the England-to-France 'Chunnel' (or on the surface aboard the ferry or boat train), travellers will find the coast of Normandy a literal breath of fresh air. There are also plenty of opportunities to enjoy the many healthy, outdoorsy activities along this pleasing stretch of seashore. The route to Paris will continue to be water oriented, hugging the coastline for some distance before heading inland to follow the Seine as it winds through the peaceful farmlands and primeval forests of the Seine Valley and Ile de France.

Calais, the host port to millions of arriving tourists each year, is less well known as a centre for handmade lace. There's even a lace museum (Musée des Beaux Arts et de la Dentelle) in town. Equally famous is the bronze 'The Burghers of Calais' by sculptor Auguste Rodin, that stands outside the Town Hall.

Following the coastal road, head south towards Boulogne along the Côte d'Opale (Opal Coast), so named for its dazzling chalk cliffs and vast stretches of sandy beaches and dunes. Along the way, stop at Cape Griz-Nez, for a soaring overview of the turbulent meeting of the English Channel and the North Sea. On the not-so-frequent clear day, you can see all the way to the English coast.

Boulogne is France's first fishing port. Be prepared for the first-rate seafood served at virtually every local restaurant. Boulogne's Ville Haut (Upper Town) represents the town's historic core, built in the thirteenth century atop existing Roman ruins.

Continue the coastal trek southward to Le Touquet-Paris-Plage, nicknamed the 'Pearl of the Opal Coast'. Despite the mixed-jewel metaphor, this chic resort is favoured by international players who come for the casino and the wealth of land and water sports, as well as for the thalassotherapy spas – the famed seawater treatments for which this region has become famous.

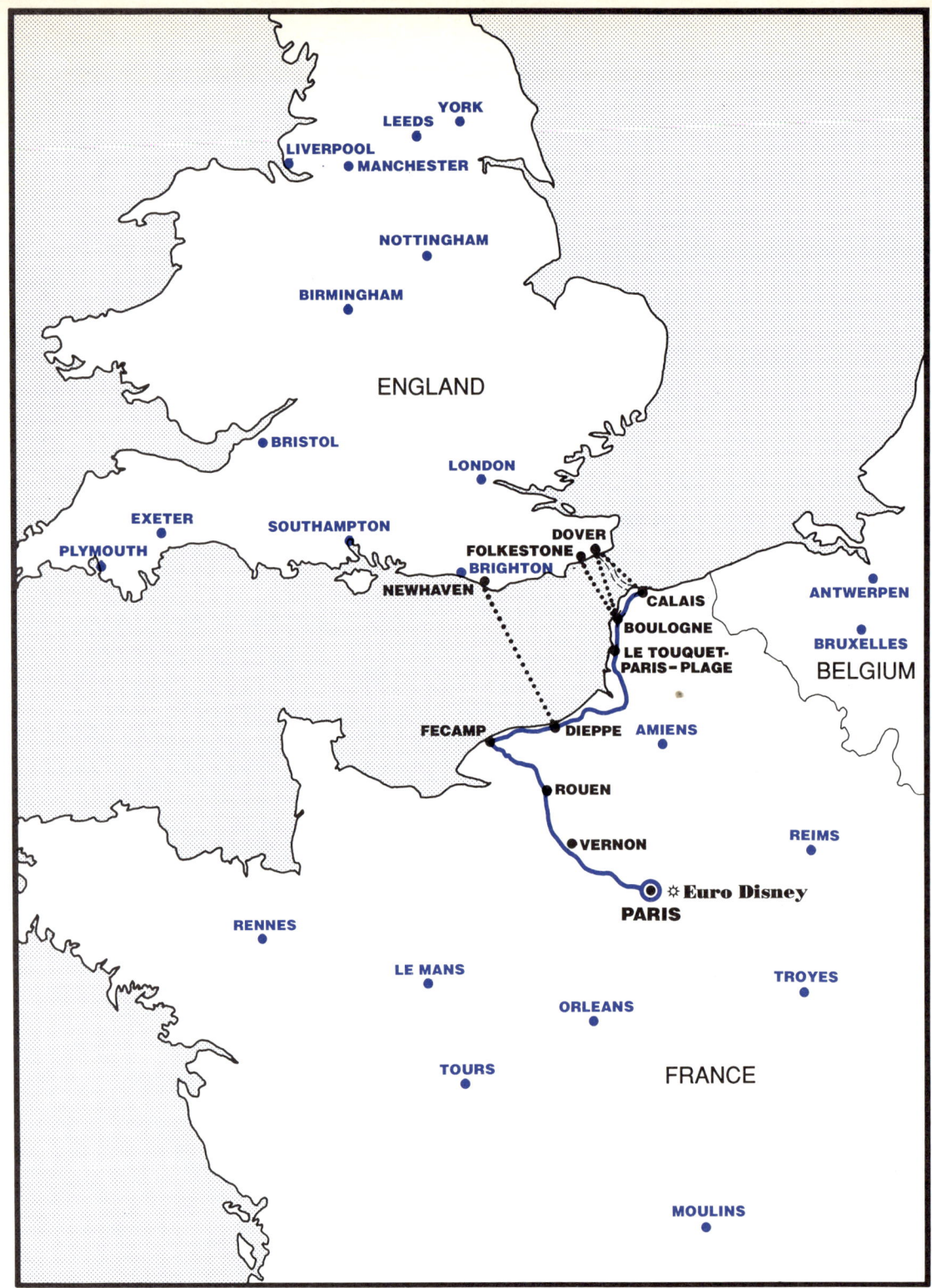

En route from England

Follow the sea road south to Dieppe which, in addition to being the closest beach to Paris, is also the undisputed *grande dame* of Normandy's seaside resorts, having been designed in 1863 by Empress Eugénie and Napoleon III. Dieppe, too, has a casino and many leisure activities, along with several historical sites to see, including the fifteenth-century hillside château with panoramic sea views and museum.

Still hugging the coast, continue south to Fécamp, a harbour and fishing port with a cathedral-size Gothic abbey church, Eglise de la Trinité, built in the late twelfth century. Another famous building in town is the Palais Bénédictine, a museum which traces the history of the famous liqueur invented here in 1510 by Benedictine Brother Vincelli.

From here, our route turns inland southeast towards Rouen. Just past the intersection of D926 and N15, watch for D982, an especially scenic route that traces the Seine. Rouen, the capital of Lower Normandy, long has been called a living museum. There are also museums that honour famous local names and events: Joan of Arc, who was burned at the stake here, as well as such important literary figures as Flaubert and Corneille, who were born here. In addition to Rouen's remarkably well preserved Old Town (that dates to the fifteenth century), the Notre Dame cathedral is one of the finest in France.

Follow the Seine along N15 as it winds along with Vernon. The countryside here is forest primeval, much as it was during the twelfth century when King Louis IX brought his hunting parties here. Although much of Vernon was destroyed during World War II, the twelfth-century church of Notre Dame escaped the bombings. Just outside town, visit the Château de Bizy, built in the Empire style, yet surrounded by distinctly Italian-style gardens featuring elaborate waterworks.

A mile from the bridge on D5 is Giverny, the village made famous by Claude Monet, the Impressionist painter. His home, where he lived and worked from 1883 to 1926, and his famous gardens and lily ponds, are all open to the public from April through October.

From here, it's only a short journey into Paris, following the Seine as it reflects its subtle transformation from bucolic waterway into urban river. From there, it's only about 20 minutes to the Euro Disneyland site.

The South of France

Perhaps it is fitting that this all-French route begins and ends with Napoleon, stretching northward from Nice to Grenoble, where the 'Route Napoleon' ends. From there your path winds from Lyon through the Rhône Valley and Burgundy, pausing at Fontainebleau, Napoleon's favourite retreat, before ending at the Euro Disney Resort on the outskirts of Paris.

The Route Napoléon is a scenic highway (N85) that follows the General's return march from Elba in 1815. It is identified by signs bearing the flying eagle symbol, inspired by his pledge: 'The eagle will fly from steeple to steeple until he reaches the towers of Notre Dame'

From Nice, our recommended route leads to Grasse, famous as the centre of the French perfume industry. Over 10,000 tons of local flowers are harvested every year, most of which are processed by the three largest factories in town. Tours of these factories are offered to the public. Also try to visit the museum devoted to local artist Fragonard, and the museum of the art and history of Provence.

Next along the General's route was Digne. Not to be missed are the dramatic views from high atop this hilltop village. From here our route leads over the mountains to Sisteron. The road actually tunnels through the

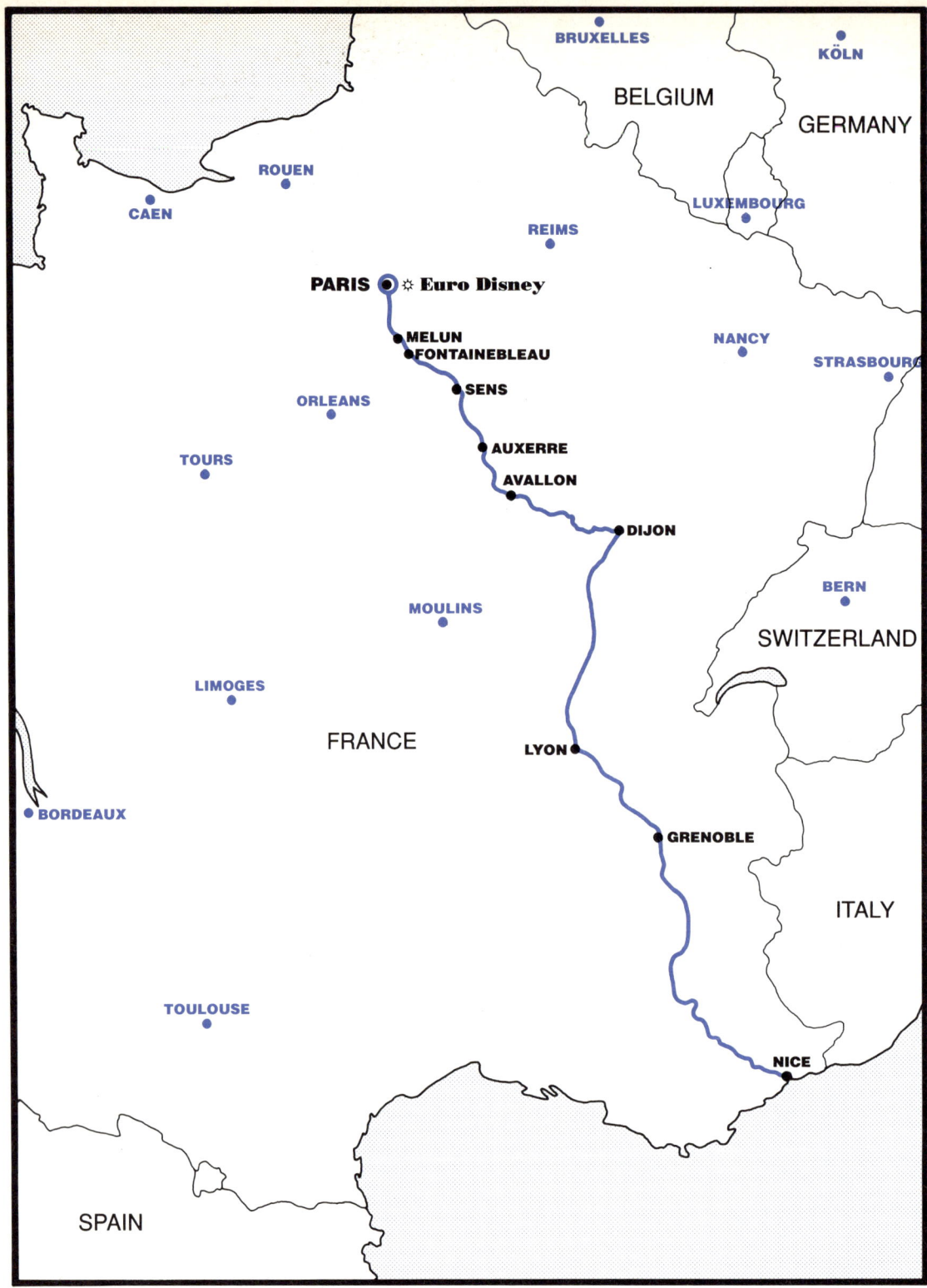

En route from the South of France

mountain on which the twelfth-century citadel stands. From Guérite du Diable (Devil's Lookout), experience even more outstanding overviews of the surrounding area.

Route 85 continues along the fertile farmlands of the southern Alps through Gap, through a valley carved by ancient glaciers, ending at Grenoble. Although perhaps best remembered as the site of the 1968 Winter Olympics, this venerable town traces its origins to the year 1 BC. It is also the capital of the French Alps, and for a look at just what this means, take the cable car up to the Fort de la Bastille, where the views seem to go on forever. Visit the Old Town, anchored by two thirteenth-century churches. Also not to be missed: The Musée de Peinture et de Sculpture, one of France's most important provincial museums, a treasure house of both Old Masters and Impressionists. Other local museums are devoted to such diverse themes as Stendhal, vintage cars, and the French Revolution. Not just for skiers and sightseers, Grenoble is also a fishman's paradise, surrounded by dozens of abundant streams, lakes, and rivers.

It's only a short drive westward to Lyon, France's sophisticated, well-fed second city. Not to imply that every one of this city's 1.2 million residents is a culinary expert, but it's practically impossible to get a bad meal here. Why else would so many Parisians willingly hop aboard the high-speed TGV just for a meal in Lyon?

Well situated at the confluence of the Rhône and the Saône, Lyon boasts miles of quays along both river banks. Take the funicular from the Old Quarter to the basilica of Notre-Dame-des-Fouvières for a view of the confluence of the rivers and Presqu-île, where the Musée des Beaux-Arts is located.

While Lyon excels in gastronomic excellence, it owes its early wealth to the silk trade. From the 1700s, Lyon supplied France and all Europe with the finest silk fabric. There are several excellent textile museums which trace the intimate relationship between this city and silk, and for a bit of living history, walk along the *traboules* in the Old Quarter, the ancient honeycomb of covered corridors which helped protect the silk cloth from the weather.

The N6 leads northward through the Rhône Valley, through the towns of Mâcon and Chalon-sur-Saône, each of which offers interesting local histories, and each of which shares in the regional wealth of the Mâconnais vineyards.

Beaune is the heart of Burgundy wine country. It is also rich in art and architectural treasures, the best known of which is the spectacular *Hôtel Dieu*, which was founded in 1443 by Nicolas Rolin, Chancellor of Burgundy, as a hospice, and which continues today as an old-age home. An excellent example of the Flemish-Burgundian architectural style, its outstanding features include the roof of geometrically-patterned colourful ceramic tiles and the fifteenth-century altarpiece, 'The Last Judgement'. Its poignant history is retold during sound-and-light shows which are presented from March through October. The wines from the hospice's vineyards are auctioned annually – on the third Sunday in November. This event is pivotal in the pricing of burgundy wines around the world; the prices here set the trend for all burgundies.

Due north is Dijon, former capital city of the Dukes of Burgundy, and a repository of art and historical and architectural treasures. The construction of the Ducal city spanned five centuries, beginning in the fifteenth. Experts consider the Eglise Notre Dame to be a masterpiece of Burgundian Gothic; the Eglise St Michel a prime example of the Renaissance style. Of Dijon's many museums, and Musée des Beaux-Arts is truly outstanding, its collection second only to that of the Louvre. And for something entirely different, don't miss the Grey Poupon Shop which, since 1777, has been dispensing that famous Dijon condiment.

Even today, residents bring in their empty mustard crocks for refills of the spicy stuff.

Head west along A38, picking up local scenic roads outside town, towards Avallon. Perched high above the Vallée de Cousin, this town was a natural stronghold during the Middle Ages. Stroll the ancient ramparts, enjoy the breathtaking views, and don't miss the clocktower on the fifteenth-century Butcher's Gate. Early pilgrims flocked to the Eglise St Lazare, the fourth-century church that housed what the faithful believed to be a relic of the saint.

Follow D957 through nine miles of valley along the scenic Cousin River into Vézelay. Once a stopover for pilgrims bound for Santiago de Compostela (see our route from Spain), this ancient city is renowned for its Basilique Ste Madeleine, a pink and ochre stone masterpiece of Romanesque design which held a relic of Mary Magdalen. About this church and its achievement in attaining the Romanesque epitome of light and space, André Malraux wrote '. . . [it] strives to release a feeling of sacredness, to express the inexpressible.'

North along D951 and D6 to Auxerre, a port city on the River Yonne. A medieval city, Auxerre is famous for several churches: The Cathédrale St Etienne, which has been called 'a first class example of thirteenth-century Flamboyant Gothic architecture', and the Abbey of St Germain, with its spectacular pre-Romanesque crypts (holy grottoes) and the eleventh-century fresco 'Christ on Horseback'. Auxerre also offers a lively market and many trendy shops along its sinuous streets.

The Cathédrale St Etienne in Sens, the foundations of which were laid between 1128 and 1130, is recognized, as the first of France's great Gothic cathedrals. Its twelfth-century stained-glass windows are important, as is the Treasury, which houses a unique collection of liturgical vestments and fabrics, shrouds and tapestries.

Follow the N6 northwest. When the woods along the roadside begin to thicken and to resemble an enchanted forest, you'll know Fontainebleau can't be far off. This twelfth-century hunting lodge, nestled in its own dense 50,000-acre forest, long served as the country retreat of France's sovereigns. It was the all-time favourite of Napoleon, who always preferred it to Versailles. The Fontainebleau Palace is, as one would expect, palatial – filled to excess with wondrous ballrooms, chapels, courts, and grand bedchambers. Equally overwhelming are the grounds, the vast Forêt de Fontainebleau, acknowledged as among the most beautiful and well-protected woodlands in all Europe.

From here, one final decision remains: whether to detour west for a plunge into the splendours of Versailles; or to set a straight course northward along the N36, directly to Euro Disneyland.

Spain

While in Spain, this route covers much of that country's diversity – from the cosmpolitan urbanity of Madrid to the seaside charm of San Sebastian – with plenty of opportunities to explore the surprises of Green Spain and to experience the wild beauty of the Cantabrian coast with its prehistoric caves, its time-warp of a medieval village, its ancient pilgrims' route, wilderness game preserves, and chic beach resorts. At the French border, our route takes a more leisurely pace, often crisscrossing the countryside in order to squeeze in as many of southwestern France's most compelling sites as possible – from the clay-red seashore through the Pyrenees into the Aquitaine and up through the lovely Loire Valley's château countryside.

Our first suggested stop, just 30 miles northwest of Madrid along the M505, is San

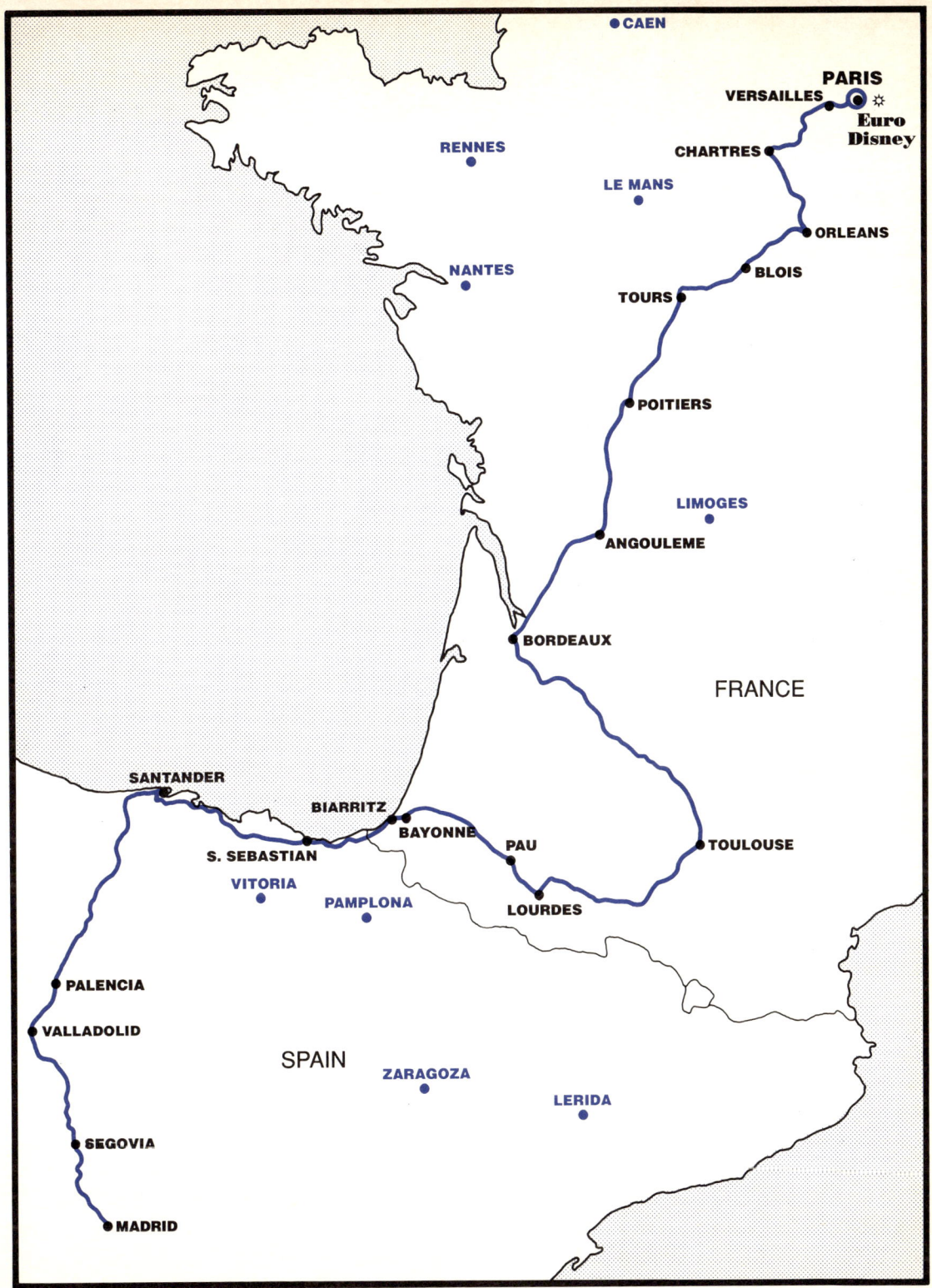

En route from Spain

Lorenzo del Escorial, King Philip II's monastery-palace monument to his father. From here, follow route C601 north of Segovia, a city so historically significant it ranks on UNESCO's World Heritage list. Don't miss the cathedral (the last Gothic church constructed in Spain), the Roman aqueduct, and the fourteenth-century *alcázar* (palace).

Heading northwest along route N601, the broad, fertile plain becomes dotted with impressive fortifications just outside Valladolid, the capital of Meseta province and a bustling university city as well. Among Valladolid's almost 50 sites worth seeing are the home of sixteenth-century author Miguel de Cervantes (who wrote *Don Quixote*), the cathedral and diocesan museum, the 1479 university, and the sixteenth-century cloisters of San Gregorio College.

Head north through the town of Palencia, which despite its more exciting past is distinguished today primarily for its Gothic cathedral known as 'La Bella Desconcida' (the Unknown Beauty).

As the route along N611 winds towards Santander on the coast, there are four significant sites that warrant detours or lengthier explorations: the Pilgrims' Way, the road which led religious pilgrims from all over Europe to Santiago de Compostela during the Middle Ages; the Picos de Europa and the surrounding wilderness of the National Hunting Reserve (head west into the Park at Reinosa); the Caves of Altamira, often called the 'Sistine Chapel of the Stone Age' because of the clarity and genius of the vividly coloured prehistoric drawings of bison, horses, boars, and stags which date from between 14,000 and 9,000 BC. (Note: reservations must be made well in advance for permission to visit these caves. Call the Director at 818102. If you can't get into the actual caves, there's a lifelike video of the interiors at the nearby museum.)

The town of Santillana del Mar, a breathtaking jewel, is something of a time warp of a town whose medieval roots seem to have suffered blessedly few modernizations since the Middle Ages. This is the birthplace of the legendary (although fictional) rogue, Gil Blas. As has been the case for centuries, most residents are dairy farmers; cows live in comfortable style under the town's houses, and cowherds still drive their flocks along the cobbled streets. Don't miss a visit to the twelfth-century Collegiate Church.

Begin your journey along the Cantabrian coast at Santander, a chic resort that boasts an exceptional variety of beaches, as well as a casino, an International Music and Dance Festival, and summer university courses at the beautiful La Magdalena palace.

From here, route E70 hugs the coast, passing through (or near) such Cantabrian villages as Guernica, a town whose horrors during the Spanish Civil War were immortalized by Pablo Picasso, and Lequeitio, Orio and Sarauz, typical Basque fishing villages with their requisite flocks of seagulls and aromas of roasted sardines.

San Sebastian remains Spain's most fashionable resort, despite some nay-sayers who label her a 'faded beauty'. Blessed by nature, this seaside town has mountain peaks, a tranquil bay, beaches, and even a river. Truly Basque in nature, San Sebastian also manages to incorporate a certain Belle Epoque charm, as evidenced in the convivial restaurant and bar scene around the central square. There's also a posh casino, and you should visit the San Telmo Museum, housed in the sixteenth-century Renaissance monastery.

It's a 20-minute ride from San Sebastian to Irun, the border crossing into France. Follow the coastal sweep of golden sand, stopping to enjoy the glamorous French resort town of Biarritz and (just four miles inland) Bayonne, where the town's Musée Basque offers a lively introduction to the elusive Basque history, culture, and traditions.

East along the N117, it's 90 minutes to Pau, the largest and most cosmopolitan city in the western Pyrenees. Among its more traditional historic treasures, Pau also claims the oldest golf course in Europe, one which, most golfers agree, can also lay claim to several of the most arresting views from any course anywhere – modern or ancient.

Follow D937 for a 30-minute detour to Lourdes. En route, the Grottoes of Betharram, with their eerie caves, make an interesting stop. Despite some cynics' claims that the best miracle would be to rid this town of all the commercialism, a visitor can't help being touched by the unquestioning faith shown by most of Lourdes's pilgrims.

From the tawdry to the rosy: head east along the N117 to Toulouse, capital city of Midi-Pyrénées, the 'Rose City', its profusion of blush-pink brick buildings making it an artist's and photographer's dream. Visit the St Sernin Basilica, renowned for its splendid Romanesque architecture, and the majestic Capitole, which also houses the city's opera. Summer welcomes many music, dance, and art festivals.

Despite the fact that Bordeaux is somewhat off the direct path of this route, the N13 offers an efficient trail along the Garonne River, one that also offers ample opportunities to experience some of the antiquities of the Aquitaine's lush Dordogne Valley – not to mention the chance to sample the region's culinary specialities that focus on foie gras, confit, or anything else made from duck or goose livers, as well as the legendary bordeaux wines, cognac, and armagnac.

Bordeaux has been called the ultimate regional centre, and with its splendid eighteenth-century Grand Théâtre, the treasures in its Musée des Beaux-Arts, its twin-steepled cathedral, its richly historic Vieux Bordeaux (Old Town), and its modern-day trendy boulevards and boutiques, this seems a fitting title for this ancient and proud city. Before venturing out to explore the treasures of the Bordeaux vineyards, check first with the Maison du Vin in town for helpful guidance, touring advice, and information.

Follow the N10 north to Angoulême, nicknamed 'the town built on a balcony'. This perched village, which overlooks the Charente Valley, also boasts several impressive sites built by man: the Cathédrale St Pierre, which dates to 1128, and several museums exhibiting fine and decorative arts.

Due north, still on the N10, is Poitiers, a renowned centre for the arts. The old town protects a wealth of churches, palaces, and houses that recall former glory. There are several venerable churches which date back many centuries: the Baptistère St Jean, the Eglise St Hilaire le Grand, and the Eglise Notre Dame la Grande.

Enter the magical Loire Valley on the approach to Tours, a city resplendent with antiquity despite its somewhat modern appearance. (Tours was heavily bombed during World War II; much has been rebuilt.) To begin to experience its history, visit the Gothic Cathédrale St Gatien, with its thirteenth-century stained-glass windows, the museum's excellent fine arts collection, and the Musée du Compagnonnage, an exhibit of ancient local craft guilds which is housed in an eleventh-century abbey.

The N152 winds eastward following the Loire River as it heads towards Blois. There are so many châteaux, château hotels, vineyards, outdoor activities, and other dazzling sights in this area that the toughest decision will be choosing when and where to stop next. Of the sublime Château of Blois, where French kings held court for 200 years, the author Henry James rhapsodized, 'this exquisite, extravagant, this transcendent piece of architecture – the most joyous utterance of the French Renaissance'.

While postwar Orléans remains less splendid than the original version, there are three treasures not to miss: the Gothic Cathédrale Ste Croix, as large as Notre Dame in Paris, begun in the thirteenth century; the Musée des Beaux-Arts in the fifteenth-century Town Hall; and the ancient history museum.

From here, it's straight to the Paris suburb of Marne-La-Vallée, where Euro Disneyland awaits. Or if time permits and curiosity urges, a slight westward detour to Chartres, the most astounding of all medieval cathedrals – the 'French Acropolis' as Rodin titled it. This is an ancient city, filled with many secular as well as religious monuments.

Sweden, Denmark, Germany, the Netherlands, Belgium

The logistics and scope of this route would daunt even a Napoleon, winding as it does across five countries on its way southward to Euro Disneyland near Paris, sweeping through Sweden, Denmark, northern Germany, the Netherlands, and Belgium. A formidable journey, but one which also provides opportunities along the way to smell the roses (or the tulips), to explore some storybook castles, to wander through enchanted forests filled with wild birds and game, and to marvel over the extraordinary diversity of northern Europe and its islands.

From Stockholm, follow route E4 south towards Norrkoping's Kolmardens Djurpark, a drive-through safari park that boasts a tropicarium, dolphinarium, and zoo among its attractions. There are camping grounds here, as well as regular boat service between the town and the park. Norrkoping is Sweden's fourth largest city, located on a bay of the Baltic Sea. It is very popular with summer sailors.

Continue on E4 westward towards Lake Vättern, where this scenic route parallels the lakeshore to Granna, a beautiful town beloved for its blossoming fruit trees. Kids love it for something else: *Polkagrisar* which, translated literally, means 'polka pigs' – the red and white striped peppermint candy for which the town is famous. Local candy factories offer tours and tastings. Granna also is the birthplace of S. A. André, the ill-fated polar explorer, whose papers and scientific exhibits are housed in a local museum.

A slight detour eastward to Vimmerby, to Astrid Lindgren's Town and the home of 'Pippi Longstockings'. A thrill for young readers, this theme town is also the location for many of the Pippi films, and is surrounded by miles of wilderness for nature hikes, golf courses, lakes for canoeing, and unspoiled campsites.

Head south to Småland, the 'Kingdom of Crystal'. Scattered throughout this forested wilderness are the factory towns of the biggest names in designer crystal, among them Orrefors, Kosta, and Boda. Tour the factories (note: glassblowers work from 6 a.m. to 3 p.m., so plan to visit early in the day) and shop in the factory outlets, some of which are the size of giant supermarkets.

Continue south and west, passing through the idyllic Skåne (pronounced 'scorner') countryside, with its fertile plains, sandy beaches, and summer resorts, plus dozens of castles, farms and medieval churches, ending at Helsingborg, an ancient port city.

Before boarding the ferry to Denmark, tour Helsingborg's thirteenth-century St Mary's church, the Town Museum, and Fredriksdals Friluftmuseum, an open-air re-creation of eighteenth-century farmhouses and buildings.

Ferries leave every 20 minutes for the three-mile crossing into the Danish port city of Helsingør (Elsinore), which dates to 1429, making it one of the country's oldest towns. Shakespeare buffs will head straight for Kronborg (often called 'Hamlet's Castle') to walk

En route from Sweden, Denmark, the Netherlands, Belgium

the inner and outer ramparts and explore other oft-mentioned sites. The bard's *Hamlet* is often performed in the castle courtyard by international troupes. Also in town: the City Museum, which is housed in Marienlyst Castle, built as a summer home for Kronborg.

En route to Copenhagen, stop at Humlebaek, the site of the Louisiana Museum, a dazzling collection of sculpture and paintings – all the diverse elements of modern art – housed in a spectacular building. The museum is set in a lovely park at the water's edge. A great picnic spot – on a clear day you can see across the sound to Sweden.

Continuing south along the coastal route, stop at Rungsted, to visit Denmark's newest museum (opened in May 1991) in the home of Karen Blixen, who, as the writer Isak Dinesen, gained international fame for her *Out of Africa*. The house, built in the 1500s, reflects the author's eclectic artistic tastes. She is buried in the 40-acre park that surrounds her museum.

It's hard not to hum the tune to 'Wonderful, Wonderful Copenhagen . . .' as you tour this delightful city, one of the liveliest capitals of Europe. It's a great walking city, filled with things to see and do – and wonderful places to eat. First stop is usually the festive Tivoli Gardens (which we suggest you omit since it will be dramatically overshadowed by Euro Disneyland), followed by a visit to the 'Little Mermaid'. (This is the *original*, pre-Disney daughter of the sea, although you'll probably have a tough time convincing today's young moviegoers of that.) A cultural capital as well, Copenhagen overflows with ballet, theatre, and other performing arts.

West along route 156 is Roskilde, Zealand's second largest city. It was a royal residence as early as the tenth century, and during the Middle Ages was an important religious centre for northern Europe. The Roskilde Cathedral, which was built in 1170 (on the site of a 200-year-old wooden church), represents a major blending of Romanesque and Gothic styles of architecture. Amid the ancient marvels is something to which growing youngsters can relate: the pillar on which such royals as Peter the Great and the Duke of Windsor have measured their heights. Don't miss the Viking Ship Museum, with its exhibits of five vessels dating from AD 1000.

Heading south, pick up E20 to Haskov for the one-hour ferry ride to Nyborg. Although all the roads on this tiny island lead to Odense, route 160 is the most scenic. Odense is the birthplace of Hans Christian Andersen, the 'Father of Fairy Tales'. His home exhibits all his personal effects, including inscribed copies of his best-loved stories, and there are Andersen plays presented each summer in Funen Village, an open-air museum nearby.

Continue across the island, crossing the bridge to Jutland and the European continent. The southward journey along route 170 leads through quiet farmlands bordered by forests. Jutland's east coast is scored with inland fjords and sand dunes. En route, visit Haderslev, which is renowned for its cathedral built in 1265. Other cities in this area still bear the scars of World War II and their close proximity to Germany.

At the border, one of Germany's famous autobahns speeds traffic into Hamburg, the country's largest seaport. Among the sights to see in Germany's largest seaport are Europe's only privately owned zoo; the Sunday morning market, which is a shopper's heaven; and a wonderful harbour tour, which provides an overview of this bustling port city.

Bremen, another major port in northern Germany, is 75 miles from Hamburg, about an hour on the autobahn. For a more leisurely drive through the region's open moors and forests, take route 75. The oldest port in Germany, Bremen is best toured on foot. Its heart is the medieval section surrounding the Marktplatz, with its inviting coffee houses and Ratskellers. Also worth a visit are the

Focke Museum and the eleventh-century St Peter's Cathedral.

Head west, crossing the border into the Netherlands, heading for Zwolle, the capital of the province of Overijssel. Among the several interesting ancient sites to see in this old fortified town are the thirteenth-century city walls, the Sassen gate (1409), and the fifteenth-century St Michaelskerk.

Choose between the scenic routes which wind along between Zwolle and Amsterdam, or the A28, which is the most direct route into the Netherlands' capital city. Although built on a pleasingly human scale, this city has some 7,000 historical structures and sites to see. Dam Square ('The Dam') is a central landmark, adjacent to Walletjes, the Old City. The Royal Palace is open to the public, as are the Anne Frank House and Rembrandt House. There's also a museum featuring works by Van Gogh. And be sure not to miss the unforgettably colourful early morning flower auctions held in Aalsmeer, just outside town.

To appreciate the diversity of this compact country, follow a route which leads through the Randstad region, from Amsterdam to the coast along the Haarlemmerweg, which becomes the N5, to Haarlem, the remarkably well-preserved 900-year-old city, south through the bulb fields of Leiden to The Hague, the country's capital and seat of government, with three royal palaces, 60 foreign embassies, and a score of important museums. And that doesn't mention the famous Madurodam, the five-acre miniature city that works almost as efficiently as the real one; Delft, famous for its signature pottery; and Rotterdam, the modern phoenix, risen from the ashes of World War II bombings.

The A16 leads south across the Belgian border into Antwerp, a cosmopolitan city founded in the seventh century that, today, is a centre of culture and industry (notably diamonds). The artist Peter Paul Rubens was born here in 1577; his birthplace is now a museum open to the public. Visitors are also welcome at Diamondland, to watch the gem cutters and master craftsmen at work.

Follow the N1 south to Brussels, the elegant capital city of Belgium, whose main square, the Grand Place, is said to be the most beautiful in all Europe. Despite the wealth of imposing historic monuments, cathedrals, palaces, and museums in town, don't overlook the small seventeenth-century bronze 'Mannekin-Pis' statue, beloved as a symbol of the country's independent spirit.

Only twelve miles south of town is Waterloo, site of the 1815 defeat of Napoleon. The nearby Wellington Museum offers insights into this historic battle.

The N5 meanders southward through the Ardennes, the mystical, magical 'Forest of Ardens' in Shakespeare's *As You Like It*. Today, this gentle green countryside, with its legends and abbeys and castles, is also the favourite of vacationing skiers, hunters, hikers, and other outdoorsmen.

Just south of the French border, jog east (N43/E44) to Charleville-Mézières, two towns in one which loop around the River Meuse. The sixteenth-century city of Mézières spans two islands. Don't miss its Flamboyant Gothic Notre Dame d'Espérance, or Charleville's elegant Place Ducale. This town is also the world capital of puppetry, with summer puppet festivals and an international headquarters.

The N51 leads south through Champagne country into Reims, considered by many to be the quintessential French city. Indeed, the two local landmarks – the Notre Dame cathedral and the prestigious champagnes – are both ranked among the world's best of the best. Visitors can visit both the cathedral and the cellars, and study the secrets of each first-hand. The cathedral possesses soaring beauty, and is the coronation choice of French kings; the champagne is notable for its incomparable excellence, around which a refined gastronomy has developed.

It's been a long journey from the Swedish coast to these fertile vineyards in Champagne. From here, there are a wealth of short detours possible to such 'worth-the-trip' spots as Châlons-sur-Marne, L'Epine, or Compiègne. But for those anxious to begin their Disney adventure, there remains only a speedy jaunt along the A4 to meet up with Mickey, Minnie, and all the gang at Euro Disneyland (signposted 'Marne-La-Vallée).

Italy

This route, which meanders leisurely from Milan to the Euro Disney Resort outside Paris, winds through some of Europe's most spectacular scenery, offering travellers a bit of everything – from the Lombardy Lakes to the Swiss Alps, through historic Alsace and the peaceful farmlands of Lorraine – with even a taste of the bubbly of Champagne.

Driving north along route A9 from Milan, head for Lugano, just across the Swiss border. Just south of town, stop at the village of Melide for a walk-through taste of what lies ahead, thanks to the delightful 'Swissminiature' – a 1:25 scale model of all Switzerland – filled with detail-perfect little cathedrals, houses, towns, the works.

Even from a distance you'll know why Lugano, with its paintbox panorama of blues, greens, and florals, is known as the 'Garden City'. In summer, dive right into the famous lake or stretch out on one of its many beaches. And whatever the season, don't miss the Villa Favorita that houses Baron Thyssen-Bornemisza's incomparable art collection and visiting exhibits.

About 90 minutes north of Lugano is Bellinzona, the heart of Italian Switzerland. The attraction here is three medieval castles. Actually, it's not necessary to visit all three; start with touring Castello Montebello, which has recently been restored. Bellinzona also boasts 350 miles of hiking trails, all with spectacular vistas. Best are the views of Lake Maggiore from high atop Monte Ceneri.

Head northwest to St Gotthard where, in fine weather, daring drivers switchback over the mountain pass. For those who prefer their roads a bit less twisting, the tunnel ploughs straight through ten miles of mountain, making it the second longest tunnel in Europe (the 'Chunnel' between England and Europe is 31 miles long). A quick stop in Altdorf yields some photographs with the famous statue of this area's favourite son, William Tell, then continue on to Lucerne which you'll probably recognize right away; it's the most photographed town in Switzerland.

There's something for the whole family in Lucerne: an historic old section complete with impressive fortifications; a famous covered bridge that's decorated with sixteenth-century artworks depicting the town's history; as well as summer music festivals and boat trips on the lake. During the daytime cruises, be sure to hop off to explore any of the charming villages that dot the Lake Lucerne shoreline; at night, feast on a fondue supper and dance to folk music as you sail around the lake.

One excursion not to miss: take the special bus (this is important, you don't want to have your car along for this adventure) for the 15-minute drive to Kriens and up Mt Pilatus. A cable car runs up one side of the mountain and a cogwheel train runs down the other, dropping you off at the lakeside where there's a steamer to sail you back to town. On top, there's a hotel, seven restaurants, and several picnic sites – not to mention nonpareil views that just don't quit.

Continue on N2 to Basel, considered the cultural heart of Switzerland. Here is enough culture and art to last for several visits: some 35 museums, including the world-class Kunstmuseum, ballet, symphony and opera,

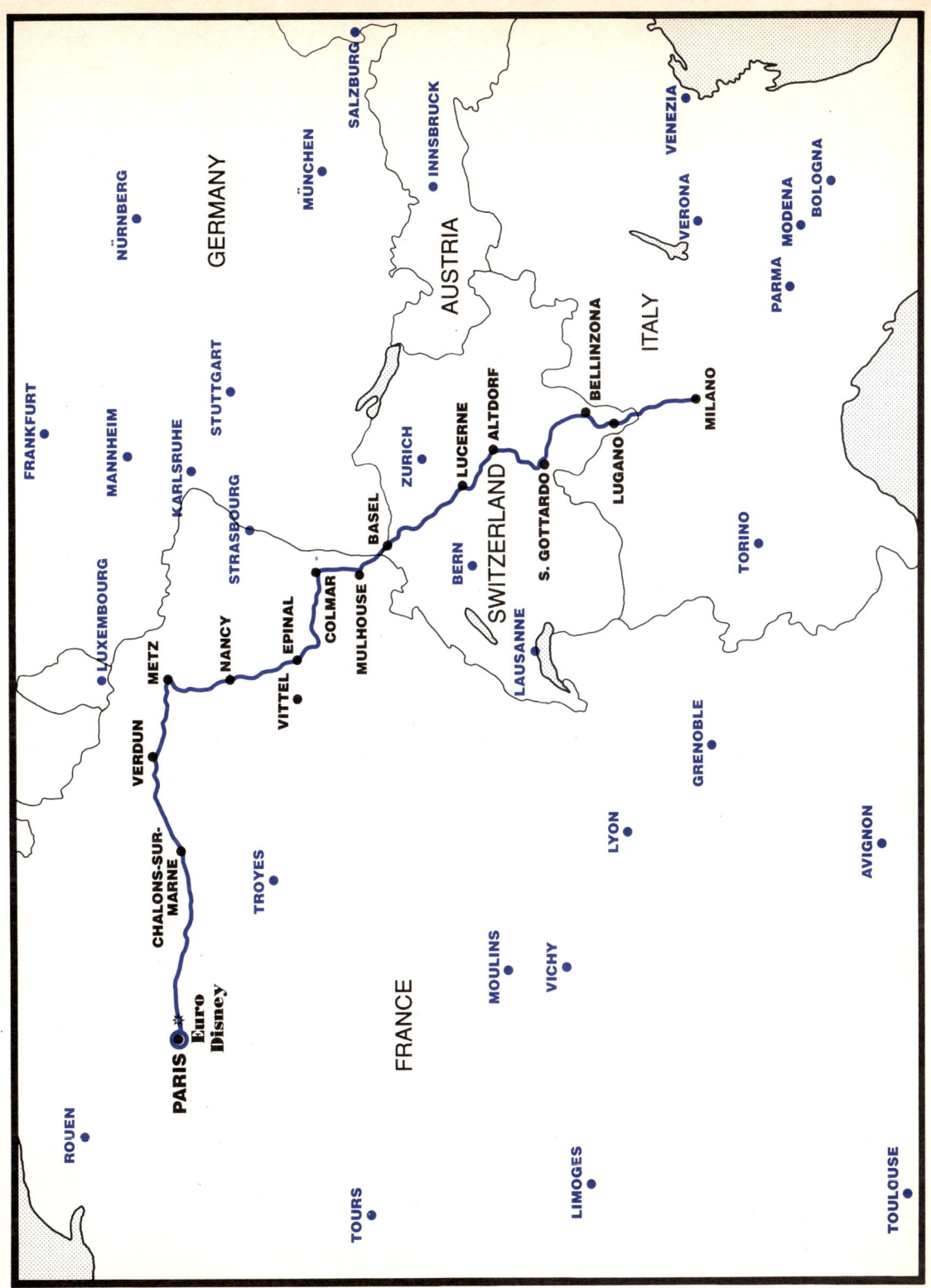

En route from Italy

an historic Old Town, and charming cafés all along the banks of the Rhine.

Cross the border into France, and head along N66 for the Rhineland Renaissance town of Mulhouse. The children (and definitely the driver, as well) will love the Automobile Museum with its collection of almost 500 of the world's most memorable vehicles – an august collection of Bentleys, Rolls-Royces, and a staggering number (123) of vintage Bugattis.

Continue north to Colmar, considered by some the most charming city in Europe. The capital of Alsace, it is also known as 'Little Venice', for its charming waterside activities and *joie de vivre*. Head east along D417, a scenic route that winds through the forests towards Nancy, via Epinal, and if there's time and some serious spa-lovers in your group, a side trip to the water-conscious town of Vittel, famous for its mineral and thermal springs, as well as for its notable table water.

In Nancy, the capital of Lorraine, don't miss the Place Stanislas, arguably the most elegant square in France. The Ducal Palace houses a museum of the history of the region. And for shoppers, the nearby factory and showrooms of Daum Crystal offer hours of sparkling entertainment.

North of Nancy is the ancient fortified town of Metz, a war-ravaged city with the Cathedral of St Stephen still miraculously intact. It's a Gothic masterpiece renowned for its fourteenth-century stained-glass windows, as well as the more modern ones of Marc Chagall. Head eastward for Verdun, a town with a slightly more recent war history. There are several routes through the surrounding countryside (D112 and D913) that tour and remember the worst of the Word War II battle areas. Continuing westward, stop at Châlons-sur-Marne for a look at its cathedral and to sample some of the famous champagne of the region as you relax on the waterfront Quai des Arts, along the banks of the Marne River.

There's also a circus school in town that often allows kids to watch the clowns and jugglers go through their paces.

From here, the choice is whether to continue to explore the cellars and vineyards of Champagne country, or swing on to the main highway (RD33) that speeds straight for Euro Disneyland.

Germany

Tracing a journey back through history, we follow a portion of Germany's 'Romantic Road', an astonishing route that links ancient walled towns filled with storybook castles and fortresses, continues on through the magically scenic Black Forest to a world-famous spa, and then into France through the historic regions of Alsace and Lorraine.

Begin in Munich, Bavaria's principal city, a town that delights in tempering the magnitude of its architectural splendours with an atmosphere of gaiety and celebration. Serious sightseers can feast on the city's wealth of cultural sites that include palaces, formal gardens (including the Englischer Garten, Europe's largest urban park), and museums. Less serious visitors can toast these sites with a stein of the city's other source of civic pride. Munich is justifiably proud of its beer (six different major brands are brewed here) and for its festive beer gardens. The old Hofbrauhaus, a vast beer hall, dance palace, and restaurant, has become virtually synonymous with this fun-loving city, where every day is a mini-Oktoberfest.

Head out of town, northeast on route 2, to pick up the Romantic Road at Augsburg. Founded over 2,000 years ago by the Romans, this city fairly resonates with fascinating history. Don't miss the Mozart festivals in the Schaezler Palace, and the summertime 'Rotes Tor' open-air opera festival.

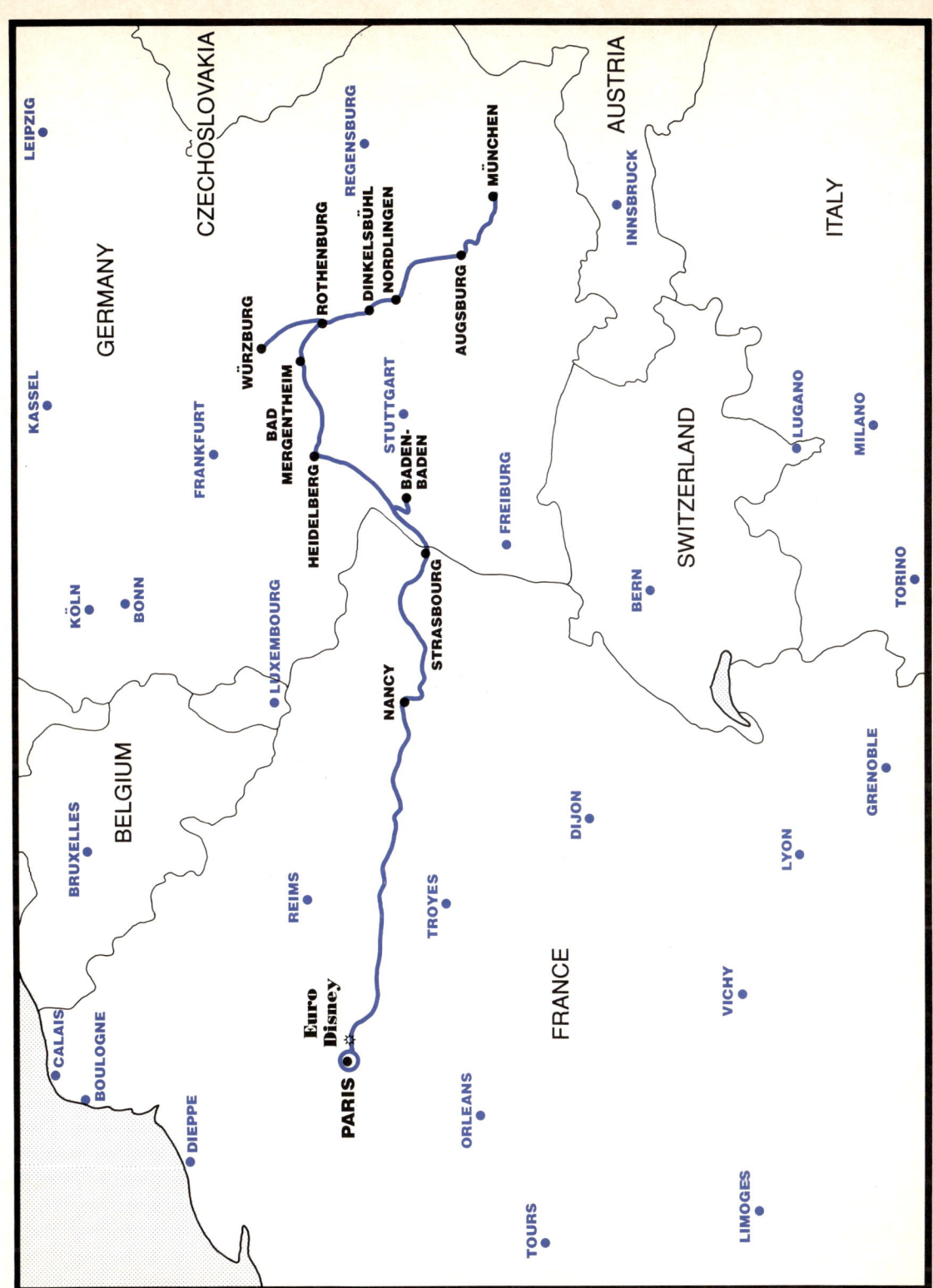

En route from Germany

From here, pick up the Romantic Road (which begins in Fussen, south of here) as it arches north and west, traversing landscapes that range from vineyards to snowfields, and passes through ten medieval towns, each worthy of a lengthy visit and inspection. Travellers face difficult choices indeed, having to decide whether to lavish time on Nordlingen, a city with a 'living' medieval culture that includes costumed residents; or Dinkelsbuhl, a picturesque medieval town complete with walls, towers, and even a moat, as well as a 'Kinderzeche' children's festival each summer; or the walled town of Rothenburg, a wealth of Gothic and Renaissance buildings that many consider to be Germany's most perfectly preserved medieval city; or Bad Mergentheim, the renowned health spa in the Tauber Valley, with its glorious Mergentheim palace, where Empress Josephine once danced through three pairs of slippers in one gala evening. Every other town along this route – Donauworth, Harzburg, Feuchtwangen, Schillingsfurst, Creglingen, Weikersheim – is packed with thousands of years of history and fascination.

The entire Romantic Road, which stretches between Fussen and Wurzburg, is 215 miles long. Although our portion is somewhat shorter, the decisions of what to see and where to linger are no less challenging.

Leaving Bad Mergentheim, pick up route 292 heading southwest towards Heidelberg. (At Mosbach, route 37 into Heidelberg meanders through an especially scenic stretch of the Black Forest.)

Heidelberg is a university city, at once vital, energetic, and romantic. The old castle, with its Gothic and Renaissance history, towers above the city, the river, and the scenic countryside. It's the perfect walking city; vehicular traffic is banned from the centre of the Old Town. In addition to the castle, sights not to miss include the seventeenth-century gardens, the museum, the Students' Jail (that once housed unruly undergraduates), and the Grosses Fass (Great Vat), with its 58,000-gallon capacity. (Local lore tells of a dwarf named Perkeo who once drank the whole thing.)

Heading south, take either the autoroute or the more scenic route 3 to Bäden-Bäden. Although the Romans were the first to tap these thermal springs, today this famous health resort has expanded to offer a bit of everything. From Roman ruins to a state-of-the-art convention center, from a glitzy casino to 300 miles of natural hiking trails, it's all set within 17,500 acres of spectacularly scenic gardens, parks, and wilderness.

Head southwest along route 36, crossing the border at Kehl, into Strasbourg. Another famous university town, Strasbourg is the ancient capital of Alsace, almost as comfortable with German as it is with French. Don't miss the Cathédrale Notre Dame, begun in 1015, famous for its architectural beauty and its stained-glass windows. The town is equally famous for its trio of museums, its covered bridges, and its Parc de l'Orangerie.

Then head west to Nancy. From there, follow the route towards Paris that's traced in our route from Italy.

INDEX

Accommodation, 7, 13, 14, 15, 17
  on-site, 24–33
  off-site, 33–6
  seasonal calendar, 25
Adventure Isle, 11, 15, 47, 52, 53
Adventureland, 7, 8, 11, 15, 17, 18, 37, 46–8, 56, 61–2
Ali Baba's Street Musicians, 56
Alice's Curious Labyrinth, ii, 15, 43, 55
Arc de Triomphe, 100, 102, 103, 104, 107
Autopia, 11, 49
Ay, 93, 94

Ben Gunn's Cave, 47
Big Thunder Mountain Railroad, 8, 11, 15, 43, 44
Blue Lagoon Trio, 56
Boulogne, 141
Buffalo Bill's Wild West Show, 12, 63

Calais, 141
'Captain EO', 8, 11, 15, 49
Centre Georges Pompidou, 100, 105, 116
Châlons-sur-Marne, 97
Champagne region, 7, 71, 84–100, 153, 154, 156
  champagne cellars, 87–8
Champs-Elysées, 102, 103, 114, 117
Chartres, 7, 79–84, 86, 150
  Cathedral, 7, 71, 79, 80–2
  Eglise St Pierre, 83
  Musée des Beaux-Arts, 82
  restaurants, 83–4
Cimitière Pere-Lachaise, 106
Cinderella, 41
Court Jesters, 55

Dieppe, 143
Discoveryland, 7, 11, 15, 37, 48–9, 53–4, 55–6
Disney-MGM Studio Europe, 25
Disney Square, 26, 37

Disneyland Pool and Club, 26
Dr Livingstone, 56
Dumbo, the Flying Elephant, 11, 15, 42

Eiffel Tower, 100, 107
Epernay, 85, 87, 93, 94
  champagne cellars, 93
  restaurants, 94
Euro Disney Information,
  Baby Care Centre, 15
  babysitting, 15
  disabled visitors, hints for, 16
  holiday packages, 13
  lost children, 15–16
  older visitors, hints for, 16
  planning ahead, 10–14
  sample itineries, 11–13
  strollers, 15
  travelling with children, hints for, 14–16
  weather, 8, 9, 10, 18
  when to go, 9–10
Euro Disney Marching Band, 54
Euro Disney Railroad, 11, 40
Euro Disney Special Events, 10
Excalibur Ceremonies, 55

Fantasia in the Sky, 9, 10, 11, 12
Fantasyland, 7, 15, 17, 18, 37, 40, 41–3, 51–2, 55, 59–60
Festival Disney, 12, 13, 16, 23, 25, 63–4
Fountainebleau, 71, 74, 78–9, 143, 146
  apartements royaux, 79
  Chapelle de la Sainte-Trinité, 78–9
  Galerie de François, 79
  restaurants, 79
From Time to Time, 11, 15, 48–9
Frontierland, 7, 8, 11, 17, 18, 37, 40, 43–6, 53, 56, 60–1

General local information, 17–19
  lockers, 17
  lost and found, 18
  mail, 18

  money, 18
  pets, 18
  tipping, 18
Grand Canyon Diorama, 11, 40

Home Run Gang, 55
Hautvillers, 94, 95

Ile de France, 71, 74–9, 141
Ile de la Cité, 100, 109, 114
It's a Small World, 8, 11, 15, 40, 41, 43

Jeu de Paume, 107, 114

Keystone Kops Saxophone Quartet, 54
Kids of the Kingdom, 55
King Arthur's Knights of the Round Table, 41

Lake Buena Vista, 37, 63, 64, 69
Lancelot's Carousel, 11, 15, 42
Left Bank (La Rive Gauche), 100, 107–9, 117, 133, 135, 136, 138
Les Halles, 105
Les Voyageurs, 56
Le Marais, 105–6
Louvre, the, 103, 103–4, 105, 115, 124, 145
Loire Valley, 146, 149
Lucky Nugget Revue, 56
Luxembourg Gardens, 108
Lyon, 113, 143, 145
  Musée des Beaux-Arts, 145

Mad Hatter's Tea Cups, 11, 15, 42
Main Street USA, 7, 11, 12, 13, 15, 17, 18, 26, 37, 39–40, 54–5, 57–9
  Electrical Parade, 9, 10, 12, 44, 54
  Character Cavalcade, 11, 12
Main Street Quartet, 54
Mark Twain Steamboat, 44
Marne La-Vallee, 7, 154
Marseilles, 113

INDEX

Molly Brown Steamboat, 44
Montchenot, 91
Montmartre, 104–5, 126
Montparnasse, 100, 108, 116, 117
Mosquée de Paris, 108
Musée D'Orsay, 107–8, 110
Musée Rodin, 108

Notre-Dame Cathedral (Paris), 100, 109, 110, 113–4, 137, 143, 150

Opéra, 104, 117
Opéra de la Bastille, 104, 136
Orbiton, 11, 49

Palais de Chaillot, 107
Paris: Information & Entertainment
  boats, 110
  buses, 112
  car rental, 112
  galleries, 116–7
  metro, 111
  museums, 114–6
  nightclubs/nightlife, 124–5
  restaurants, 125–40
  shopping, 117–24
  special events, 113
  taxis, 112
  telephone codes, 110
  Tourist Office, 110
  trains, 112–3
Pearly Kings and Queens, 55
Peter Pan's Flight, 11, 15, 41, 42
Phantom Manor, 11, 15, 45–6
Pinocchio's Daring Journey, 8, 11, 15, 41, 41–2

Pirates of the Caribbean, 8, 11, 15, 40, 46, 56, 62
Pirate stuntmen, 56
Plaza Garden Trio, 55
Place de la Concorde, 102, 103, 114
Place Charles-de-Gaulle, 100, 102, 110
Pratfall and Son, 54
Provins, 75–8
  restaurants, 76
  Tour de Cesar, 75

Quartier Latin, 108, 114, 116

Reims, 13, 85, 93, 94, 153
  Cathedral, 80, 85–6, 91, 92
  Champagne cellars, 87–8
  Palais du Tau, 86
  restaurants, 88–91
Restaurants/Eateries, 26, 27–8, 29, 30, 31, 32. See also under individual city/town
Right Bank (La Rive Droite), 100, 102–7, 116, 117
Rio Grande, the, 37
River Rogue Keelboats, 11, 44–5
Rivers of the Far West, 11, 40, 43, 44, 45, 61
Rouen, 143

Sacré-Coeur, 100, 104–5
Seine, the, 103, 107, 108, 110, 132, 136, 141, 143
Sept-Saulx, 92
Shakespeare and Company, 122
Shopping, 26, 28, 29, 31, 32, 33. See also *Paris*
Skull Rock, 40, 47, 56

Sleeping Beauty Castle, 7, 8, 11, 15, 37, 39, 40, 40–1, 51, 55
Snow White's Adventures, 8, 11, 15, 41
South of France, 143–6
Sports, 33, 69–70
Spyglass Hill, 47
Star Tours, 11, 15, 48
Stromboli's Marionettes, 55
Swiss Family Robinson Treehouse, 11, 15, 47

Travelling by Air, 15, 16
  classe affaire, 22
  vols vacances, 22
  vols visites 22
Travelling by car, 13, 20–2
  petrol, 21
  rental, 20–1
  tolls, 22
  driving rules, 22
  sample driving times, 22
Travelling by train, 17, 23–4
  BritFrance Railpass, 24
  France Rail and Drive Pass, 24
  France Railpass, 24
Troyes, 85, 98–9
  restaurants, 99
Tuileries, the, 103, 104, 114

Versailles, 71, 71–4, 146
  Chapel, 72
  Grand Apartments, 72
  Gardens, 73
  Museum of French History
  restaurants, 74
Videopolis, 11, 55–56
Vertus, 96, 97